DAUGHTER OF DAMASCUS

MODERN MIDDLE EAST

LITERATURES IN TRANSLATION

SERIES

Daughter
of
Damascus

taken from *Ya Mal al-Sham*
by Siham Tergeman

English version and Introduction
by
Andrea Rugh

Center for Middle Eastern Studies
University of Texas at Austin

PJ
7864
U76
Y3/3
1994

Library of Congress Catalog Card Number: 93-072705

ISBN 0-292-78126-1

Printed in the United States of America

Drawing on cover by Douglas Rugh

Cover Design: Diane Watts

Editor: Annes McCann-Baker

Table of Contents

Acknowledgments

The Center for Middle Eastern Studies at The University of Texas at Austin is proud to publish the English version of *Ya Mal al-Sham* by Syrian author Siham Tergeman. Anthropologist Andrea Rugh has worked persistently over the years with a number of translators of Arabic to make this work available to the English-speaking world. Her preface and foreword to the English version put the story, originally written for Damascenes, in context for a Western reader.

I would like to thank those at the Center who have helped produce *Daughter of Damascus*, especially Diane Watts for the cover design and Virginia Howell for the final computer formatting. Free-lance artist Douglas Rugh studied the text and created the fine drawing for the cover.

And I send warmest gratitude to author Siham. When I was in Damascus last year, she helped me understand the background of the book through the hospitality of her wonderful city.

Annes McCann-Baker
Editor

Preface for the English Version

I first became aware of this book while living in Damascus when, despairing of the dry and boring materials I was using in my Arabic classes, I took the suggestion of a friend that I might find *Ya Mal al Sham* more interesting. It was, and from then on my Arabic lessons become much more enjoyable.

I was impressed by how a cultural "insider" could so unerringly pick out details of her own society in such a way as to convey the uniqueness of its flavor to an outside reader. The book was not intended for a foreign audience. It was for Syrians, locally printed by the Syrian Military Press as a favor to Siham and at her own expense, and written in a local dialect best understood by a Syrian audience. The book was distributed by Siham herself, appropriately, through a sweet seller in the Bizuriyya Suq.

It was a book passed on hand to hand by Syrians who found in it an echo of their own sentimental attachments to their city and the memories of their past. My Arabic tutor's response used to run the gamut from tears to laughter during our lessons, and it was clear he enjoyed the book as much as I did. His reactions and those of others assured me of the book's authenticity. I remember how he would comment in admiration, "My God, Siham, you are really something!" when a detail would suddenly touch him.

Sabah Qabbani, the diplomat and man of letters, wrote to Siham after reading her book, saying:

> In your book I saw myself, my babyhood, and my early childhood in the quarters of Madinat al-Shahm, Bizuriyya and Ma'awiya. In your book I heard again the voice of my father, the phrases of my mother, the quarreling of my brothers, and the calls of the people in the quarter. I smell the nice scent of jasmine and incense and the *mada'af* and remember the wonderful people who gathered together in our homeland.

Looking back, I see that part of the savoring of the book was in the slowness with which we painstakingly translated the text. We had time to digest the minutest detail, to absorb the vivid imagery, before proceeding to the next word picture. When someone foreign to the culture skims over the English text without mental images to tie descriptions to, there is the risk of losing important underlying themes. For that reason, I have included a fairly extensive foreword, the purpose of which is to highlight details the reader should look for in the text and to offer some general observations that might be lost in too rapid a reading of the book. I hope these comments will help the reader savor the insights that come from a more careful reading.

Each country of the Arab world has unique characteristics that differ from other Arab countries. We need to remember those differences. But we also need to recognize that, like the glittering straw Siham describes binding the mud of old Damascene houses, there are strands that draw the countries of the Arab world together into a culturally sympathetic confederation. Siham skillfully describes details which show the uniqueness and the universality of Syrian Damascene life.

This book, in its own way, is a labor of love and friendship for all of us who have prepared the English translation. Working together has enhanced some established friendships and has helped to develop others. We have all worked on it, I believe, because we feel there is genuine value in providing the English reader with primary source materials from the Arab world. Siham Tergeman has provided us with the original rich Arabic manuscript and a great deal of enthusiastic support. I have provided the managerial function of gathering together native speakers of the regional dialect to help in producing a rough-draft English version and explanations of key words for use in footnote clarifications. The final English version and the foreword are my responsibility, and any errors found in them due solely to my errors in understanding.

I must therefore acknowledge the large debt I owe to a number of people. First and foremost, my thanks are due to my Arabic professor, Ibrahim Aude, who translated a great deal of the text with me. Where he left off, the bilingual May Roustom took over, providing wonderfully colloquial texts that needed little changing in their final form. The late Ibrahim Hanna, a man who cherished the English language more than most native speakers, in the short space of a few weeks, gave me a first draft of a very difficult section on proverbs, which in the final version has been cut for production reasons. Suad Dahr, in turn, helped me with the meanings of the proverbs, the peddler's calls, and the final understanding of difficult passages. I owe thanks to other people who from time to time helped out. Siham's niece, Sawsan Shareef, and Leila Martin of the American Institute of Yemeni Studies, a native Lebanese, stand out in this respect. Selwa Zaher, also in Yemen, read the entire text with me in its final stages to insure the correctness of the translation and the transliteration system.

I want to thank my sons, Nicholas and Douglas, who typed parts of some of the chapters, and also Jean Britton and Zakiya Saleh, who typed most of the final manuscript.

Finally, I want to thank William, who always retains enthusiasm for my projects, even when they take so much of my time and attention away from our mutual interests and activities.

Andrea B. Rugh

Woods Hole, Mass.
June, 1988

Foreword

"I long for the past, for its purity, and for the child who was two children, one who played and one who watched the one who played," says Siham Tergeman in the early pages of this book. She goes on to portray Damascus, the city, like that child, as both actor and acted upon, as subject and object, as the one influencing and the one being influenced by its inhabitants. There are times when the two realities merge for her, and it is difficult to separate where the people end and the city begins. The point is that to Siham, like most Syrians, the city is more than streets, houses, monuments and quarters. It is people, traditions, history, proverbs, peddlers' calls, sights, smells, weddings, births, and humor. It is what people do in their houses, their material surroundings, how they spend their leisure time, their daily schedules, and their holidays. It is how people respond to each other. It is past events that leave a residue in modern minds. It is today's relentless advance of other cultures' presence, and the importance of evaluating what directions the future will take before it is too late to stem the tide of what many Syrians feel is the enemy of cultural traditions, internationalism.

Siham's attachment to her city is at times emotional and uncritical like the eye of a lover appraising its beloved or the mother watching her child. At other moments, her honest pen includes those touches that reveal the imperfections of human organization and the foibles of human nature: the watermelon rinds among which the children play in summer, or the naughtiness of Siham and her sister who refuse to reveal the reason for the worn spots on the toes of their shoes. As a real daughter of Damascus, Siham has trouble separating her own identity from the city that has had such a formative impact on her life. In this she is not unique. It is this inability to separate the self from the city that is what the book is all about. It is the story of Damascus as it was emerging, like much of the rest of the world, into full international connection. More specifically, it is the story of the formative effects on a people growing up during that time.

How does one present the essence of a city to an audience that may never have seen a street or building in its quarters, or who may only have come in contact with its people in other areas of the world? The approaches are as numerous as the writers who attempt the task. My personal preference is through the words of the people themselves, in primary source materials that are not too heavily didactic. I like this book because it is at the same time both broadly descriptive of life in Damascus, and yet narrowly informative on specific aspects of the society. Siham reports on details of life that one could only come to know if one lived long and intimately in Syrian society, and then only if one had a deep commitment to know its people. She offers the reader the sights and smells, the outlines of a world view, the complex workings of human relationships, and all in a form that is easily digested.

Siham's purpose in writing this book is not wholly the same as mine in presenting it to you. Hers is the task of preserving for later generations the traditions of the recent past and the fast-retreating present. She expresses the sadness some people feel over the passing of a way of life that, despite wars and other disruptions, fits the human condition like a comfortable shoe. Others see only the fleas, vermin, and unsanitary details of the past and their reminder in the old city. These detractors generalize their feelings to traditional people, and would like to see them disappear, much as if, as Siham puts it, an old grandmother who no longer had any use were buried in her grave.

Siham wants to remind us of the beautiful monuments, the human interaction in the dusty suqs, the charming houses designed for human comfort, the soothing splashing fountains in tree-covered courtyards, and the intimacy of narrow alleyways. Yet, she is enough of a realist to admit that she herself has moved to the "cardboard carton" houses and broad boulevards of modern Damascus to escape rats, lizards, snakes, and other entrenched inhabitants of older quarters. Her experience in only realizing what she has missed when it is gone is one she wants to help the present generations avoid. She knows she cannot turn back time, but she would like to leave a record of the details of this period for generations of Syrians to come. This theme of rapid change in the Arab World, exemplified through the changes that have occurred in the traditional quarters of Damascus, is the main message of this delightful book.

The widely varied vignettes cover decades within the life span of most present-day Syrians, a period that spans most of this century from its first decade to its seventh, when the book was first published.

Traditions in the Middle East form slowly and die slowly. Many of the customs she describes in these pages still exist today, though perhaps in truncated form, or hidden away in remote corners of the city, or sometimes only as a trace in the memory of older people. To know the flavor of original customs is to know where people are coming from and what values still retain their potency. It is also to penetrate the world view of a people and find that larger store of conditioned response that observation alone fails to reveal. We hope Siham will forgive us for seeing in her book more than the preservation of a rich and varied historical record, and allow us to glean from it, in such a palatable and entertaining way, an insight into the workings of a whole society.

There are several reasons that this book is valuable. First, it is the story of ordinary people and events. Though the author's experiences and descriptions are limited to people among her acquaintances and relatives, these people are neither of the destitute poor nor of the highly aristocratic classes whose experiences may be unique in a society. The persons described in her book are well chosen to portray the life of "everyman" and "everywoman" as they can be defined in the social sense.

Second, songs, poems, peddlers' calls, games and proverbs provide a richness to this account that cannot escape notice.

Third, the book mingles the traditional and the modern, if these terms can be defined to have real meaning. Arabs accuse Westerners of focusing too much attention on the old in Middle Eastern societies. But it would also be unreasonable to concentrate only on the modern, without understanding how older customs inform the manifestations of the new. Both old and new, whether we like it or not, merge in the people of today in ways that make their separation a futile task. Siham has nicely balanced the two in her presentation, even though she clearly indicates in which direction her preferences lie.

Fourth, some of the formidable changes that have occurred in this century are portrayed clearly in the book. For example, we can see significant changes in the economic life of Syria. During the youth of Siham's father, the silk trade occupied "more than half" of the workers in Damascus. The trade later suffered in competition with synthetic fibers until today, even with a renewed interest in natural materials, production has fallen to extremely low levels. The complicated process and the number of workers involved in producing silk undoubtedly explain why few people are attracted to the industry now, when wages are better in other sectors. Much the same can be said for wool production, which apparently was largely a home industry at the time of World War I. Siham, working in the public relations section of the Syrian Military Office, represents the modern educated generation, involved extensively in clerical and service oriented professions.

Syrians are known for their skill in commercial and middle-man activities. Some of the population's ingenuity in this respect comes through in the descriptions of how women left behind during the war organized ways to generate income to keep themselves and their children from starving. In times of necessity, these usually sheltered and protected women were quite capable of managing their own affairs. The same ingenuity is found in the exploits of soldiers who, badly paid and outfitted by the Turkish War Office, set up ad hoc merchandising operations along railway lines on their way to the front. War was not a totally negative experience for Siham's father. During his military period he continued his schooling and received training in telecommunications, allowing him to move out of unskilled work in the silk trade and into skilled work within the postal service when the war was over. The whole family presents a case history in economic and occupational change.

Educational changes are portrayed in the book as well. Siham's father learned to read and write in a *kuttab*, a mosque-related religious school which emphasized memorization of the Koran. Later, as mathematics and the Turkish language became useful to him, he enrolled with a tutor, and eventually completed his schooling in the War College. Siham's mother studied, as was the more acceptable form of schooling for girls of her time, in a private school run by a woman teacher. As a young woman she enjoyed reading the books she borrowed from relatives. Later, as a married woman, her household duties precluded time for reading, but Siham comments that her native intelligence did not depend for knowledge on books. Education comes through as a useful though not necessary skill for those of Siham's parents' generation. By the time she herself goes to school, however, the educational system has become formalized with most urban boys and girls attending schools, and many continuing on to university.

Most important, the book provides a glimpse into the Syrian world view of past and present, and the system of values that was and still is its foundation. As is true for all societies, Syrian values are played out in all aspects of daily life, echoing what become familiar themes in descriptions of the 'Azm Palace, dress, food, feast days, holidays, people's relationships, song, stories, almost in every detail. By looking at the past, not as some quaint remnant, but as a living context that enriches present thinking and modes of actions, we can better understand what is still vital and what is losing its vitality in contemporary life. It is worth a few words to point out some of the most obvious values we find here.

Siham refers again and again to the old Damascene homes, and they, perhaps more than any other material aspect, reflect the deep-seated values of home and family in Syrian society. Because so much time was spent inside those inner walls, care was taken in the past to make them as much like worldly paradises as possible. This was true whether the houses were as large as the 'Azm Palace or as modest as the one where Siham grew up. The entire household complex was organized to entice family members into congenial meeting spaces. In winter, people sat in rooms on the upper story that projected above the rest of the house and, like a solarium, attracted the sunlight's warmth. In summer, the sitting area was an alcove in the sweet-scented courtyards, open to the sun and air, where the splashing fountains and the foliage of flowers and trees provided a cool and soothing place to relax from the heat and the dust of the outside street. Everything was well situated in such a house: stairways were strategically placed to allow women to move about unseen by male visitors, small ventilation openings were located near ceilings, specialized windows high up on the walls let sunlight in by day or moonlight by night, storage areas occupied empty areas in stairwells, and so on. Each house was built with similar requirements, but each, as is the case in any artistic creation, emerged as a totally unique configuration.

The builders of that time did not neglect the aesthetic needs of human beings. Every wall, every cupboard, every ceiling, every floor, received its own independent decoration, in what might appear at first to a Westerner's eyes as a "busy" treatment. After the eye becomes accustomed to the endless variety, the subtle shapes and colors blend into a pleasing and eye-entertaining whole that seems the measure of aesthetic beauty.

The totality of the old Damascene house aims at pleasing its occupants in body and mind; it does not strive toward a public competition with neighbors next door. It hides its charms from outsiders with blank, rough walls facing the street, and saves all its creative energies for the inner parts that serve to satisfy the family members. This kind of house implies a certain kind of household organization where women devote full time to housework, and where the most efficient work group is the extended family with many daughters and daughters-in-law to share the tasks.

One feels that the people who built the old quarters of Damascus were more attuned to their psychological and physical needs than modern people. Perhaps they were less distracted from their physical requirements by extravagant entertainments, or less able to compensate for discomforts with air conditioning and central heating. Even though old quarters in Damascus develop organically and haphazardly, in the end they emerge as a design admirably suited to a human population.

In these quarters long narrow alleyways connect at odd intervals with broader arteries where cars can pass. The narrow uneven pavement of the alleys discourages the access of vehicular traffic and makes residential areas more peaceful places to live. Pedestrians pass under the shaded arches of houses bending toward each other to take optimum advantage of space. The next level of branching lanes, more often than not, ends in blank walks that are not apparent until one turns a corner and suddenly finds nowhere to go.

With gentle admonition, they discourage the passage of any but residents, and in the process preserve the privacy and intimacy of neighborhood and family life. This life is of higher priority than providing time-saving throughways with direct access to main arteries. Such a complicated maze brings a new dimension to physical space. Without the usual cues to distance, the mind imagines spaces with larger-than-life proportions.

I remember going to see what remained of an old quarter that was bulldozed to make way for modern buildings. The shock of seeing an empty field where once there had been one of the most beautiful old quarters of a Syrian city was great, but not as great as the realization that an area which had seemed to contain endless houses and people piled on top of each other in randomly scattered alleyways could be reduced to so small an acreage of empty space. Perhaps it is this unpredictability and the knowledge of its illusionary power that makes the Middle Eastern city mysterious and delightful, beyond the capacity of a rational mind to measure too exactly.

I know, and one sees it from Siham's book, that Syrians do not always make strong distinctions between things, persons, events, and places, and their emotional feelings about them. It is not an inability to distinguish the difference rationally, but rather a preference for feeling emotional attachment to animate and inanimate objects and a hope that the feeling is somehow reciprocated. It makes the world of objects come alive, imbuing them with a vitality worthy of the feeling expended on their behalf. It is a part of the culture that is important to convey even though at times it may appear overdone.

In 1981, when bulldozers suddenly descended on the lovely old leather suq crowded against the walls of the Citadel, and leveled it rapidly to the ground, the story went around town that a large serpent had been found in the ancient walls of the suq. Belief has it that serpents of this magnitude often guard a treasure of some kind. So, after the beast was duly slain, the story goes, workmen searched the walls where it had been found and came upon an old chest of gold Russian coins. I have the story from the daughter of a shopkeeper who saw the serpent, and because she is a reliable informant, I feel the story has some basis in fact, however remote. In its magnified form it can be seen as an allegory of the kind Syrians like, where the treasure is the suq, with its protector, the snake, slain by the unconscionable actions of a city government that destroys the heritage of the past. The story certainly symbolizes the unspoken feelings of the dispossessed shopkeepers.

Serpents who live in the walls of the old houses are harmless, some Syrians have told me. You can hear them breathing at night, and as long as a bit of food is left for them they stay in their place and do not harm people. I know of at least one person who ritually leaves an offering for the snake in her wall. Are the walls breathing, or is it the snake? Is it the walls that look down benignly on people, or is it the contented snake? It would be dangerous to take these analogies too far, for it would violate the image of a people who in general are well planted in reality. But it would be a mistake not to recognize the strain of, if not animism, at least a strong emotional attachment to familiar objects. It is the deceptively complex and private world of their dwellings and cities that lends itself to such imaginative musings and obscures the full knowledge of reality to even those who command complete access to their inner world.

The love of material objects comes through in Siham's book in her loving attention to the details of architecture, the furnishings of houses, of dress and jewelry, the accouterments of the bath, and the elaborate variety of food. For the most part, this form of materialism is less an obsession with value or costliness, and more the desire of people to surround themselves with objects that improve the quality and aesthetic pleasures of life. Women want to feel feminine, and want to clothe, bejewel and perfume themselves in a way that brings out their femininity. The descriptions of the bride's apparel and the numerous changes of clothing during the wedding party is a case in point. Similarly, people like their houses filled with the material objects that connote a luxurious, ideal and coveted way of life.

In the introduction to the Arabic version, Siham includes a letter written by Dr. Sabah Qabbani in praise of her book. In it, Dr. Qabbani made an analogy between her work and a piece of Persian carpet his uncle once rescued from his burning house. For Dr. Qabbani, Siham's registering of an old way of life that was fast disappearing was similar to his uncle's rescue of a precious work of art. Better than any other example, his story illustrates the urban Syrian's appreciation of beautiful objects:

> I don't know why your lines remind me of a valuable Persian carpet which was at my uncle's house. This uncle of mine used to live in the time of the Syrian Revolution in Sidi Amud lane, where Hariqa is today. His house was a masterpiece of genuine Damascene art with its decoration and skillful craftsmanship, and contained as well other works of art, Chinese bowls, and Persian carpets.

> When the French shelled the quarter and the Great Fire took place, the blaze destroyed his house and swallowed up all it contained faster than the wink of an eye. My uncle, with others fleeing in the dead of the night, ran to save himself

and his family but before he passed through the door of his house he stopped for a last look at his burning house. In that look was all he felt of sadness and grief and love and memories. Suddenly, a burning piece of the hall carpet flew up and landed at his side. He fell on it with his two hands, not caring about the fire, and extinguished the flames. Clutching it to his breast, he ran with it as if he were embracing the treasures of the earth.

Days passed, and the situation of my uncle worsened. He lived in a humble cement house in the suburb of Mazze but that piece of burnt carpet was given a place of honor in his home as a living symbol of the house which was lost. For him, it represented the decorations of his beautiful Arabic house, the spacious living quarters, the pots of flowers and jasmine, and the melodious fountain that were all part of his former residence—for my uncle that carpet he rescued was home.

This underlying strain of materialism supports a romanticized version of reality. Material objects of high perfection help to create the fantasy of a more palatable world. Yet underlying this romanticism, as noted above, is the pragmatic nature of Syrians. They see all too well the darker side of reality. Siham looks through the glitter and glamor of the bride and remembers the borrowed finery and difficult adjustments that are ahead of her. Wedding songs frequently note the irony of a perfection that falls short of the ideal. People are fearful that everything will not work out as well as they hope, and their sarcastic jabs at themselves and life protect them from too painful a disappointment when dreams do not come true. Note the mother-in-law who immediately after the picture-perfect wedding of her son, starts casting aspersions on the daughter-in-law she has so painstakingly selected. She mentally prepares herself to go out and start all over again in case this bride does not produce children within the year. She does not feel confident enough that all will go well, and prefers the pessimistic preparation for worst eventualities.

Or read through the proverb examples, and note the theme of warning against the possible pitfalls of life. This note of pessimism, of what can go wrong, leavens the descriptions in the book just enough to keep them from an unnatural and overly sweet romanticism.

Syrian humor, in significant part, is based on this dark view. Note the sarcastic witticism of the peddler bargaining with his customers. Or read the two small Damascene dramas: one, the story of Aiwaz and Karakuz, is based on two shiftless characters who will go to any length to avoid work, even, as we find in the end, to marrying a rejected wife who appears to have some property. The humor in the other drama, which takes place in a dentist's office, is based on the characterizations of the patients, the familiar types of everyday life who drive others mad with their exaggerated penuriousness, their literalness, their circuitous reasoning, and their virtues magnified to vices.

The book provides us with valuable insights into the science of human relationships, an interest and a field in which Arabs in general have developed a level of expertise and sophistication hard to find elsewhere. The chapter on pigeon keeping, for example, is a disguised explication of the types and qualities of relationships between human beings, in this case described in the context of bird training. The detailed rules and understandings that govern the flock keeper's behavior and the form negotiation takes in the case of conflict can all, without resort to very much imagination, be generalized to human intercourse on a broader scale than the isolated example of the birdkeeper.

From the keeper's perspective, his relationships are of three kinds: accord, buying, and hunting. "Accord," or exchange, is a relationship well established in Syrian society. In the rest of the book we see the importance of exchanging visits, gifts, help and solace. It is almost mandatory that an emotional sense of connection be cemented with some material token, whether it be the dowry payment for the bride, the gift for a new mother, or food distributed at the appearance of a baby's new tooth. In this book, perhaps the most unusual exchange of all is that provided by Um Husni, who parlays her possession of an elaborate set of jewels into a lively social life for herself, as she is invited night after night to lend her jewels to brides and enjoy a continuous stream of weddings.

"Accord" in social life generally, as with the flock keepers, takes place between those who are well acquainted—friends or relatives, and is based on a rough equivalence of position. Though the act appears altruistic and in fact may be just that in any one transaction, the expectation is that over the lifetime of those involved there will be rough equivalence in the exchange of goods and services. "Buying," on the other hand, is a relationship based on payment for goods and therefore is a completed act with no deepening of personal relationship or feeling of long term commitment. And, finally, "hunting" is an activity where a person sets out to increase his own gain by depriving another. It is an activity designed to create animosities, and may lead to continuing transactions of the negative kind.

In a certain sense this modest chapter maps out a model for personal relationships. It is fascinating to see how a Damascene hobby that on the surface appears nothing more than a matter of training birds, meticulously mimics the approved rules of social behavior.

Proverbs go a step further by explicitly setting the rules for human behavior, defining what should and should not occur. Like proverbs everywhere, however, there is a great deal of contradiction, so that people of opposite frames of mind can always find a saying to support their point of view. What matters in the end is the purity of the intent more than the actual behavior itself.

Syrian society accepts a great deal of latitude from professed ideals of temperament and beauty so much lauded in poetry and prose. People like to build illusions around themselves and significant events to give the less-than-perfect the momentary appearance of perfection. Elaborate staging of traditions with vast supporting casts of rich costuming, dance, song, jewelry, prayers, apt expressions, and foods, surround the rites of passage in births, circumcisions, weddings, and death to help the centrally concerned figure assume the proportions of the role. Thus, the bride becomes the perfect example of beautiful femininity, the groom of handsome masculinity, through the support of props. The aim of course, in weddings, is to create the best possible appearance for this first meeting of the couple in hopes they will be attracted to one another. Not incidentally, the desire is also to create distracting activity to alleviate the nervousness both are bound to feel. And, meanwhile, all the supporting cast are amply compensated: potential brides parade their charms before the mothers of potential grooms; young men display their exquisite manners and thereby show their families to advantage; older men and women meet socially with their friends; and the scale of the wedding's entertainment and hospitality supports the family's reputation for years to come.

Yet on the other hand there is no attempt to hide with stage sets the discomforts of the woman in childbirth. The same beautiful bride becomes a physically distorted crude-tongued wench, and only elicits the sympathy of onlookers for her externally applied affliction. Her audience has come in a kind of bonding ceremony to experience this trial with her. People understand the attachment that grows between individuals who share joy, sorrow, anger, and mutual help, and take every opportunity available to co-opt others' friendship through these means. The Syrian proverb expresses this sentiment well when it warns, "Never take a friend, until you have quarreled." A person who remains true through a period of trial will always remain true.

By the time the young mother receives congratulations on her new son, she is restored to her original beauty (and her bridal dress) and, if anything, is more beautiful in the flush of her new motherhood with her sleeping baby lying at her side. The capacity of Arab audiences to stage events as they would like to see and remember them is infinitely supportive of the human actors momentarily cast in leading roles.

There are subtleties to all these human relationships, of course, that don't appear onstage. Everything is not all finery and roses. Family conflicts and jealousies emerge in the aftermath of the birth over the question of which women in the household are the best childbearers. No one criticizes the new bride or her relatives for raising victory cries over her proven abilities—it is expected, especially in the face of her mother-in-law's doubts. Similarly, at the time of marriage, the two faces of desire are recognized when the young girl is taught what she must say to the bridegroom in their bedroom. She must weave a delicate line between showing her intent to please him, and exacting concessions from him at a moment when, so theory goes, she is in the best position to get what she wants. The older women teach her how to make the most of the situation without losing advantage in an emotional abandonment to love.

In the description of the family picnic to the Ghuta, we see Siham's subtle eye for picking up the details of the psychologies of various age groups. There is the nice image of the little girl forbidden from swimming because she's a girl, and pleased with the punishment of her boy cousin who has fallen in.

The most loving attention to human relations in the book is of course devoted to family relationships, which it is well known are the basic glue of Arab societies. Siham's descriptions of family life are worth a study in themselves—her analysis of her mother's and father's behavior and the sophisticated way they bring up their children to feel secure and loved without undue pampering is an exemplary case in the child psychology of any society.

We learn a great deal about the actual details of bringing up children in this book. This is important information, and contrasts in many respects with societies like ours where children are brought up to be independent and self-reliant, and to depart the parental nest by the time they reach their early twenties. In Syrian society the object is different, to incorporate the child as a good, devoted, and lasting member in the family group until death. One can see how Siham and her siblings are carefully and sensitively drawn into mutually caring relationships. Through family gatherings she learns her place in the complex web of kin: where she stands, the degree of relationship, the obligatory people to whom invitations and support are required, the degree of trust she can expect. As a child she assumes responsibilities in the household early, learning where the best shops for particular items are, and knowing how to obtain a good bargain. She recognizes the sacrifices made for her by her mother who refuses to let her spoil her hands washing dishes. Yet, intuitively she knows that her mother's sacrifices are a way of holding the other members of the household in a loving captivity where they depend on her and she remains indispensable.

Children in most Syrian families tend to be well organized and disciplined, as can only happen in a culture that firmly knows the boundary of right and wrong, or correct behavior and incorrect behavior. Children are gently sensitized to the limits of these boundaries. A range of choice is not normally available within such definitions. Experience and age know best, even in such important matters as the choice of a marriage partner. The consensus of a group of highly educated Syrian women I once heard discussing these matters, was that parents' dispassionate choice of their children's spouse was far more likely to result in a successful marriage than the irrational choice of a child in the heat of love. When appropriate characteristics match in the partners, the marriage is expected to work. If they do not, the marriage is doomed.

Siham's description of the mother seeking a bride for her son is one of the best I have seen for recording the important details in spouse selection. It is not too far off the mark from the process used by most Syrian mothers today. The difference now is that the couple might be allowed greater freedom after the engagement to get to know each other before the wedding. And of course, in some instances now, the young people themselves may have seen a likely candidate and need only go to parents for final approval to initiate the marriage negotiations.

The text is full of examples of how children are drawn into active participation in family life. Note how summer holidays are spent with relatives, as are weekend excursions, and in the nicest example of all, children stay up late to join the big family gathering on a wet winter evening. At all these events the sexes of every age mingle. The entertainment moves smoothly and sensitively from one activity to another, so that no one's interests are long ignored: people may all join in the general game of the moment, or for a while the children may turn to their own games; an older woman sings a song she particularly likes, and then an older man starts up the proverb game. Each age group or individual feels responsible for entertaining the others, and in turn is indulged in his or her preferences. No one is allowed to monopolize the center of attention for long. Such a gathering is meant to be fun for everyone, and encourages all those present to concentrate on the larger group's activities rather than splintering for long into separate age or sex groupings. The ultimate result of course is cohesive family groups who come to enjoy each other more than outsiders or competing groups of nonrelated peers.

There is a kind of gentle conspiracy between adults in the bringing up of children. A Syrian once explained to me how Syrian fairy tales end with a line that translates roughly as "Well, that is how the story goes! Were you pleased with the way it ended or not?" As he explained it, this line provides the parent with an excuse for not telling another bedtime story. If the child answers "yes," the parent says, "Good, then you can go to sleep." If the child answers "no," then the parent says, "Well, you didn't like my stories, so you'd better go to sleep."

Another way of putting off a child is incorporated into known games and rhymes. When a mother is busy and a child is underfoot, she may tell him, go to your grandmother and tell her "to tie the sheep" or "to hold with molasses" or "the beans remain," all phrases that in the secret language between mother and grandmother mean "keep him entertained for awhile." The grandmother usually begins a stock song or story that the child thinks he or she has ordered up. In all these cases there is a firmness yet gentleness in the way the child is directed.

Children like those in the book that participate to such a large extent in the adult world learn early in life about the mysteries of that world—about sex, birth and death. They can put off the knowledge if they are not ready for it, as Siham does with her horror of death, and her confusion over some of the details of what goes on in the wedding, but eventually, slowly, even these unknown aspects are revealed to her and she learns her responsibility with respect to them. Children are rarely prevented entirely from knowing. For them, adult life is the fascinating center of existence around which the action of daily life takes place. They are like gaily colored butterflies fluttering near the attractive glow of adult activities but not fully engaging in them until they pass the rituals of marriage. To become an adult and share fully in those central activities becomes an obsession which shapes the behavior of children growing up.

A few points should be mentioned so they are not overlooked in the text. There is first the unusual custom in Lebanon and Syria of calling a child by the name the child should call the person addressing him or her. For example, the mother calls the child "mama" and the father the child "baba." Other relatives may call the child "uncle," "aunt," "grandmother," or "grandfather." Even complete strangers may call the child "aunt" or "uncle," as appropriate to the speaker's sex. It is a curious appellation that Arabs themselves find hard to explain. In the context of family values, however, it is a constant reminder of a familiar relationship that extends between the two persons involved, unlike a given name that stands for the individualism of a person. Much the same can be said for terms of address like Um Ahmed or Abu Ahmed, mother or father of Ahmed.

Family origin is a topic that surfaces continuously throughout the text. Siham describes the acutely embarrassing evening when her father tells the story of his boyish "bad" behavior in front of guests whom Siham and her mother think should be told stories to impress. Siham stresses the visitors' high status and the honor they bestow upon the household by the very fact of their visit. At another point, when Siham's father applies for work with the post office, the letter of inquiry asks about his origins, which presumably play a part in whether applicants are acceptable for jobs or not. Clearly, origins are significant in the appointment of high officers who are all addressed with the honorific Turkish titles Bey, Pasha and Affandi and who carry family names still recognized today in Syria as some of the best. There is significance, too, in belonging to a battalion where all the companies are commanded by the relatives of Siham's father, Fahmi.

Typical of Syria more than most other Arab states is the mosaic origins of its inhabitants. Even after centuries spent in the region, people are still considered Turkish, Algerian, Kurdish, Armenian, Arab, Circassian, and Assyrian. In a single family, such as Siham's, the origins can be diverse. On top of these distinctions are also the important distinctions of origin within the country. People are recognized as typically from Homs, Hama, Aleppo, Damascus, Dair al-Zur, or Suwaida. An even more fine-grained distinction is that of origin within Damascus itself. A family may be known to come from a certain area of the city, from Maidan, Bab Jabiyya, Suq Saruja, Bab Sharqi, Muhajjarin, etc. One result of modernizing trends is that families who once came distinctly from these different quarters now live side by side in modern apartment buildings, and no longer maintain the distinctions of their places of origin.

For those readers who are not familiar with Arabic, it is necessary to make a few comments about Arabic in translation, and about Siham's style and use of the language. About the latter, Sabah Qabbani in his letter praising the Arabic version writes:

> Boldness is the most important characteristic of the book—the way you describe Damascus and the Damascenes in colloquial Arabic. Many considerations must certainly have occurred to you, yet didn't stop you from writing this way. You must have imagined what the polite doubters would think, "How can a person who holds a degree in philosophy

write in colloquial Arabic, an educated woman writing in an
unrefined language just as it is found in the street, suqs and
baths?" All this I think occurred to you, and yet you decided
to ignore their "Oh how terribles!" and went on writing about
Damascus spontaneously and in a language as sweet as the
pure water that flows from brass lions into Damascene pools
with their floating melons and jasmine flowers.

Literary works are generally produced in a formal classical language
that, though usually modified now into a modern literary style, still remains
a far cry from the language of the street. Each geographical region within
the Middle East and even each region within a country may have different
dialects, different word usage, different expressions. Siham uses a
combination of modern literary Arabic accompanied with a large dose of
colloquial language, and on top of that some very specific Damascene
usages. The book as it stands in Arabic is very difficult for any non-
Levantine Arab to understand well, and in detail for any but a Syrian to
understand completely. I noticed that younger Syrians had some difficulty
with words that expressed the experiences of an older generation. Of course,
Siham's bold venture in trying to give as authentic a picture as possible of
Damascene life by expressing herself in the language of the person in the
street is lost in the English translation.

Also lost in translation is the beauty of written Arabic that cares a great
deal for the sounds of language, almost more than for the specific content.
Time and again I came up against sentences that sounded well in Arabic but
which in English, where greater attention is paid to logic in meaning,
produced contradictions not easily resolved. For the sake of the English I
have taken the liberty to reconcile these specific bits of content.

There are other difficulties in translating into English. Arabic repeats a
point several times in order to make a simple declarative statement, and
approves of using some of the same words repetitively. English prefers
parsimony, and if repetition is necessary likes to find new words to express
the same thing. Arabic loves the long sentence connected periodically with
"and." English prefers the staccato punctuation of short sentences and active
verbs. Arabic similes and analogies are often mixed, and may not be
technically consistent. English notices the inconsistencies and finds the
argument of the author weakened. Arabic exaggerates to make a point.
English prefers understatement. Arabs call on the name of God continuously
to support veracity in cases where Westerners might say "really" or
"indeed." In the same way that the Arab's world is pervasively filled with
God, so is language ever a reminder of that omnipotence. The English

language more readily compartmentalizes religious expressions and may even consider religious terms out of context blasphemous. For the Arab, use of such phrases as "God be with you," "Blessings on you," "May his soul rest in peace," and so on lend a grace to the language of everyday intercourse.

Arabic romanticizes and tries to appeal as much to the emotions as the mind. English prefers drier, less emotionally involved discourse. In Arabic it is the intention that counts as much, or perhaps more than, the actual outcome. It is important for the author to show sincerity and pure intent. A work is judged in large part by whether the author's motives and feelings are sincere. This is not true in English, where it is the logical structure and rational force of the argument that is primary.

In dealing with this problem of different styles in writing, I have made compromises. Where it is a question of making the English easier to read, I have made shorter sentences out of longer ones. I have cut some of the repetitiousness, and where there are two ways to express the Arabic meaning I have often chosen the more understated way. In the text itself, I have dropped out a number of pages from the author's preface which seemed redundant without adding much new content. I have kept enough of the preface, however, to show the strong feelings and attachment of Siham to her homeland. Overall, even though it is not always a completely sympathetic style for English readers, I have tried to retain enough of the feeling of the Arabic to provide an authentic context. Sometimes, my desire to retain the flavor of her work may have resulted in use of a slightly archaic-sounding English which I felt necessary to capture her Arabic phrasing, the play on words, her emotions and the sincere good will intended in the expressions used for greetings and wishing people well. One of the purposes of translating this work is to preserve in as authentic a way as possible a Syrian view of life. I would ask the reader to absorb the style of writing as part of the presentation.

The more the style and content appear alien, the more confidence we can place in its authenticity. This book was not dressed up for an American audience, nor was it written by someone who is familiar enough with American culture to know what would "sound good." Remember, this is a book written for a younger generation of Syrians so they will not lose the feeling for what is "authentic" in their culture. The greatest difficulties of translation, as one might expect, are found in the songs, proverbs and peddlers' calls which, more than simple prose, depend on rhythm, rhyme, and cultural understandings. At first I felt I should omit them all as meaningless in translation, and in fact I have omitted eight pages of poetry.

The proverbs and peddlers' calls were too extensive to include in the body of the book, so they can be found in annexes. Chapter Two in the original, Siham's story of her efforts to save the old city, have unfortunately because of space had to be left out. And I have dropped a chaper of definitions of Damascene Arabic terms, most of which appear in other chapters.[1] With the exception of these materials, however, I have included all other material with as accurate a rendition of meaning as possible. Choosing meaning as the most significant aspect to convey, of course, has meant a sacrifice of rhyme and rhythm, and in these respects the text is deficient. The most powerful and important reason for inclusion of these materials is that Siham has presented them within the settings in which they are used and appreciated in Syrian life. The vignettes are not complete without them, nor they without the vignettes.

A final point on style is one related to most artistic creations in the Arab world. They originate in a world view that is less linear than ours and thus, in certain ways, more complex and sophisticated. An artistic creation is like the geometric pattern that serves as the basis of decoration in the Middle East. The design extends infinitely in imagination beyond the frame that encloses it, with no identifiable point of beginning and end. This book is similar; it is episodic, with parts brought in here and there like a mosaic. There are few logical connectors between the parts, but together they contribute to a larger whole that gives a meaningful picture of Syrian life. There are few rising crescendos or dramatic climaxes that characterize Western literary pieces, and if anything the writing moves along in a continuous series of high and low points. The endings in many vignettes characteristically finish where the story began. This fusing of beginning and end provides the harmony and continuity in each episodic piece. Moreover, it is a statement about life that goes on and on with no clearly demarcated divisions outside of birth and death, and even these become obscured in the flow of human generations.

Nowhere is this more clearly represented than in Siham's juxtaposition of her chapters. In the first parts of the book, she tells us about current-day discussions on the fate of the old quarters of Damascus. Her last two chapters cover her father's experiences during the Balkan War and World War I. A linear mentality would have located these two chapters in reverse

---

[1] Siham and I also decided to omit the final part of the book, which describes an imaginary young woman musing about life. Sabah Qabbani and others felt these parts were not as authentic as earlier sections. The book is, in fact, two books in the Arabic, each standing independent of the other.

position, with the historical chapter preceding the contemporary chapter. There is design in this kind of presentation.

In these historical chapters which, by the way, are very valuable as personal accounts of a period for which little documented evidence exists from the common soldier's perspective, Siham's father relates the defeats of the Turkish-Syrian forces, and sensitively describes himself watching the British and seeing their disgust at the Turkish lack of discipline and organization. In his observations are some of the seeds of that ambivalence Arabs feel toward the West—the shame they feel in their inferior technical knowledge and their inability to organize themselves effectively. At the same time, they show the attraction Arabs feel for certain aspects of material Western society. The Arabs know they have much to offer to the science of human condition, but where in the modern world does such a science hold a premium? Where is it considered an art to know how to celebrate well and sensitively, to know how to contribute responsibly to group welfare, to welcome guests hospitably, to perfect the arts of cookery, and build houses that conform with bodily and spiritual needs so harmoniously?

In Fahmi's observations on the battlefront come clear the futility of war, of human life flung away so carelessly by superiors whom the common soldier has no choice but to obey. To what purpose? The objectives of war appear insignificant compared with the loss of so much human potential. The recounting of these war experiences partly explains the desire of people to keep up their festive feast days and their holiday family gatherings, creating a life of happiness and enjoyment that obliterates the empty days of war and occupation. "Our life wasn't always fun and games," Siham's mother says. "We lived through a lot of bad times and now want to make up for it."

By positioning the chapters this way, back to front, it is as if Siham is saying, "Look, in our history you find what explains us—our complexes and our sensitivities—now you can understand the hardships we have lived through and our pragmatic approach to life. You see how we make do with what we have, why we are ambivalent toward foreigners, hating their treatment of us in the past but admiring their material technology and their organizational skills. We are not convinced yet that we want all you have to offer. Our history explains how we have learned to live on two levels—one where we have open communication with our intimate circle of family and friends—and another public level where we might say one thing and do another. It is our defense against the psychological and moral dilemma that you outsiders originally presented us. Now that we have learned to behave that way we can extend those modes of action to the 'strangers' or oppressors within our own society, so that in the end no one can completely come to control us."

Though I put these words in her mouth, I think Siham would agree with me. She states the same thing in so many words when she criticizes the foreigners who come with plans to demolish certain parts of old Damascus, and the pervasive foreign influences that bring a taste for blue eyes and pinching buttocks, or modern dancing in underground velvet caves. She notes also the contradiction inherent in a situation where foreign tourists come to Damascus not to find an imitation of their own culture, but for a return to a simpler way of life and the appreciation of what is genuinely indigenous and rooted in its own values. It is the rapid disappearance of what she calls "our genuine Syrian culture" that prompts Siham to write *Daughter of Damascus,* so that the record of her family's and others' experiences with those traditions and customs may be preserved. It is a story of change that is being repeated again and again in the Middle East of today.

Note About the Transliteration of Arabic

In this book Arabic words for which there are no direct English equivalents are transliterated using the Middle East Studies Association system outlined in the International Journal of Middle East Studies. To avoid what to publishers is the tedious task of providing diacritical marks, simplifications have been made. Thus, in English, no distinction is made between the Arabic letters <u>siin</u> and <u>sad</u>, which express lighter "s" and heavier "s" sounds. When accepted English equivalents of place/names exist, these have been used. Care has been taken to avoid mistakes but because of the difficulty in transliterating Arabic into English, some may have inadvertently crept into the text. Those that appear are the responsibility of the translator.

Andrea Rugh

Siham Tergeman in her old neighborhood in the Suq
Saruja, 1978

About the Author

Siham Tergeman was born in Damascus in 1932, in what was the conservative environment of a traditional quarter. Women primarily fulfilled the roles of wife and mother, and few at that time carried their educations, if they were fortunate enough to receive them, to higher levels. Because her parents were more liberal than others of the quarter, Siham was one of the fortunate women to attend the University of Damascus and eventually to receive a Bachelor of Philosophy degree in 1955. After university, Siham says, she was the first woman of her generation to take up journalism as a profession. Now she is the Director of Planning in the Media Branch of the Ministry of Defense in Damascus.

Her book translated here, *Ya Mal al Sham*, which means literally "the treasure (wealth) of Damascus (or Syria)," was published first in 1969 and later reprinted in 1978. In September 1985, the Tlas Publishing House published a second book called *Ah! Ya Ana* (Oh Me) and late in 1985 a third book called *Jabal al Shaikh fi Baiti* (Al Shaikh Mountain in My House).

Author's Preface

I hope that my book will refresh the souls of lovers of Damascus in the way a cup of *fija*[1] water from the good, pure, fresh Barada revives the spirit on a moonlit evening in the hottest part of the summer. I hope it will perfume their souls in the same way that a few drops of flower water[2] flavor our glasses with the tang of *naranj*[3] and lemon blossoms in those old Arabic Damascene homes of ours that are aged like kegs of wine in ancient Arabic churches.

The water of Damascus is the most tasty in the world. I became accustomed to drinking it with a few drops of flower water, as my mother, and my mother's sisters and my father's sisters did. It is a Damascene tradition that I want to keep alive in my home and in the homes of the people of Damacus. I hope I will be able to perpetuate the custom, maintaining its continuity from the old Damascus that was, into the new Damascus that will come.

I do not remember ever offering a cup of coffee on a tray to a guest without also offering with it a glass of cold water and a *qumqum*[4] of flower water. Next to these was always another coffee cup filled with water, not coffee, containing a floating blossom of jasmine or iris if my guest came in summer, or one red Damascene rose, the color of the setting sun, a white carnation or some violets with tender leaves if the guests came on a rainy day in winter. How confused my guest would be! Should she drink the coffee or the violet, or the flower water or the Damascus water?

My mother's aunt, Um Jafr, sister of my mother's mother Um Aziza, used to pray the morning prayer correctly as it should be done and then she would drink her morning coffee in the courtyard of her house, sitting among her pots of pampered plants and plucking at the jasmine as the morning light was dawning. I too would drink my coffee with one jasmine blossom floating in it. Between the two of us, my aunt and I, exists a thousand and one jasmine blossoms.

In my aunt's courtyard and at my house, there were a thousand pots of jasmine and in the courtyards of my older relatives another thousand.

---

[1] Much of the water for Damascus originates in the Fija springs, flowing down the mountains behind the city and feeding the homes through the seven branches of the Barada River. In the old city, public taps are called "fijas."

[2] An essence distilled from blossoms.

[3] A citrus fruit.

[4] A brass bottle used for sprinkling flower water.

1

Honoring our house now on the modern cement, one last tin of jasmine remains to remind me of my mother's smell...it is her jasmine. I water and indulge it and am anxious that it live.

I try to make it up to the tins of jasmine which my father cared for with his own hands, trimming them and bringing them up as he brought us up with patience and indulgence. My mother watered them with cold sugarless tea and fertilizer she brought from "Biru al-Atar." She fed them from the depths of her heart just as she fed and watered us. I try to turn back the time by watering my mother's jasmine with the water of my heart in a moist spray of flower water tears. And in so doing my soul returns peacefully to my breast. I imagine myself back in the Damascus that was and try to repay the debt I owe by blowing in the breasts of young Damascenes, the spirit of the great Damascus which sanctifies and loves God and people and life and love and land and animals and plants and water and sun and moon and mountains and river.

The pilgrims who passed through to the holy lands to Jerusalem and to "Mecca the bountiful" on their way to fulfil the obligation of Pilgrimage called her "Damascus, the honorable." The pilgrims discovered she is a generous city, because of her inhabitants—those who sought refuge in her as a second homeland and are filled with pity, love and generosity.

Through her passed prophets, holy messengers, and saints. To her south, exactly at the village of "al-Qadam," the Arab Prophet Muhammad, peace be unto him, stopped. On the way to Damascus and in the "Straight Street," St. Paul walked, passing through the East Gate to spread the religion of Christ in the world. Because she is a beautiful city with a natural attractiveness, she appeals to tourists, poets, artists, scientists, researchers, historians, kings and all those who attend to the heroes of history. She attracts them through her panoramas that include her old Arab houses, her alleyways and quarters, her markets, mosques and churches, all the way to the gardens of the Ghuta,[1] that world's homeland for the spring season, to the river Barada with its seven branches, to Qasyun Mountain, to the waste lands and the deserts of Damascus that surround the Ghuta, to the blue sky embracing the city and to the sun with the heat of life and warmth of love.

My feeling for the city has dominated the three stages of my life, so that Damascus is my past, my present and my future. As far as the fourth stage is concerned, following my life on earth, I will be united with Damascus in an everlasting mortality. It will be a "living" period in which I will feel affection for Damascus in the same way as in the first three. I have

---

[1] The fertile agricultural land near Damascus.

the same love for Damascus that I have for the mother-of-pearl and the bone and metal decorating my mother's cupboard, the one crowned with a high board on which is written in Arabic script the saying I love: "Fulfilling a need." It is the same feeling I have for the pieces of mother-of-pearl glittering like diamonds on the furnishings that were prepared for the wedding of my mother 'Aziza and the chest of drawers of my grandmother Um 'Aziza, or like my love for Koranic passages and popular Arabic poems and sayings, for "lucky" decorative wood carvings in my "book and notebooks" that are really the walls of the "fortress," that high room in which my father Fahmi slept. My feeling for Damascus is like the strong affinity golden bracelets and rings of pearls, diamonds, carmelians, emeralds and turquoise have for the fingers and wrists of the beautiful young girls of Damascus.

I feel also that Damascus...the old city...is attached to me in the way that the trailing branch of the jasmine clings to the worm-eaten wood of the bannister on the staircase of our tall, vine-covered house. Damascus permeates my life as that vine permeates the walls, the ceiling, the windows and the houses of our quarters, or as the "water weeds," dahlias, magnolias, and blossoms of Indian apricot, sour lemon, citron, sweet lemon, naranj and the zaini[1] and black grape vines love the pots in the courtyards of our good neighbors-for-life—our beloved "relatives," that are like family but even more so, in the home of my "uncle" Abu Majid, 'Abd al-'Aziz al-Kilarji. Wall attached to wall and heart attached to heart. There lie the houses of the Sabbaghs, the Murtadas, the 'Awads, the Limunis, the Qanis, the 'Ashas, the Tarabzunlis, the Zarifs, the Affandis, the Dalatis, the Saqa Aminis, the Quhfs, the Pash Imams, the Dairis, the Nahas', the Fawzi Sabri Beys, the Ghala al-Halibs, the 'Asasa, the Zazas, the Turks and the homes of many more whose doors I remember but whose names escape my memory.

The incline of Qaramani[2] starts from Suq Saruja facing Quli Lane. Our street, Qaramani, is curved. On the right side is the shop of Uncle Abu Rashad, the grocery of Kamil al-Ahmadi and his brother Manzur al-Ahmadi. Our street ends with the public bath, also called Qaramani, and with the shop of Majid al-Fawwal[3] and Suq al-Atiq on your right, and stops at the other end at the houses of al-Murtada and Zirif Affandi on your left, and

---

[1] A variety of sweet grape.

[2] Qaramani is the name for a part of the old city, taken from the street of the same name that is the major throughway bisecting the area.

[3] A *fawwal* is a person who sells cooked and spiced beans, a staple of popular areas.

3

with Khan al-Zait[1] and al-Qatran next to the Dalatis' house. From Khan al-Zait, the street continues through the Suq al-Atiq and Suq al-Tibn[2] and from there emerges into Suq al-Hal[3] at the railroad track. Before Khan al-Zait on your left, our street penetrates Suq Saruja at the Turkish bath and the 'Azm Palace, ascending to Suq al-Hal and al-Samani lane.

In the very heart of the Qaramani district at the point where three roads cross, was the strategic place at which the famous old beggar of our quarter, "Abu Da'as," used to compete with the beggar "Abu Abdu" and exchange worries about life, wife, and children with Abu Anwar, the sellar of *tirmis*[4], and the seller of sweets, Abu al-Saleh. Abu Da'as used to compete for the place at the Qaramani crossroads with the female begger of our quarter and all the quarters of Damascus, the crazy Ikram and her mother. Sometimes he would become disgusted with the goings and comings of those crazy beggars and would ask in poetry for a "good deed" holding in his hand a bird[5] decorated with wax flowers as he sang:

> Bird, oh bird, passing without knowing where she goes,
> Getting on, getting off trams,
> Travelling from Marje square to Shaikh Muhai-al-Din in Salhiyya Street,
> To Muhajjarin to al-'Amara, to Bab Tuma to al-Qasa'a and Maidan and Duma

Still today the beggar Ikram roams about in her dirty patched wrap through the popular quarters of old Damascus and the modern streets where the bourgeoise live. I still give her "good deeds from the wealth of God," and she returns to me a "May God compensate you." I smile at her, my eyes filling with tears, and feel uplifted for the price of a "good deed" at a Syrian penny from my pocket money or a pound from my salary, the difference one that comes from two periods separated by 33 years, and two quarters of the city, the old popular quarter called Suq Saruja and the modern aristocratic area called Abu Rumani.

---

[1] A place name meaning the commercial center where oils were sold. A "Khan" usually contains shops on a lower floor and storerooms and places to sleep up stairs.

[2] The Suq for fodder.

[3] Where vegetables are sold.

[4] A chickpea-like legume.

[5] A bird symbolizes one who has gone mad.

4

That crossroad in Qaramani, near where the public drinking fountain went dry, is still overlooked by the protruding lattice work windows of five neighboring houses: the homes of the Tergemans, the Kilarjis, the Murtadas, the 'Awads and the Sabbaans. The heads of the girls, young women and wives of these houses, appear and then disappear watching the passers-by, listening to their conversations, or looking to see who is hammering at the brass knockers of their front doors. Those who knock can not make out their forms above, as though they were beautiful, Eastern ghostly beings for whom hearts beat, or shadowy veiled women, or Arab spirits mad at their lovers and in turn driving their lovers mad.

All my being loves this old city Damascus in the same way that ladies love moon-shaped small windows high in their rooms, or passageways or salons, or the way I love the residential areas where my family and relatives live in the old quarters: Bahsa, Shala, Quli, Mufti, Ward, 'Ubaid, Bunduq, Samana, "The Place where the Monkey Lost its Son," 'Amara, Madhnat, al-Shahm, Shaghur and Bab Barid, Qanawat, Baridi, Suwiga, 'Asaglan, Bab Misala and Maz al-Qusab.

It is the love the pidgeon keeper has for his neighbor's roof-top in our quarter, or the love of the rain for the holes in our red, mud and straw-covered roof. It is the love of our small pampered kitten "Shama" for sleeping and snoring and gurgling in the folds of the quilt on rainy winter nights under the leaking ceiling, or her love for playing with thread spools, or with our hands or between the little seedlings in the flower beds, or for sleeping and being lazy or stretching or sucking on the white hair of the sheep skin cover where she stretched out on our wooden bench, cushions, carpet or straw mat. It is like the love she had for eating the thin film of tissue covering the meat or for stealing a piece of meat or fish from the neighbor's kitchen when she became bigger and began jumping the wall that separated us from the house of the neighbors.

My spirit loves Damascus as the hornets and wasps love the bunches of grapes hanging from the vines of our arbor, and as the dry wood loves the fire madly thundering inside the pot-bellied stove—that dear stove—which roasted chestnuts in the ashes under its open door in the middle of December in our sitting and night rooms. It is as the smell of the frying eggplant on the kerosene stove loves to drift through the air of the orchards lining the pure waters of "'Ain al Kirsh" when we go there with our mother and father on Friday, the day we have a holiday from school.

And Damascus loves me in exactly the same way as her charming bygone summer evenings love the chords of the lute, and the melodies of the special songs called "Basharif," songs like Basharif "Tatyus," Basharif

"Hijaz Karkarada" and Basharif "Uthman Bey" and Basharif "Sama'i" and the melodies of rounds, solo recitals, poems, and songs wafting through the air from lutes made by the best lutemaker, and from the best of the selections of the Damascene composer and musician "Subhi Sa'id."

Damascus loves me—before my birth, during my life and after my death. Damascus is my spring, summer, autumn and winter. Damascus is my mother, father, sister, brother, husband, lover, son and daughter, grandson and granddaughter, grandfather and grandmother, friend and neighbor. Damascus is all the people of "Sham" who live in her and have died in her and all those who will live there in the future.

Damascus is my relatives: my aunts and uncles both maternal and paternal. Damascus is old respectable families from the East, like the one to which I belong on my father's side—the Tergemans.

Others include the Basrawis, the Sadats, the Halabis, the Shainis, the Qatans, the Idlibis, the al-Sharifs, the Talu Aghas, the Safis, the Tahhans, the Barakats, the Mushtashims, the 'Albis, the Ustaz, the Nazirs, the Jililatis, the Shalabans, the Jabris, the 'Ijas, the Istawanis, the 'Audas, and the Murads.

Damascus is also families from the West—from Algeria, to which I belong on my mother's side from the quarters of Maidan and Suwiqa: the Habbals, the Yanyuis of Algeria, the Bahluls, the al-Sharifs, the Khalifawis, the Yahyawis, the Yalaqubis, the Zubyans, the Dubas, the Tawils, the Hashamis, the Majids, the Barakats, the Jumas, the Sarijas, the Tayyibs from Morocco, the Tayyib Mubaraks, the 'Ammars and the Shaikh Mishriqis.

Damascus is the genuine old families of my neighbors and relatives, and the many families of acquaintances and friends. The families of Damascus are linked through marriage as is the case for the Qabbanis, the Sukirs, the Jabris, the Nuris, the Mahaynis, the Habbabs, the Mahmaljis, the Ashmars, the Bitars, the Midanis, the Taba'as, the Qawadris, the Qawatlis, the Bakris, the Zains, the Kharsas, the 'Abids, the Lahhams, the Qssabs, the Diabs, the Baqdunis, the Zahras, the Qashlans, the Shaghlils, the Qadamani, the Hamuddas, the Murads, the Hakkis, the Adlibis, the Jalads, the Qatriyyas, the Akribuz, the Halabis, the Bunis, the Trabulsis, the Qurbis, the Qallis, the Luwstans, the Sharbajis, the 'Uwaishaqs, the Muluk, the Shamis, the Shammas, the Abu Shalar, the Sab'as, the Asbars, the Luwis, the Khabbaz, the Qashishus, the Shalabys, the Farahs, the Malaks, the Qandalifts, the Kassab, the 'Absis and the Mishaqas, and many others.

Damascus is the Syrian people and my people.

6

My mother 'Aziza gave birth to me in the 'Amara quarter in the month of December 1932 when the earth was covered with snow. My "mother" Syria gave birth to me the second time in the Subqi quarter on the fifth of June in 1967 with a world at war. Between the first and the second births, Damascus was born inside me and assumed its shape. Between the two points, the two houses, and the two times was born my calling as a writer about my old Arabic city. At some point between the quarters of the old genuine Arab Damascus with their Eastern character: Suq Saruja, Maidan, Qanawat, Shaghur, Qimariyya, Salhiyya, Muhajjarin, Bab Tuma, and Hamadiyya, and the quarters of modern Damascus with their western character: Abu Rumani, Subqi, Mazr'a, Malki, the new Mazze, Baghdad Street, and Tijara, Truth was born out of contradiction. At the same time my book *Ya Mal al-Sham* was born out of a sense of danger that the Arab personality of Damascus would be lost both to the threat of a hostile Israeli occupation and the menace of civilization's axe forging a modern age through elimination and destruction.

The genuine Damascus was born out of the womb of my spirit and I became the mother of the biggest daughter. My fate presents me with the dilemma of whether I am a daughter of Damascus or the spiritual mother of Damascus, or whether I live in Damascus or whether Damascus lives in me or whether I am a human body whose spirit is composed of a city with Arab houses, gardens, rivers, and mountains or whether I have become a city that once upon a time had houses made from mud, water, wood, straw, colors, stones, marble, colored glass, flowers, poetry and love, and now builds them from cement, iron, aluminium, tar, tiles, selfishness and a love of money. This old city/new city settles into the breast of a woman made of flesh and blood, and the woman becomes herself a city embraced by its spirit, a woman representing all women.

My responsibility to Damascus is the responsibility an Arab knight has to defend his genuine origins. If it is my fate to record every word and wisdom said about Damascus, then out of my love and admiration, I will accept this mission.

My book *Ya mal al-Sham* is a billboard dedicated to the love I feel for my homeland and the sanctity of Syrian culture expressed in Damascene life. This billboard drawn with a paint brush dipped in my heart, my mind, my past and present is a spontaneous creation of my emotions and my beliefs.

7

Daughter of Damascus
Ya Mal Al-Sham[1]

Chapter One

Oh treasure of Damascus, Oh God, my treasure. The time is so
long, my beauty, come here to me.
The time is so long and in my mind's eye, I see a beauty mark
appearing high on her cheek.
The time is so long and it grows longer, the beauty paces
back and forth, Oh God, bring back that wonderful day in the
past that escapes me.
The time is so long, my eyes spill tears and my heart is so
full I can't talk, Oh God.
If my lover becomes my own it will be a day too wonderful to
imagine; it is so long since we have seen each other.
It was a dark day when we said goodbye to them, Oh God, how
I wish you could bring us together again, such a wonderful day
I can hardly imagine.

This authentic old Damascene song was composed and set to music by
the Damascene artist Abu Khalil al-Qabbani. The late excellent artist is still
and will remain immortal, a treasure of Damascus as undying as the immor-
tality of Damascus itself.

The older we grow the more we feel nostalgic for our childhood and the
playgrounds of our youth. Whenever I walk in the modern streets of
Damascus, my longing grows for the old quarters. When I am overcome
with emotion for my childhood, I see a small girl holding a ball in her hand
and wearing little colored wooden clogs on her feet. When I go back to the
old quarters where our ancient house sleeps or to the suqs with their smell
of age, I find that my attachment to things that are old is stronger than to
modern ones. I discover that the only pure reality in my soul is the reality
of childhood, as if childhood is a being, aware of what goes on around it,
clinging to what is most genuine in order to keep it from changing. This
reverence for the past reassures me that my knowing, attentive, pure childhood will reject anything false that tomorrow might offer.

I long for the past, for its purity, and for the child who was two children, one who played and one who watched the one who played. I see that

---

[1] The original title of the book in Arabic was "Ya Mal al-Sham," the "Treasure
of Damascus," or of Syria (Sham can mean either). The name of the book was
taken from the song translated here.

child clearly, that child who loved the past and stored it for my sake, jewel-like in its purity without imitation as though it were an old precious gem passed on to my mother by my grandmother from her grandmother and from her grandmother's grandmother, an amulet warding off the surprises of the future.

That child loved playing and jumping rope with the girls of the quarter on stone streets running between the worn walls and low nail-studded wooden doors of Suq Saruja. In summer she played near heaps of watermelon rinds and garbage and in winter in mud and pools of water left from the rain. In the narrow alleys the walls of the houses of the quarter inclined toward one another in an ecstasy of love, forced to kiss each other from the pressure of crowding. High windows, hidden by wooden lattice work, concealed the charmingly curious eyes of the women.

That child who has now become a teenager, and rationally convinced of the laws of development, nevertheless rejects the rows of new high buildings like cardboard boxes, the wide smooth asphalted streets with smart villas set far apart from each other and neighbors who pass by without even a "good morning." I am a daughter of the old Damascus that sleeps shyly and quietly and contentedly there in the lap of the Ghuta under the eye of Mt. Qasyun... that mountain that used to carry on its peak, its face and its slopes those landmarks that aroused the people's faith and awe: the "Chair of the Midwife," "Sayyar's Dome," "The Forty," "People of the Cave," and the grave of Shaikh Muhyai al-Din, son of Araby.[1] The Midwife's Chair flew apart with the cannons of the French, the people of the Cave—the Forty—sleep in a deep sleep, and the Sayyar's Dome was transported away from the terraces of prickly pear and in its place buildings were planted. Modern streets extended up to the holy place of the Shaikh, Son of Araby, and on the bald head of the mountain in place of the "Midwife's chair" rose the high antenna of Syrian television with a light that winks like a red eye in the night.

I am one of those daughters of Damascus who planted their footsteps since childhood on the ground of her stoney quarters... on the cobblestones poking out like hard boiled eggs in the narrow pathways of her suqs, the Ghuta and her orchards—tracing a map of sheer joy in the attachment of the people for the suqs of their country: Suq Hamadiyya and its smaller suqs of Khuja, Hariqa, Asruniyya, Harir, Qishani, Silah, Miskiyya, Khayattin, Bab Barid in Suq Midhat Pasha, and its small branching suqs like the Wool Suq

---

[1] These were all landmarks on the mountain that provides a back drop for the city of Damascus.

10

and the Cotton Suq, the Ladies' Suq and the Bizuriyya Suq; in Suq al-Atiq and its smaller suqs of Khan al-Batikh, Khan al-Zait, and Ali Pasha, Juza al-Hadba, Suq Saruja and Suq al-Hal.

My childhood is inseparable from the old Damascus quarters of Maidan, Shaghur, Qimariya, Qanawat, Suq Saruja, 'Amra, Bab Tuma, Q'sa'a, Shaikh Muhyai al-Din, and Muhajjarin and the districts of Sham...Quli, Ward, Shalla, Samana, Siti Zaituni, Aqiba, Bawabat al-As, al-Saba'a Twala'a, Nufara and in the Bahrat al-Dafaqa, Manakhliyya and Bab Sarija.

Until now I still long for our house in Suq Saruja which they used to call "Little Istanbul" because of its people's origins, its beauty and genuineness. In this quarter of respectable origins I was created. My mother became pregnant with me in the Quli quarter, bore me in 'Amare, nursed me in Manakh and we lived in a number of houses, the last of which was our beloved house in the Qaramani quarter. Our relatives lived in Ward, Shala, Bahsa, Samana, Aqiba, Maz al-Qasab, Dawragha and the Madhnat al-Shahm quarters.

As was the case in the majority of the old houses, we did not have facilities for bathing in our home. For this reason during my childhood I had the pleasure of frequenting the famous public baths of Damascus. The weekly visit to the bath in the suq was as enjoyable to my sisters and myself as a picnic. How we used to love to slide on our knees in the bath on tiles covered with soap suds and endless streams of soapy water! Our innocent laughter echoed in the big chambers of the bath, rising with the steam to nestle in the ceiling like a fog and then return to us. The domes of the bath were illuminated with "the light of God" streaming through the many moons of colored glass. The reverberations of our echoing laughter only encouraged us in our determination to produce more playful sounds.

The bath of Qaramani was a permanent stage and an excellent playgound for the games of our childhood. But I musn't neglect to mention the baths of Ward, Juza, Fathi, Khanji, or Malika in Darwishiyya, the most beautiful bath in all Damascus. Sadly, I was deprieved of its pleasures because it was reserved for men. But I used to enjoy looking in at the door when I was a little girl. I would call out to my father to say I needed to speak to him, and as I hesitantly opened the door of the Malika Bath, a marvelous sight appeared before me, striking my soul as if by lightening with its charm. That image always stayed with me, even when the memory of the rest of the Darwishiyya quarter had faded from my mind.

Before going to the bath, we used to love the careful preparations for the enticing trip. We always carried a bundle[1] of clean clothes to the bath and another with things needed for the bath: a cup,[2] an Aleppo bath mit,[3] laurel soup from Aleppo, a lufa sponge, perfumed red powder, also from Aleppo, a wooden comb, another comb we called "white fish teeth," and a soft black pumice stone used to clean our heels, and clogs. Also we carred a bundle of clean handerchiefs, wine-colored towels striped with glittering threads, and white linens which we spread on the benches of the bath to sit on. When we came out of the bath, we put on our clean clothes that had been watched by the woman caretaker. This was all we took with us except for the special bundle mother carried for us with all kinds of delicious foods that we ate ravenously in the bath: oranges in winter and slices of bread with oil and spices, black olives and pickled turnips. Our favorite of the dishes we took was *mijadara*[4] with olive oil. In summer my father used to send us water melon and a jug of cold *'arqsus*[5] to revive our spirits in the burning heat of the bath. For a few piasters the attendant helped Mother wash our hair and scrub us all over. During the bath the woman in charge would pass by several times to make sure we had everything we needed. She greeted her customers warmly, addressing herself to the large white bodies draped in bath towels with a corner thrown over the shoulder. This arrangement of the towels added to the charm of the beautiful bodies which looked like statues of white marble wrapped in wine-colored draperies, lined with threads of gold. The atmosphere in the bath was one of pervasive well-being.

Over here stood a chaste bride and at that basin an old woman working henna into her hair. From her, across the floor of the bath, flowed a black disgusting stream that we avoided with quick leaps like those we used to jump over the narrow irrigation channels of the orchards. Next to the hottest chamber in the center of the bath, with the doors of rooms forming a circle around it, a woman who had recently given birth[6] sat impatiently. She had finished the two weeks of her confinement. They called this the "bath of

---

[1] "Bundles" were often wrapped in carrying cloths called "buqja" which were usually embroidered by or for the bride as part of her trousseau.

[2] A cup for dipping water and pouring over the owner.

[3] Like a wash cloth.

[4] Mijadara is made of lentils, rice and fried onions.

[5] A licorice drink.

[6] Two weeks after birth she is brought to the hottest section of the bath to sit on the scalding tiles.

separation."[1] Her body was painted a strange yellow color which emited a penetrating oder.

A trilling cry of joy came from the bride's chamber. A violent quarrel erupted between several women around one basin and came close to ending with a war of bath cups. At the neighboring stone basin a customer sat alone with her children, enjoying the water and ignoring the problems of the others. She had paid a high price for a "protected basin" that was hers to use alone. A child wailed in the lap of its mother when soap got in its eyes. A woman poured several final bowls of water on her head and then washed for prayer.

A mother took her child to the drain, hopeful that he might learn to do his duty and encouraged him with... Uh, Uh! By repeating this encouragement, she hoped he would learn to stop the habit of making "it" in his diapers. In her mind, she was prepareing a new conspiracy to wean him away from her breast; she would rub her nipple with aloe or coffee so he would find it disgusting and start eating food instead. Next to her at a nearby basin, a mother poured several cups of water on the last of her children, signalling that the bath was over, and said to him: "Your fingers are ten and your toes are ten, healthy heart and happiness."[2] A fat woman stood up to chase after her daughter who was running away. She beat her, pulling her by the hair and brought her back to the basin. She forgot her towel in her haste, and concealed "what should not be seen" with her bathing cup. A pregnant woman passed by, walking heavily—in what appeared to be her appointed month.

The cold water abruptly stopped in the basin of the mother with ten children so she shouted, "Cold...cold...cold." The attendant came running barefoot with a pitcher of water in her hands that were still black from the henna-dying operation. The pitcher she brought was filled from the outside pool of clean water.

A young woman hit a head of kohlrabi against the tiles of the bath splitting it in half. Two girls threw cold water at each other. A mother said to her son, "May you bury me,[3] come, you still have two more rounds, I've only washed it once." The hair must be washed the first round, the second round and the third round before the whole course is completed. To be

---

[1] Or they call it the "bath of nullification," to return the woman to her former condition.

[2] The expression is said as a protective charm or blessing.

[3] This is a commonly used expression of endearment. She implies that she doesn't want to be alive if her children are dead.

clean, all three rounds were necessary but the child could play and rest between the rounds.

In the room across the way, the women were beating on bath cups and clapping with wet hands, dancing and swaying from side to side. There were loud cries from several women when a new customer entered the bath with, among her children, a boy of ten, that they demanded must leave the woman's bath.

"It's not right for him to enter the women's bath... He's no longer little."

"Sister, by God, he is little!"

"No, not little. This one little? Better get out, boy, before we start screaming and bringing all the men of the quarter."

"By God, he isn't even seven yet."

"Dwarf... he's not still sucking at his mother's breast, is he? Go marry him off."

"No, better go and get his father."

"Get out! Go outside."

"I won't go!"

The insults became more intense until they reached a point where curses were exchanged between the boy's mother and a customer with a sharp tongue.

"Get out, I tell you!... Damn you, you insolent one!"

"I'm not leaving."

"May a bullet pierce your throat, if you come in here, we will tear you apart."

"If you dare even lay a hand on him! Don't think you are so important. Do you think he is alone with no one to stand up for him?"

"Curse your father and the father of the one who let you come in the bath! Get out, by God!!"

"Shame on you, what kind of gipsy are you, aren't you ashamed?"

"You are the gipsy, they should cry about you, what kind of civilized person are you, bringing men with you into the woman's bath?"

"By God, if you or he puts even one foot inside I will make drums of your skin."

"What is this problem all about, daughter, between you and her. Don't let the devil win out. Go out, boy. Get him out. God bless you, you are going to drive all my customers away. Send him back with his father in the morning, he has become a man, God save and protect him from the Evil Eye."

14

"Come, my son, come, even the head women has sided with this dirty tramp. Never in our lives will we step into this bath again."

"I'm a dirty woman, am I—God be with you—may obstacles block your path."

"Yo-oh, may evil strike you and your logic, *inshallah*."[1]

"God willing, the same to you and to ten others like you."

"Yoo-Yoo. May you bury this woman. You know, the best thing is not to answer at all and leave her barking uselessly like a dog. Come on son, may a fever strike her. She has infuriated me. Yo, may a fever consume her!"

"That's enough. Break it up. Haven't you had enough? My, how excited and stubborn you are! Come on, everyone, back to your basins. Come along with me outside. I don't want to make you angry, sister, but really it is difficult, the women naked and your son big, 'may you bury me,' and understanding everything. It's not right and you yourself wouldn't want it. You, dear, go home and tomorrow come with your father to the men's bath. You've become a young man. Soon you'll be growing a mustache. (And to the woman). Please don't go away angry. The whole bath is at your disposal. By God, I don't want you to be anything but satisfied, come in to the bath, you and these little children, and I know you will be glad you did!"

The boy went out and the violent scene ended.

The one thing that used to frighten me in the baths of the suq was the big red cockroaches that covered the walls, the ceilings and the basins and around the drains. Also, the sight that shocked me and made me run away to my mother was the sight of a woman hung with leeches at her breast or on her legs sucking her blood and dangling from her body, fat and thick, exactly as the men hang the leeches, they purchase from the barber, close to their ears. These barbers, the city's doctors at that time but no longer existing any more used to collet the leeches in large glass bottles. I would ask my mother:

"Why does she hang those worms on her boobs, mother?"

"Mama,[2] maybe she has phlegm in her chest, what business is it of ours? God help her. Why are you running away. Come here, let me wash your hair. We want to go home! Stop, you've had enough playing. Call your sisters and come right way."

"Oh, mother, God keep you, just a little more. We are sliding on our knees on the tiles in a place where there are so many soap suds!"

---

[1] God willing.

[2] She uses "mama" to address the daughter, a common usage in Syria.

15

"Come, you've had enough, evening is here." And I would go to call my sisters, keeping close to the wall to stay clear of the "leech woman" in my path. God be merciful, the sight of the suction cup used to cure coughing, with small pieces of paper on fire in it almost burning the flesh of a person's back is awful enough but this sight doesn't compare with the sight of the leeches.

Every Thursday when we finished school, we were happy because of the holiday that extended from the rest of Thursday and through all of Friday. We used to begin getting ready for the bath trip after lunch. Our hearts filled with anticipation of the pleasant time sliding on the suds, blowing soap bubbles to the ceilings of the bath, throwing cold water at each other, and playing with the other children. These enticing dreams crowding our minds made us willing to carry the loads; each one carrying a big or little bundle. But the eternal problem would be the one that emerged at the end of each bath. Who would carry the bundle of dirty clothes? I would start fighting with my sisters as we came out of the bath. Mother would be settling her accounts with the head woman who sat cross-legged on her bench behind the door of the bath, receiving all newcomers with *"Ahlan wa Sahlan"*[1] and all those departing with, "May this bath be a bath of pleasure." She counted the heads of old and young and decided the payment appropriate to the size of the family, and to whether the person was a regular customer or just a passing guest.

Our quarrel would come to an end with mother's order that each of us carry a bundle for a part of the time and distance and then exchange them so that the other must take it the other part of the way. We would be out of breath from the exertion when we reached our house, and go immediately dead tired to bed, happy that we had arrived safely at home.

Our house...no matter how much older I become, I am sitll homesick for our house...our spacious old Arabic home...and homesick for those things that still sleep and wake up in its courtyard: lemons, *kabada*,[2] naranja, grape vines, figs and tall jasmine climbers which drop blossoms like snow. You will find a central fountain there where water splashes from the Barada and Fija springs and water melon and jasmine flowers float in its pool.

In the planters of our house grew roses, hortense, perfumed 'atra, green ferns, shamshira, geranium, snapdragons and yellow jasmine etc. Beautiful

---

[1] Words of welcome.

[2] Kabad are like over-sized lemons the skin of which is used in the preparation of preserves.

fat pampered cats jumped fearlessly on to our house from the roofs of the neighbors. In my mind I see the kittens of our dear, beautiful, olive-colored cat "Shama" playing all over our old Damascus house. There were "Antar" the light colored one, "Fula" the white one, "Zaitun" the spotted black and white with a mole on his cheek like his mother, "Atra" the grey devilish one, "L'yba" the playful one that "read" at night, and "'Abdan" the black one that should bring luck but instead was eaten by "Harun" before he had a chance to grow up. Harun killed it in the evening without our knowing and then escaped by way of a platform to the roofs of our neighbors. My tears fell copiously on the body of the small kitten as I asked my visiting grandmother,[1] "Why grandmother, did Harun eat our kitten? Didn't you say he was his father? How could he eat his own children?" My good grandmother, May God be merciful to her, answered in a calm voice that convinced me, "Because Harun doesn't want to bring up his children to eat at the banquets of others."

With skill and the help of the wind my brother used to fly his beloved colored paper kites on long strings from the roof in great circles around the house. The little neighbor children ran around the balconies of their courtyards to see them soaring high in the sky.

We girls used to tie short cords to the legs of beautifully colored dragonflies, "flying" them on the balconies or playing with them in the courtyard under the grape vines or in the glare of the sun...those dragonflies...kind and gentle with their beautiful buzzing sounds. It was a different story with hornets and bees. They were our bitterest enemies when we tried to climb the grape vines for bunches of sweet native grapes in the courtyard of our house. I can taste them still. For bee or hornet stings we needed no other medicine than a clove of garlic.

I hate to mention the rest of the animals and insects in our house. We used to see snakes, scorpions, spiders, centipedes, lizards, rats, chameleons, mice, snails, ants and cockroaches, which I hate more than snakes. We fled from the snakes in our beautiful Arabic house to a modern house where snakes don't come out of the walls, and neighbors also don't bother to greet each other. There in that old house lies my true essence which I can never relinquish for the sake of a smart, clean, luxurious street in a new Damascus where houses rise high over the roofs of the city. I am attached to the old Damascene house whose land is the land of my beloved Syria. Today, I pay a price for rarified air, a price in longing and homesickness for the old house there...our house in whose walls slither snakes and over whose vines arbors

---

[1] Mother of my mother.

fly hornets, bees and wasps. It seems as if I mature toward a childhood of the past. I will never forget our old house.

Our old quarter lives in my consciousness like the pearl and coral in a popular song I used to sing with the neighborhood girls who were my companions. We would hold hands, singing and dancing in a circle in front of our houses, just as our mothers and grandmothers used to sing before the doors of their houses:

> Oh Grandmother...limping, limping
> The key to the pistol I have hidden behind the box
> My brother came and stole it
> He decked me out in ear rings
> Ear rings, "smear rings"
> The ear rings make me lose my mind
> Oh you daughters of kings
> They are coming to marry you
> On a piece of clay they built a city
> A city, a city, a city
> What brought you to our quarter
> Our quarter is pearl and coral
> Our quarter is lice and fleas[1]

And we would sing another song, never tiring of singing:

> Father, Father
> In the mosque repent
> We won't give her to you
> Unless you pay a thousand plus one hundred
> Oh cakes and cookies
> Expensive Damascene cakes
> Keep safe the beard of my uncle
> My uncle is in the country eating *tamariyya*[2]
> I ask him to feed me some
> He said, "wait until evening"!
> I came in the evening
> He beat me with a *tatariyya*

We would circle and sing and sing:

---

[1] In these songs the rhyming sounds, which are lost in English, are often as important as the meaning. The songs are included here for the snatches of meaning that give an insight into family relationships.

[2] A sweet.

Oh grandmother, our grandmother
In the gardens
Are sour pomegranates
Pick them and give them to us to eat
We swore we would not eat
Until father comes
Father is with the soldiers
Bringing me a dish of sugar
Melt it and give it to us to drink
Eat your lunch and follow us to the cold bath
May God harm you, you second wife, like you harm us!
I saw my uncle from far away
He spoke to me in Turkish
And made me cry

From the wooden lattice that screens our window, I used to lean out to see the reason for the children's noise in the alley. They would be running in circles about "Dabdabit," calling "Dabdabit, Dabdabit." I never knew his real name because he was only known by this name which means "an approaching storm." The arrival of this man Dabdabit was indeed like the approach of storm and God's anger. Dabdabit, the crazy man, loved his stomach. He would walk the narrow street asking everyone who passed "When master?" by which he meant "When will someone of you die so we can eat at your home?"

The people were superstitious about his arrival, but they would laugh anyway. Dabdabit had a wonderful memory and knew by heart all those in the city who had recently died, with their addresses. Indelibly printed on his mind were...the fortieth day after their death, the first year aniversary, the first Thursday after death and the first three days.[1]

In winter when it snowed—there was nothing I loved better than snow—the favorite food was *suwiq*. Suwiq is snow mixed with orange juice or molasses. We nearly collapsed once from laughter at a joke of one of our relatives. It was a stormy day with the snow covering all of Damascus to the height of a meter, and they sent us a big cake in a tin as a present. The whole family stood around it with each child holding his plate and waiting while my father began to cut into the cake. What a surprise to find under the cream topping, a cake of snow!!

---

[1] These are all occasions when it is appropriate to call on the close relatives of the deceased.

They say in Damascus not to eat the snow when it first falls. A popular saying goes, "First time is poison, second time blood, but the third time eat without worry."

When the snow fell mother would say to us, "Bless you, may you bury me, I hope it will be a 'white'[1] year," and we would run to the door of the street in our clogs. If one of us slipped and fell, the others would laugh at him. We would walk in the light snow cautiously, afraid that we might fall and provide amusement for the others. We would watch the groups of children roaming the streets and suqs in the snow singing and collecting money.

> Oh God, rain, Oh God send rain
> This year is white, Oh white
> God willing white, Oh white
> May God send material blessings
> Amen
> God Provides
> Amen
> God conceal the bad things about his wife
> Amen
> This year is white, Oh white
> God willing white, Oh white

There was one child playing "Baba Hassan," who according to my father would take off his clothes and paint himself with molasses[2] and then appear naked, except for white cotton stuck to the molasses on his body. It made him look like a white jinn or bear or snow man. He would wander around led by someone holding a rope attached to his neck repeating, "White year, may it be a white year," while the poor children of the singing group chanted in refrain "God willing it will be white, white." Each covered his head and back with some protection against the snow. The covering looked like a burlap bag worn as the hood of a trench coat protecting its owner against rain. People enjoyed this troop and welcomed them, responding generously to their singing with gifts of money.

They would not move from a spot in front of a store in the suq until they were paid. The owner of the store was forced to pay a "tax" for the cold, and the snow and their prayers. And of course the naked snow man

---

[1] "White" is equated with good.

[2] The molasses was a "dibs" of thick jam made usually from raisins but with a molasses-like taste and color.

who suffered more from exposure than his companions who took half the profits.

We would shut the door and climb up to the balconies of the courtyard to make a snow man from the accumulated snow there. We decorated him with a *tarbush*[1] and made him carry our father's cane, the one which with his tarbush he used to leave frequently at other houses or at the barber. He finally gave up the habit of wearing a tarbush and carrying a cane because of this problem of leaving them behind everywhere but he continued to forget his umbrella, often taking a long time to remember where he left it!

It was impossible for a person to pass under our windows without being struck by a snowball from the windows or roofs of our neighbors. I'll never forget how the French Sengalese Soldiers in a snowy year tried to imitate the people of Damascus when they played in the snow. They started putting stones inside snow balls and hitting the people in the street as if playing a game of imperialism with the white snow covering the blackness of the core inside. Winter in Damascus is a rich world of deep dimensions, in which the philosophical nature of man comes together with the wisdom of nature.

When it rains or hails in my city, "God brings good" and the children in the quarter sing this nice song:

The rain beats down on my niece's bald head
My niece bore a boy and called him Abd al-Nabi
She put him in the brazier and up sprouted a lemon twig
She put him in a cooking pot, and out came mijadara[2]

In the month of September they say:

September's tail is damp.

In October and November:

Between October and November, summer comes again.
golden things come in these two months.
The bleat of the kid and the blackening of the grape.

---

[1] Hat of a stand up pillbox style, colored red and earlier used widely throughout the Ottoman Empire.

[2] This song, of course, uses symbols reflecting the aspirations of parents for their children. The potential of this son "germinates" in any context where he is placed. The song also demonstrates the responsibility of the parent in locating this explosive potency in the right context.

In December and January:

> If grapes and figs disappear, resort to water for two months.

December is considered the barren month and January the dead month.

> Go back home and bury yourself.[1]

In February:

> You can't depend on what it says.
> It's wild and stormy but the smell of summer is there too.
> The borrowed time[2] eliminated the 'Aad.[3]

In March:

> Hide your biggest pieces of charcoal for your great uncle in March.

In April:

> The rains of April revive the hearts of people.
> The scorpions of April.

In May:

> As long as the Christian woman fasts, the cold lasts.

In June:

> The worm,[4] the head of grain, and the apricot.
> June cooks the apricots.

---

[1] Go home and keep warm.

[2] Between February and March... a time of bitterest cold.

[3] 'Aad-an ancient tribe in the old Testament.

[4] Worm here refers to silk worms.

In July:

July boils the water in the jug.

In August:

August is on fire.
When August comes, summer is shamed.[1]

Winter in my city includes four periods[2] as described by the people in their sayings. In the period, "Sa'ad[3] the slayer," not even a dog barks.[4] In Sa'ad the swallower," The sky rains and the earth swallows.[5] In "Sa'ad, the lucky one," water flows into the dead branch and every cold person becomes warm. In "Sa'ad, the concealed," young maids circle around the town.

Winter begins in Damascus with what are called "the forty days," followed by another "fifty days." At the end of these 90 days, altogether the three months of winter, spring appears and we celebrate *"nairuz"*[6] in the orchards of Damascus and the Ghuta. Everywhere the opening blossoms of spring appear, on the ground, on the branches, in the eyes and the hearts and on the lips of the people. White and yellow flowers, red poppies between the green blades of grass...apple, pear and apricot trees blossom in the Ghuta. All summon the picnickers with irresistible perfumes that are impossible to ignore, luring all Damascus to the seductive charms of the Ghuta. Chunks of snow melt from the heat of the sun and the reflections of love and flowers.

If you have lost a person in the spring time, you are sure to find him in the Ghuta.

It is impossible to go to the Ghuta and come back without a spray of flowers. It is a gay symbol of spring to hold the branches from the car's windows and greet the cheerful city with the news that summer soon will come. It is like the small snowman in winter who sits on the hood of each

---

[1] That is, summer will soon depart.

[2] These are short periods of time with names that describe the characteristics of the weather; the periods are called literally "happinesses" in Arabic.

[3] Allegorical name meaning Chance, Luck, or Happiness.

[4] It is bitterly cold.

[5] The ground is thirsty for water.

[6] A day to enjoy the out-of-doors.

car returning from the picnics beloved by Damascenes: outings to the desert plains, to the mountains of the Barada River source, to the mountain towns of Zabadani, Bludan or Abu Zad[1] covered with snow like the cream that covers *qanafa madluqa*.[2] This small snowman signifies to the Damascenes that snow is falling in the high summer resort towns even though winter has not yet brought rain to the city.

Oh my, how hot it is! Summer starts with a pervasive heat and we escape to the orchards. We set out from our house on hot summer days to the orchards nearest our quarter. We leave our house with our "herd" to make a picnic in Bustan al-Mazra at the Kirsh source from which springs an excellent, pure, cold water. We spread our rug on the grass of the orchard and lay out on it the utensils taken from the brown leather suitcase my father brought especially for picnics. Mother and women relatives begin to fry eggplants and zucchini in frying pans on the primus. The smell of eggplant frying in the oil perfumes the area along with *fattush*,[3] salads, *kibbi naya*,[4] and watermelon which my father cuts for us, piece by crescent piece, leaving the round center part for himself and his guests and saving the black seeds for mother to fry for us during long winter evenings.

The Kirsh spring is not the only place where we went for picnics. Almost every Friday would be spent in a different place; we invited relatives in a big procession out to Sidr al-Baz or Shadarawan or Rubwa or Dumar or Hama or the banks of the Barada. We would spread out, roaming a long way between the popular and willow trees of the river, and spend the happiest days of our lives. We played, rode the swings, hung from the limbs of trees, gathered walnuts and broke them with stones to eat them. We would forget and rub our eyes with our stained hands... never mind! We would turn from the fig trees to the pomegranate trees like locusts, climb up the mountain of Dumar and climb down into the canals of Mazze to swim until we overcame the heat and killed our childish enthusiasm for swimming in cold water on a hot summer day.

Oh how I wish I could return to that time...to my childhood and hear the grown-ups of our family say to each other at the end of the picnic: "God willing, by the time the next moon comes, we will go on a picnic again together."

---

[1] Above Bludan.

[2] The name of a Syrian sweet.

[3] A salad that uses greens, tomatoes, and dried broken pieces of Arab bread.

[4] A ground meat and spice dish that is eaten raw.

In our old house in Suq Saruja I got to know the folk traditi
Damascenes in the blessed month of Ramadan[1] and 'Id al-Fitr.[2] Not
the children in our quarter would break the fast. The moment the ‿‿‿
announced that we could eat,[3] was an intense time filled with many
memories for me. The best of these was the image of the members of our
family gathering before sunset around a table filled with food: compote, a
thick apricot drink, cooked dried fruit, and soups. In the suq the dishes
almost flew over the heads of the pushing crowds at Majid's, the bean
seller, or at Humusani's at the end of the quarter where we bought *tasqiyya*[4]
with ghee and a plate of *masabaha*.[5] The baker pushed hot loaves into eager
hands, and at the drinking water tap children fought over who would fill
their jugs first. A little girl would return to her home happy, in her hand a
plate of *jaradiq*,[6] "Oh transparent bread, blown by the wind,"[7] delicacies of
Ramadan sprinkled and decorated with threads of molasses so they would
taste delicious when crushed between the teeth. An old father would return
to his house from the store, carrying in one hand a pile of *ma'aruk*, a bread
of Ramadan, and in the other, a handkerchief filled with some fruit, while
under his tarbush hat, another wet white handkerchief cooled his brow.

The gun would go off and all the lights of the minarets would be
illuminated to announce the sunset prayer. The children in the suqs and
quarters shouted at the top of their lungs "Hurry up, hurry up!" and ran in
their little clogs to their houses and closed the doors. Cooking pots were
turned out onto plates, primuses were extinguished and there was total
silence over the empty streets and passageways of the cities.

A week before Ramadan came, Damascenes would go out to the
orchards to say goodbye to the days of eating and picnics and to consecrate
Ramadan before it became Ramadan. In Ramadan people had to pray the
'asha prayer[8] and participate in the extra prayers in the Umayyad Mosque.
There was also "Abu Tabla"[9] the waker at Ramadan, who made his rounds

---

[1] Ramadan is the Islamic month of fasting from sunrise to sunset.

[2] 'Id al-Fitr is the feast of celebration at the end of Ramadan.

[3] This occurs at the time of sunset.

[4] A chick pea, bread and yoghurt dish.

[5] Chick peas and tahina sesame paste.

[6] Sweet pancakes made for Ramadan.

[7] This is the phrase of a song.

[8] This prayer comes one and one-half hours after sunset-the last prayer of the
day.

[9] Literally "Father of the Drum."

of the streets singing and beating on his drum and banging on doors to wake[1] Abu Muhammad, Abu Yasin and Abu Azat. After the gun for the evening meal went off, he knocked again at the doors to collect food for his children, for his poor relatives and for his acquaintances. It was well-known that the children of the quarter dreamt about the special song Abu Tabla sang to them just around their supper time:

Shurumburum, I feel so miserable
Because of the second wife and the first wife
They give me a boil on my heart
And because of their tyranny I sold my drum
I'm going around miserable
God made a calamity for me
When I married an old bald woman
With teeth like a hyena
She became pregnant and bore me seven
Three cats[2] and four mice[3]
Shurumburum, I feel so miserable
I took one from the village of Jisrain
She eats only nuts and figs
They said "Go away you pitiful creature"
Tomorrow you will end up with no woman at all
Shurumburum, I feel so miserable

Abu Tabla made his way through the streets with children following and chanting "Abu Tabla, his wife is pregnant, what did she bear, she bore nothing, only a walking rat!" This Ramandan Waker of Damascus in the evenings and before dawn was accepted as part of religious tradition, awakening people gently to the fullness of their faith.

You sleepers, "God is One"
You sleepers, mention the name of God
Get up for the last meal before dawn
The Prophet is coming to visit you
You fasters, "God is One"
You fasters, get up, "God is One"
Pray to the Prophet 'Adnan
You believers who love God and the Prophet
Get up, worship and pray to the Prophet
The month preferred by God,

---

[1] At about 3:00 a.m.

[2] Girls.

[3] Boys.

A month of worship and love and forgiveness
You who hear the call of God is Great and pray to the Prophet
You sleepers, "God is One"
You sleepers, mention the name of God

*   *   *

You sleepers, "God is One"
You sleepers, mention the name of God
How happy is the one who worships God and observes the
fasting...
Ramadan flies like a bird...
Oh God, forgive the believers...
Oh God, make Islam and the Muslims victorious...
And you who have missed fasting and prayer...
Get up, renew your pledge with God and the Prophet...
You sleepers, "God is One"

*   *   *

My tears spilled down my cheeks like tiny doves' eggs. Oh this month
entrusted to us, "Peace be unto you."

After a long period of anticipation "Standing Day"[1] would come. We
would hear the guns announcing it had come and Mother would say: "They
have confirmed[2] it, children! Happy feast day! Run kiss your father's
hands," and we would run to kiss the hands of our mother and father,
touching them to our heads[3] and wishing them a happy feast. We'd start by
repeating the well-known song "The light went on and then went out; the
guns said 'boom, boom, boom,"...then we would go up to sleep early, to
sink into our dreams. But the night was long and the new shoes and new
dress and new ribbons laid carefully on the pillow of each child made us
await the morning and the first appearance of the feast with anxious,
disturbed sleep. We dreamt of the presents from our parents and relatives and
the freedom to enjoy enticing amusements, and good food.

When we returned with our mother and father, from the dawn visit to
place myrtle branches and roses on the graves of our relatives, we stood
with others in Nasr Street near the entrance of Suq Hamadiyya to see the

---

[1] The day that ends Ramadan with its fasting.

[2] That is, they have sighted the new moon.

[3] A sign of respect.

27

salamlik.[1] On our return, our dear mother went to the kitchen to cook the traditional specialities in our house for the first day of the feast: leg of lamb, rice and *mulukhiyya.*[2] My father would receive the men who come to make formal calls on the occasion of the feast:

> Welcome! May every year bring you good health.
> May God grant you many more years to come.
> Every year, may you be well.
> God willing, next year we will be in 'Arafat.[3]

And coffee would be passed around to the guests—my mother knocking on the kitchen door and father taking the tray of coffee cups from her because she shouldn't appear in front of strangers.[4] Then from inside there would come another knock and he would take a tray of plates and dishes of sweets: ghuraiba, sesame seed cookies, small cakes stuffed with walnuts and pistachios or cakes stuffed with figs, sweets, and cigarettes. My father would leave the house for a while to return the calls. If someone came while he was gone, mother would take their calling cards from behind the door.

We children would fly free in a charmed world. No one asked where we were going. No one accompanied us to watch where we went. We opened the door and left, without permission, to ride "the carriage of rosy dreams," drawn by a donkey or a human, it made no difference. The cart belonging to the porter was decorated for the feast with colored paper and arranged with two seats on which the children reclined. Holding tightly to the wood sides we flew with the cart on a round trip to Seven Fountains' Square, by Baghdad Street and then returned through Suq Saruja. We loved the song "Oh Children Warriors," that accompanied the cart on every trip we could afford to take for a piaster.

The owner of the cart would say and we would repeat after him:

> Oh children warriors, Juju; Push the molds, Juju;
> Chinese molds, Juju; In the shape of corks, Juju;
> 'Ali didn't die, Juju; He bore girls, Juju;

---

[1] A colorful horse guard of honor.

[2] A boiled green.

[3] Arafat in Saudi Arabia near Mecca is where Standing Day is celebrated on the pilgrimage.

[4] Men outside the circle of close relatives who are eligible marriage partners because they are strangers to a particular woman.

His daughters are white, Juju; Like devils, Juju;
His daughters are black, Juju; Like monkeys; Juju;
Oh children warriors, Juju; Oh children warriors, Juju.

It was a devilish song that we repeated like parrots after the man. It had no meaning other than that it was a song for the feast in Damascus, but a child who hadn't climbed on the cart or sung "The Children Warriors" was a child who hadn't celebrated the feast. The children would demand politely that the owner of the cart go quickly and repeat the song, "Make it go quickly and we will pay you again." And the man would run...and we would pay him again and only climb down finally with great reluctance.

No sooner did we get off the cart than we would climb on the swings. We bought toys from shops whose fronts had been extended by long tables out beyond the pavement. Sitting on rush-bottomed low stools we ate *foul nabit*[1] with salt and cumin, pickles, cakes, sweets, grape paste and *malwa* that I used to prefer spicy hot. There were a number of kinds: with honey, with lemon and with cinnamon. We used to go also to Harika Square to ride camels and visit tents erected for the feast where you could see a hyena or a disembodied head that talked or hands and legs without a body. In this way we passed the three days of the feast refusing to accept the fact that it would eventually end. On the fourth day, called "mule" of the feast, the tears flowing on our cheeks signalled our sorrow at the end of this "short feast."

On the blessed Adha Feast,[2] a sheep was slaughtered, tempering our happiness with a sadness for our friend, the sheep, who had lived with us in our house for more than a month. We fed him grass and swept up his dirt and walked him in the street and tied him to a bannister of the stair leading up to the balcony. Then one day we awakened to find him slain. They told us they had killed him and that we were going to eat some of the meat and give some to the poor. But, since that day, I have hated meat. In the cooking pot of stuffed zucchini they used to stick straws in the top of those that were stuffed with rice instead of meat for "the one who doesn't like meat." They laughed at the dining table saying that I didn't eat any but the zucchini of Um Amna.[3] I didn't laugh because I knew that they had killed my friend the good sheep!

We spent the "Big Feast" with Damascus illuminated by colored lights, awaiting the return of the pilgrims from Blessed Mecca. The women "cut"

---

[1] Sprouted beans.

[2] This is the long feast after the pilgrimage.

[3] An expression meaning that only one particular kind satisfied her.

themselves new dresses from cloth bought in the Hamadiyya Suq to welcome the pilgrims and they decorated the doors and the quarter with carpets and branches of eucalyptus leaves. There were also willow branches, colored paper leaves and lights, and people sent gifts to the houses of pilgrims who were aquaintances and relatives: sacks of flour, rice, sugar, tins of ghee and oil. They would kill a sheep for the pilgrim's return...at his feet...and I would run away to our house and close the door at the sight of the fountain of blood. The pilgrim's wife distributed gifts: Koranic beads, fans, kohl holders[1] and a quantity of dates and bottles of *zamzam*[2] water. The young men at the pilgrim's door chanted "The Mecca pilgrim returns to us..." And the women greeted the white clad pilgrim with trills of joy:

> Welcome, Oh Guests
> If we knew you were coming
> We would have prepared mutton
> Hello and welcome, you with your dark eyes
> You tall and stately palm tree blocking the high door
> Lya Lya Lysh
> Oh dear apricot, we walked the streets of your quarter
> With our heart bleeding from your absence
> If someone would come with the news of your safe return
> I would bestow all the gifts I have for you on him.

There were so many picturesque scenes of life that I saw when I looked out our little window jutting out over our humble, simple quarter. These images are dearer to me than pearls or diamonds. They take me back in memory to the time when a little girl, energetic and bold like a boy, carrying a wicker basket, ran, to buy fruit from Abu Mistu's store, and yoghurt, cream, sugar, tea, cheeses, *halawa*,[3] molasses, butter and oil from the famous Abu Rashid's grocery in Suq Saruja, thin "mountain" bread from Abu 'Ali in Suq al-Atiq, *foul madamis*[4] from Majid, the foul-maker, near Qaramani bath in Suq al Atiq, vegetables from Salah the vegetable man, meat from Abu Amin in the upper part of Suq al-Hal, and Arab bread and *mashruh* from the bakery of Abu Salah facing the Ward mosque. I would pay like a grown-up for a sack of dried wood which a porter would

---

[1] Kohl is a black powder used as a mascara by the women.

[2] Zamzam is the holy well at the Great Mosque of Mecca. Its waters are thought to have special properties.

[3] A sweet made from sesame paste.

[4] Cooked bean dish.

carry for me from the wood suq to our quarter. I used to buy a bag of charcoal as Father directed me to do from the one whose name I don't remember who sells broken pieces of charcoal by the Qaramani bath, near the man who sells milk and yoghurt, Hashim. Also, I used to buy the twigs we boiled for stomach complaints and flax seeds, flower tea, castor oil liquid used as a purge—awful stuff—and ointments, as Mother would direct me, from the "essence man" in Suq al-Atiq. If there were holes in our tin water jugs, our containers for oil or the pail for 'arqsus, I would take them to the iron monger in Suq al-Atiq. Eggs, chickens, baskets, brushes, brooms, and sacks with handles, I knew how to choose from the best sellers in Suq al-Tibn.

Straw!! The houses of Damascus were built from straw and mud. Before winter came and before September presented us with its "wet tail," we would smell the odor of mud piled in the narrow streets. They carried it by hand on foot to the house tops to thicken the roofs with new mud against the "challenge of winter" until there were no more leaks in bedroom ceilings and we were no longer obliged to place cooking pans and bowls next to our sleeping mats, or endure the noise of the dripping water disturbing our nights.

I need only close my eyes to bring back the sounds, the images and the smells of the plasterer with his rolled up pants, covered with red mud that he had mixed with his feet, carrying a basket on his head from the alley to the house. He entered the hallway from the main door, shouting at the top of his lungs to warn the women to make a path for him:[1] "Oh God, here comes the plasterer!"

I am grateful to my parents who without knowing it permitted me this precious experience. I am grateful to my father for coming from Suq Saruja and my mother for coming from Maidan. Because of them I lived the most beautiful days of my life in the old quarters of Damascus.

Damascus in my mind's eye…is an Arabic house with an open courtyard, in its center is a small pool from which 70 brass pipes pour out cool water. A beautiful woman sweeps the courtyard with water, holding in her hand a pail and a straw broom. Her wooden clogs ring on the stone tiles and her narrow gold braclets jangle at her wrists…her laughter pierces through to the depths of the heart…her whiteness is the pure white of Arabian jasmine and her eyes the color of honey. She fills her pail from the pool and throws the water on the tiles, sweeping it with her broom. Meanwhile, her friend fills a second pail with water to sprinkle the flowers,

---

[1] The women hide themselves from him.

31

and water the plants and trees. The smell of eggplant frying in oil fills the house and the houses of neighbors. A clever woman beats *kibbi*[1] in the stone mortar especially made for kibbi, while her sister-in-law[2] plays on the 'aud[3] in the cool sitting room, the soft golden bracelets moving gently on her wrist as she picks out the chords with a feather. Her mother-in-law peels garlic in the shade while the daughter of her mother-in-law pushes at the handle of the pump to fill a large jug of water for washing dishes. The second wife to her mother-in-law climbs a ladder to pick tender grape leaves from the vine in order to make stuffed grape leaves for the next day's meal. A devilish boy pounds on the door, and runs away.

The murmuring of running water from the stream that passes through the courtyards of the houses casts a soothing sound over the scene. A dove clucks happily on the balcony saying as the old women understand it "coo-coo, coo-coo, God is great, coo-coo, coo-coo...God...God." The daughter-in-law suddenly remembers her dispute with her mother-in-law and says to her sister-in-law from the bottom of her wounded heart: "I'm like the wild doves; no one dares harm me or God will blind him. May God take revenge on her for turning my husband against me." With her clogs, a little girl breaks on the black stone of the stair almond seeds that she gathered from yesterday's meal and eats the inside. Several children play hide and seek in the big courtyard. A young girl of the house, like an opening rosebud, plucks jasmine flowers and threads them with a needle into a necklace for her breast. Maybe suitors will come to ask for her hand in marriage today. She doesn't forget to pick a sprig of budding jasmine to tuck in her mother's hair.

From his nearby shop a man calls out his wares, then counts the money he earned today. He dreams of closing the shop door and returning to the coolness of his house where he can recover from the hot day by sitting with a pail of 'arqsus at one side and on the other, water melon. A rebel hides behind the trunk of a tree in the Ghuta, in his hand a gun with which he will hunt the French colonizer. In the Umayyad Mosque a shaikh prays, asking God to give Islam and the Muslims victory. Women in *malayas*,[4] black as ink, fill Suq al-Harir and al-Qishani. Lengths of material are their only preoccupation. The fanatics among them wear black and white malayas

---

[1] Meat and grain mixture.

[2] In this case the wife of her brother-in-law, who by the old custom of wives moving to the homes of their husbands would put them in natural proximity.

[3] Lute

[4] Cloaks.

while the more modern wear black coats with scarves on their heads, covered in addition with a black head cloth having two veils. From the street a man shouts, "Cart man, look behind you!" and he tries with his whip to flick a boy hanging on to the back of the horse-drawn cart. The two horses leave their dirt behind in the streets and a bad odor pervades the air. The sound of two horses' hooves is heard travelling on an errand of pleasure out to the fresh air in the Rubwa and lunch in Dumar. The call of noon prayer drifts down from a nearby minaret and little children in black smocks burst out like Arabian jasmine buds into the streets, leaving school for their noon break. The street car clangs and the commissary[1] blows his horn and the Barada flows...and a velvet curtain descends suddenly, making me aware that Damascus lived behind it, unconscious of how unique its happiness was. That old Damascus fades into the shadows.

I wonder why people do not worry about the authentic roots of Damascus...how they can run away from them to new cardboard boxes...how they permit those imitation boxes to invade our genuine past, and the images of a deeply rooted authenticity. I wish I could press the old quarters of Damascus, with its suqs, its baths and its people to my chest in an embraace that would protect her from the invasion of pretension and the claws of superficial imitation, as a tender mother fearful for her child protects her from a crushing flood. Never mind, I was your baby, Damascus, and now you have become my favorite spoiled child. I love you, Damascus, more than anything in the world even though I have not seen all the world yet. You, Damascus, are greater than any image any one could have fashioned!

---

[1] Ticket taker.

Chapter Two

Sumayya, Hind and Kulthum

Fire! Fire!

Damascus turns its head in sorrow to watch the red flames that threaten what remains of the houses in the area and spread down as far as the end of the walls of the old "Dak al-Bab" Mosque on Salhayya Street. My child's heart turns with Damascus, leaping like a frightened rabbit in the direction defined by the fearful pillar of black smoke. When they opened the street, still wet from the hoses of the fire brigade, I went with the others, fearful of what I might see. Everything in me warned me to go back. No one knew that I possessed a great treasure there near the mosque and I feared that the malicious, stupid fire had removed it. But no...it was as if the flames sympathized with me and with the generation who accompanied me on the long trip to obtain this treasure.

The people pushed against each other, weeping, and I smiled at the small marble sign hanging over the old wooden door. The people ascended the three steps to the door and entered into my paradise. The sign smiled back at me, that one remaining word smiled at me: "Zubaida." And I was still rich compared with those prayerful believers whose mosque had burned or the peaceful inhabitants made homeless by the collapse of their houses.

It was still mine, Zubaida, and would remain mine, my childhood that didn't burn.

Oh, dear! See there...the smoke...the smoke!
Where?
There, where it is burning.
Near Zubaida!

This time, I walked slowly with dragging feet like an old woman without a cane to ease her way. And suddenly I was a little girl again, wearing my black school smock with its white starched collar and a wide red ribbon waving on the top of my head like a rooster's comb. The pocket of my smock was stuffed full of nuts and under my arm I carried a leather case whose color had faded to a pale brown from being handed down from my sister to my brother to me. I arrived, *al-hamdu lil-lah* before the fiery area had consumed Zubaida, and before its walls had been transformed into a raging ash, blinding the eyes of the passersby.

This accident had given the engineer an extraordinary opportunity to carry out his plans to make Damascus beautiful. All those piles of debris would be transformed into a beautiful square, joining all the most important streets of Damascus together. The son of the last house overlooking the garden of Abu Rumani would be able to see the girl of the last house overlooking the garden of "New Mazr'a." And when the son of Muhajjariin district looked out from his balcony, he would see a beautiful young girl looking out from her balcony on Baghdad Street and she would smile at him.

But...what do I care for this spacious square! Have they forgotten me, this committee for city planning, and have they forgotten the first half of their lives or of complete generations whose lives were woven in Zubaida!!

I will to have to accept the news I've heard recently that there is no way to avoid the destruction being planned in the name of urban renewal. Zubaida is included in those plans.

Why do they want to pull down my golden palace? Why do they swing axes without mercy at the head of my happy childhood? I spent five years in Zubaida elementary school for girls and graduated in 1945. It is now twenty-three years later and the memories of the most minute details of my life there still pass before my eyes. Zubaida to me...is a big wooden door, at the side of which was another iron door with many small holes. Behind this iron door we small girls used to hide, watching happily when the big boys, rebelling against France, came to our school to encourage the girls to demonstrate with them. It was an old, old door that as far as I can remember was never opened while I was a student in Zubaida.

If I stop and think about it...I find myself remembering a school yard in winter with a dark staircase leading up to the upper floor where I spent first grade, second grade, and fourth grade. Third and fifth grades I spent on the benches of the inner rooms overlooking the school yard of this big Arab house converted into a school for little girls. The school's kitchen faced the office of the headmistress and in this spacious, simple, damp kitchen I got to know the meaning of socialism for the first time in my life. My friends and I used to share our food. I would feed Haifa crushed black olives and boiled eggs and from one of the layers of her brass lunch pail, she fed me kibbi with yoghurt, or mulukhiyya with chicken. Haifa, as an only child, was spoiled by her mother but I was only one of five sisters and brothers. I used to love Haifa and still do. She remained my friend throughout our education from first elementary grade until we graduated together from the Faculty of Arts in the Department of Philosphy. Haifa Jamal is now an important and successful inspectoress in the Ministry of Education.

My memories stay with me, taking me back to the playground of summer school, and the place near the water taps for drinking and washing for prayer. At the right of the playground we used to play jump rope and over there on the left near the windows of my third grade class, still alive in my imagination, is a corner we fought to reserve for ourselves early in the morning. There we would draw squares on the ground with chalk and play "stone."[1]

How I used to laugh with my little sister over our secret when my father, at a loss, stood before al-Bazm, the famous seller of children's shoes in Suq al-Hamadiyya. He was unable to explain the phenomenon to the good skilled merchant when the two of them stood looking in astonishment and surprise at the shoes on our feet.

"I would like to know how the front of the shoe can wear out like this so quickly. By God, brother, I gave you shoes of the best quality leather! How can it be that the toe is worn away in only one week? And why from the right foot only?"

And both my father and he would examine the toe of each shoe, including the one which had changed to white. He would throw up his arm in a gesture of bewilderment, and he and my father would ponder the question for a long time…with no explanation!

The stone game, my father! The stone game! Oh, if you had only known it on that day you would have given us such a beating. We would kick the stone, you see, with the toe of our right foot to win a new home square against our friends.

Oh, those doors and windows of Zubaida, how I held tightly to their wood so as not to "die" when someone chased me and tried to touch me in the game of "life." We would become bored with "life" and play "hide and seek," ranging far and wide after secret hiding places until the school bell deprived us of the pleasure of continuing our games.

But…where are those dear friends? Where are Sumayya Habbal, Khulthum Nuri, Hind Hakim, Su'ad Hafez and Haifa Jamal? The roads of life have made me lose them. I'll never forget how Kulthum forced me to be friends again with Sumayya and how Hind pressed Sumayya in turn to be "sisters" again. In the very middle of the road there was a point we selected to repair the damage caused by our childish haughtines and rebelliousness, and there we built on our willingness to compromise. I feared and Sumayya feared that eventually Kulthum and Hind would despair of our pride and discontinue their efforts to reunite us. So we gave in, and made up by touching the tips of our right forefingers. Thus the quarrel vanished that had started when the grasp of the little finger of my right hand broke from her little

---

[1] "Stone" (hajar) is a game similar to hopscotch but with different rules. In it the players kick the stones to the appropriate squares.

finger with the words "I am angry with you," each thereby announcing the state of animosity and the break in the relationship.

In my school Zubaida I knew injustice for the first time in my life. That day it was the teacher Hayat Khanum's[1] turn to ring the bells of the breaks between classes. Hayat Khanum was a tough teacher, born with a stick in her hand. It was my bad luck to get the highest marks in the first examination of the second grade. My kind, beloved, respected teacher called me before the whole class to appoint me prefect in the place of Bakaza, the cruel, black, tall, stupid previous prefect.

In the playground, after the ringing of the bell and after everyone stood in line, Bakaza took her revenge. She stuck her foot out from the straight line of obedient, orderly pupils, despite all my threats to use a ruler against her mutinous foot that was destroying the perfection of the line I had so carefully formed for the admiration of Hayat Khanum when she made her tour of inspection. When my warnings to Bakaza failed, I called out in a voice audible to all the silent classes assemble there, "Hayat Khanum, Bakaza has put her foot out of line!" To everyone's surprise, Hayat Khanum pulled me by my hair to the middle of the school yard to make an example of me for all the pupils of the school, especially those who might feel inclined to defy their respected teachers. And she began to complain about me:

"You, impolite child! Am I *your* comrade! Am I *your* colleague! I'll teach you good manners. Stand here next to the wall and you will see what I will do to you after all the pupils have passed by and looked at you. Your punishment will be harsh. I will hang a paper donkey's head on your head, and you must stand on one foot, with your face to the wall and your hands above your head."

Days passed with streams of tears, and my good, cruelly treated, wondering soul was still ignorant of why I deserved such a punishment. Finally, I learned from my good headmistress, who loved and valued me, that my guilt was for uttering her name "Hayat Khanum." I should have called her "Teacher Khanum." My headmistress defended me, and in the end had the last word, for the school didn't see me for even a week, wearing the donkey's head with its two upright ears...

I could never forget...even after all these years, that good deed done to me by my respected, cherished teacher Saniyya Qabbani, owner of the most beautiful face, the kindest heart, the most accepting personality. Or could I forget my dear able teachers Mary Sab'a'a and Adiba Shakush, and 'Aziza

---

[1] Khanum is a respectful term of address that loosely may be equated with "Miss Hayat." Hayat was the teacher's first name.

Kilani and Ulfat Ghuzzi and Wusal Mulawi and the now deceased Raifa Nashid! I cannot forget the face of the good old Haj[1] with his white beard who guarded the door of the schoolyard nor will I forget the sympathy of the kind attendant, Um Rashid.

No! I could never forget their understanding or their small kindnesses. I shall never forget either the first word of thanks this little girl heard from a teacher when I returned the world map to the lab where she was in charge. And I shall not forget how our beautiful, capable, pious, religious head-mistress who never left off praying and fasting forbade the teachers from beating the students, and how she severely punished our cruel teacher, Thurayya Khanum, when she beat the palms of my little sisters with a stick until the blood flowed. I won't forget very soon how I fell down on the school ground one winter when the snow had piled high on the tiles and turned into ice. I twisted my finger and the memory of that pain and of falling down is still with me twenty-five years later.

I will never forget the faces of the berry seller or the one who sold Damir ice cream or the peddler who sold popcorn, dried humus and nuts, or the seller of notebooks, copybooks, tablets, rulers, pens and nibs. I will never forget standing with my friends, long mutinous minutes, under the water spout of the school on a rainy day in the good old days of Damascus in a generous downpour of the past.

How could I forget? How could anyone forget?

Where are Sumayya and Hind and Kulthum and Haifa and Su'ad? You, my now grown up and far away comrades, hurry to me, with your childish hearts like mine that never forget. Let us stand together at the door of our beloved school Zubaida and open our now big-little hands, each one taking the hand of a friend in hers to make a wall of faithfulness and love that will prevent the axes from destroying the playgrounds of our childhood and the cradles of our minds. Hurry to me, my comrades, and grasp tightly the old wooden door of the school to play the game of "life."[2]

---

[1] Haj is a term of address indicating that a person has made the pilgrimage to Mecca.

[2] In the game of "Life", the home base confers life on the person who touches it.

Chapter Three

I Delight in My Mother

In the end my mother grew to dominate my feelings, thoughts and concerns. Even from the beginning she was the fertile red dirt of my soul and all the plants, branches, flowers and thorns that flourished on its surface. My whole personal being drew its life from the efforts of my mother. She was the warp and the woof of my existence, while all that is embroidery and decoration was from some other source. My mother was central in my life. Whenever I returned from work, tired physically, mentally and spiritually after struggling a full day to earn the wherewithall for tomorrow, I found her at the door waiting to receive me with bright, comforting words overflowing with the eternal joy of the mother seeing her children again after a long or short absence. There is nothing sweeter, more sincere, or more delightful than my mother's welcome at the door. Always, however late I was, steaming hot food was waiting for me. Mornings I always returned to wakefulness with the sound of her flowing sympathetic voice from behind the barely ajar door...that voice that I love and wish would never change.

My sister came once...opening the door with a shove and shouting loudly, her words tinged with impatience for a number of reasons: because the sun had already risen, birds were singing, buses were screeching, and the clock hands threatened boredom and scoldings and the need for haste. "Really, it's very late. Get up...this time I will leave you behind and not come back to get you."

I felt full of disappointment and pain. The turmoil inside me waited anxiously for the soft way my beloved mother interrupted my sleep to reassure me that my pampered childhood would continue as before: "Come, 'mama,' come my daughter, God be merciful to you...get up, 'mama,' so you won't be late, I have your breakfast and tea ready for you. Wash your face. Come talk to me, I have missed you." Being away from her while I slept made her miss me...as if she wished she could stay with me and do away with her own nights and the nights of her children in order to double the time she could be with them!

The time I spent with my mother was short but intense. I enjoyed being with my mother in a way quite different from the time I spent with other people. I would observe her carefully...looking into her eyes...at her hair...at her old dress which emitted the odor of the kitchen...at her good smile...I would consider her hopes...those obvious and those concealed...her way of walking...see her at sleep...and she didn't realize that I was watching her. She doesn't know how I drank from her divine beauty and how I stored inside myself pictures of her that were endless in number.

I used to enjoy watching her play with my brother, kissing him on the back of his neck. Then she would ask about the health of my other brother, and wait expectantly with pleasure and anxiety while someone read to her the last letter that arrived from him. I enjoyed watching her answer the telephone with a soft hesitant voice. I liked watching her grilling meat and frying vegetables, washing dishes and cutlery, and nearly melting from fatigue at the washing machine, or hanging out or gathering in the wash from the clothesline. I would reach out a hand to help her but she always refused with an oath. And since I had learned to respect the religious Islamic fanaticism of my mother, I would be silent and withdraw from the place of her activity.

My mother tired herself, breathing heavily, yet never complaining of the daily work she did for our sakes and for the sake of the children who, though grown up, are still children returning to the house and the lap of the mother who embraces them all. When I approached her to whisper in her ear the secrets of a daughter to her mother, I felt she was happy. She listened to me and loved me and considered my opinions and attitudes toward things. She believed that I was the most beautiful girl in the world. I used to laugh at this assessment and her compliments, reminding her of the well-known Damascene saying that makes light of a mother's evaluation of her own children. The proverb says that, to the eye of the mother, the monkey appears as a gazelle. She laughed with me over the saying but never retracted what she said. And a happy pride would grow in my heart.

Once she said: "I worry about your hands. For their sake I will never let you wash dishes!" I looked at her rough, worn, veined hands at that moment and smiled sadly at the mockery of time. I will never forget that the luxury of my hands owes a debt to the misery of her hands. But she would answer with overflowing tenderness, "I'm not spoiling you, just saving you for the future."

"But, Mother, you are tiring yourself and I worry about you."

"I will never stop working for you and your children until the day I die."

And I stopped arguing with her, afraid that I might start weeping uncontrollably. After that, I said something totally unrelated to our conversation, and returned to my room and to myself.

I have discovered the secret of the happiness of my mother and of all mothers through her and understood why she became angry when I entered her kitchen. My mother was happy because she could exhaust herself working for our sakes...because, despite her growing age, she could still offer us something wonderful, something that people might consider an ordinary daily duty in the guise of a plate of kibbi in yoghurt, or a washed and ironed shirt, or the clean tiles of the floor. I used to see them not as trivial duties but as the great deeds of my mother, for which she never asked any compensation but the pleasure expressed in our faces and words. Her first interest was to serve us.

On more than one occasion I felt the inward rebellion of my mother toward what others might deprive her of. What would be left for her to do, for example, if I took away the work of cooking the food? She was determined that I should remain a small child continually banging at my empty bowl with a little spoon demanding a dish from the hand of my clever mother. How could I deprive her at that age from making her contribution to life, she who had already given to life men whom she had taught to live their days with love and honor? I could never do that...in my heart I worried about her, and I wished that I could increase her life and strength through my own youthful energy.

During the day my mother looked for things with which to wear herself out...she never sat still for a minute. If there was no more work to be done in her house, then she created more work to do. She was always working like the laborer who climbed the wall of the new building opposite us with the crowing of the cock and didn't come down again until the call to prayer at sunset. Mother always sacrificed for us...and we were always heavily indebted to her.

Mother was naturally intelligent, a fact that attracted attention even though it had been many years since she had had time to read books. She possessed the most sensitive of feelings, a clear, limpid soul bursting with emotion, and Algerian[1] blood from North Africa which poured out vitality and rebellion. Her innate feminine intelligence was charged with cheerfulness, love, and understanding. She advanced along the path of life, a human being richly endowed with the traditions of the past, the inventions of the present, holding tightly to yesterday, accommodating to today, and awaiting tomorrow. She understood you by your eye, with her heart. She would embrace you, and with her sacrifices she would enslave you. I always cry when I hear Fairuz singing part of her song, "Don't Blame Me," the part that goes:

My mother made me swear not to talk to anyone.
My mother told me to beware of enemies.
You are not anyone, nor are you the enemy.
In my eyes you are a hill of flowers.

---

[1] Her mother's ancestors came from Algeria.

41

And I am choked with tears every time Faiza Ahmad sings the part from her song to mothers which goes:

You, the beloved of all beloved.
You, who are more precious than my soul and blood.
You, who are all tenderness and goodness.
May God keep you, my mother.

I rebelled one time against my mother, because she put something on my desk that didn't belong in my room. And after many arguments from my side and few from hers, I slammed the door in her face and retreated to my bed shaking with anger and overcome by a pain that threatened to annihilate me. In my bed I tried to sleep but the attempt failed. I felt remorse because I knew my mother had not done anything to me. I wished I could go back to her to kiss her hair, face, eyes, hands and feet and say to her with a love that knows no comparison, "Mother, I don't mean it. I am sick...the pain is killing me but I tried not to let you know so you wouldn't worry...that is all."

But she was ahead of me. After a few minutes, with her rare intelligence she stuck her head in my door and full of tenderness she said in a smiling, comforting, sympathetic voice, "May you bury me...can I bring you a cup of hot tea, or would you like a cup of mint tea...hot?"

I will never forget the nice tale my mother used to tell me and my brothers so we would go to sleep. The story, to the contrary, used to make us more wide awake because it was so entertaining and we would want to hear more songs and stories. My mother's story, designed to satisfy our insistence, is not a real story but a nonsense rhyme that every Damascene mother tells her children:

I'll tell you a story.[1]
My daughter's pacing back and forth on the tile floor of the bath.
In the bath is a chameleon, on the ceiling, on the ceiling.
It requires a ladder but the ladder is at the carpenter.
He wants an egg but the egg is still in the ass of a

---

[1] This is comparable to our "I'll tell you a story of Jack and Margory and now my story's begun, I'll tell you another of Jack and his brother, and now my story is done." The rhyme is more important than the sense of the words. As a result, the "story" does not translate well into English. It is included here for what it reveals of the quality of different kinds of family relationships in its nonsensical snatches of verse.

chicken.
The chicken wants grain but the grain needs a mill.
The mill is closed and the water cut off.
I went to my mother's sister Um Hussain.
She gave me two apples. I ate one apple and hid the other.
My father's sister, the thief, came and stole it.
She ran away and I ran after her.
Our feet slipped on her shit; her shit is made of dates and henna.
Really, I wish the daughter-in-law would die.
I would raise a resounding shout at her burial
Climbing up on the pulpit and saying "God is Great."

When my sister refused to sleep, my mother would croon to her until
she finally closed her eyes. She slept in a cradle which my mother rocked by
pushing with her hand once and then pulling several times on a rope. She
would repeat the sweet lullaby which I shall never forget:

> Awala O awlani (First, O First One)
> O God, don't forget me
> Please, O Merciful One.
>
> *
>
> Awala O awlani
> The Haj[1] has left me,
> Left me in the country
> The women Siti Zainab and Ruqayya
> Ruqayya went down to Damascus,
> "Give something for Allah, O Shaikh Rislan.[2]
> You, the Protector of Damascus and its environs.
>
> *
>
> Awala, O awalati
> Thanks be for the day that you[3] came
> Your mother was happy
> And broke the good news to your father.
>
> *
>
> Awala hadabu nadabu
> A small cat
> They cut off her tail.
>
> *
>
> Sleep, my son, sleep
> I'll kill a dove for you

[1] In this case, "Haj" refers to her husband in a slightly more respectful way than
saying "My old man".

[2] Ruqayya with this phrase is beseeching the legendary Shaikh whose tomb sits
on one of the mountain peaks overlooking the city.

[3] The feminine is used here.

Oh, dove, don't believe it
I only tell him lies so he will sleep.

*

They shook the lemon tree and she couldn't sleep
She's spoilled and pampered and cannot sleep.

*

Awalala, O "mama," awalala
Sleep, my son, sleep.
The eye of God doesn't sleep
Our loved ones travelled, my son
Oh God, how our hearts long for them.
Awala, O "mama" awala
My grandmother and my daughter
The moon has set; where are you?
The moon and stars have set
And nothing sheds light on me but you.

*

Awala, O "mama," awala
You dwellers of the countryside
The ladies Zainab and Ruqayya
Lady Zainab carries a load
Lady Zainab with a scarf covering her head.

*

Awala, O "mama," awala
My mistress, mistress of all
With your bridal payment, I will do and undo things
From your bridal payment, I will clothe the naked
From your bridal payment, I will feed the hungry.[1]

*

Sheep, O sheep, sleep
I hope you will not be troubled
Awala. O awalani
God, don't forget me
Please, O Merciful One.

How often, too, Mother would play our favorite game with the three of us, my sister, my little brother, and me. How we would laugh and enjoy ourselves with our nice game "Timshi Manimshi." We would kneel on the floor before mother with our little hands on our laps and wait until mother touched the hand of each of us, saying:

"Timshi Manimshi"
My mistress sent me to buy onions
The jug fell and broke

---

[1] This verse makes fun of good intentions.

My mistress swore to hang me from a tree
The tree is full of drops of money
Hide your hand, you good little bride[1]
You, the owner of earrings and pins.

When she touched the hand of one of us with the word "pins," that hand had to be put behind the back and the game continued until there remained only one left from all the little outstretched hands. Mother would continue singing "Timshi Manimshi" with the last hand and its owner's nose. We would fall on the floor with laughter and mother would laugh with us, her laughter still fills my ears.

One of the nicest games and stories of my mother was the one of:

Ya bah, Ya bah, the branch of apples
A bird came to wash for prayers
He found for himself a silver jug
She caught the bird and slew him
She cooked and ate him
Tell me where I am to sleep
I embrace you and want to sleep.

And then mother would tickle our necks and we would roar with laughter, demanding to have the song and game, "Ya bah, ya bah" repeated, so that Mother would touch each of our fingers again. "This one caught the bird and this one killed it," and at the end Mother's finger would move lightly over the sensitive small wrist of her child until she reached its neck for the tickling. Oh, how good and kind my mother was!

My mother once said to me, while I was stirring yoghurt on the fire with a ladle:

—"Mama," be careful…stir the yoghurt well so it won't separate.

—Mother, teach me how to cook kibbi with yoghurt.

—I wash the burghul well, and strain out the water leaving it just barely covered with cold water. Then, I sprinkle a little salt on it and leave it to swell. Then, with my hands, I knead into it well-ground meat that has no fat, some salt, pepper, and two handfuls of flour or a little cornstarch. I pound the mixture together in a stone mortar or else I put it in a machine that grinds it well. On the side I have prepared the stuffing for the kibbi: beaten fat with walnuts, onions, salt and pepper, and I stuff the little kibbi with this. Meanwhile, I have soaked the rice in hot water and salt for half an hour, and afterward washed it with cold water, and then dropped it into a pot

---

[1] Little girls are often addressed affectionately as "bride."

45

of boiling salted water. When you see the rice swell, not fall apart—only tender—you take the pot off the fire and put it on the ground.

Stir the yoghurt while cold with egg and a little cornstarch and some water and put it on the fire until it boils not leaving it for one minute. If you leave it thinking it will boil by itself and don't stir it constantly with a spoon, it will curdle. When it boils pour the rice over it, but if the rice begins to stick together like mud I pour a little cold water over it and stir it so the grains won't stick together before the yoghurt boils. When it boils, you drop in the kibbi and slowly stir with the ladle from the bottom of the pot. Don't ever cover kibbi with yoghurt, *shaikh al-mahshi*[1] or *shakriyya*[2] with a lid—remember that, daughter.

Before all this, you have soaked dried tarragon and squeezed the water from it, or if it is still green, wash it and put it on the top of the yoghurt and kibbi and let it come to a boil four or five times. Remove one kibbi to a plate and tap it. If it sounds hollow it is done. Be careful, though, because if you boil it too much the kibbi falls apart. You need to test the yoghurt by tasting it a little; if it is too liquidy turn down the gas to low and sprinkle over it, little by little, starch diluted with water, stirring slowly so it won't stick. If it's easier, you can put the pot on the floor and stir it so it won't stick, because if you let it stick there's no way to fix it!

Next, put the pot on the ground and heat a spoonful of ghee until it begins to smoke but won't spoil the taste of the dish. Pour it on top of the yoghurt. Take the ladle to dip out the kibbi before the rest and put them in bowls or in a pan or on a tray. Then stir the rice and yoghurt and pour it on top of the kibbi.

My daughter, kibbi with yoghurt is only one of many ways to serve kibbi: there is kibbi served on a tray, kibbi fried in oil, kibbi roasted on the coals, with *babaghanuj*[3] or with fried eggplant and salad.

Kibbi served on a tray is easy. Oil a shallow platter with ghee and form the kibbi into several large disks; spread a layer of kibbi in the bottom of the tray, and sprinkle the loose meat, pinenuts, onions and walnuts fried in ghee over the kibbi layer. Pat this layer down firmly and them put a second layer of kibbi on top. Dissolve some cornstarch in water and sprinkle it evenly on top of the kibbi, pressing the mixture firmly together and smoothing it. Sprinkle a little saffron on the top, and again smooth it with your wet hand. Draw a knife through the kibbi to make pieces in the shape

---

[1] A dish that consists of small zucchini stuffed with meat and pine nuts.

[2] Rice and yoghurt dish.

[3] Babaghanuj is a dip made from eggplant, tahina, garlic, lemon and salt.

of *baklawa*,[1] and then after you bake it until it browns on top, sprinkle it with a little water, Heat ghee and, when hot, pour it over the top.

For a soup that goes well with the kibbi dish, put lentils, onions, a spoonful of ghee and a little salt in a pressure cooker half full of water. Leave it on the heat a quarter of an hour after it whistles, then take it off the burner and put it under cold water. Pass it through a food mill until very soft, and then add a handful of flour dissolved in water and stir it. Over the mixture sprinkle ground sweet red pepper, saffron, salt, black pepper and ghee drained from the tray of the kibbi. At the last minute the ghee should be heated before it is poured over the soup.

Another way[2] is to mold the kibbi into balls and take the meat, pinenuts, walnut and onion mixture and push it into a hole formed in the center of the kibbi. This is how it should be done when you make the big kibbi: heat oil until it smokes and turn down the fire so the kibbi won't burn on the outside and then fry them until they are a golden brown.

Fried kibbi[3] doesn't require a lot of work either, my daughter! You make a hollow in a flat disk of kibbi and place on it the mixture of sheep fat, walnuts, onions, salt, pepper, and added to them, the seeds of the sour pomegranate. Then make another disk-like dome on your palm and place it over the first seeing that the two stick together and the joins are smooth. You can bake the disks, "mama," in an oven like they do now or else you can roast them on the metal rack of a brazier over the charcoal as we used to do in days past. How delicious they used to be!

—Mother, I want to learn also how to make babaghanuj and *fatush*.

—Yi...there's no work involved in those dishes! Babaghanuj is a good dish to eat with kibbi. Kibbi without babaghanuj, in fact, isn't kibbi! Roast an eggplant over the fire and then dip it in cold water immediately and peel off the burnt skin under water so that the color of the eggplant remains as white as the Arabian jasmine. Pound the eggplant in a mortar and sprinkle it with lemon, salt, garlic, oil and cut parsley. For fatush, break up dry, hard bread into pieces and soak it in water. Strain out the water and put on top of the bread diced cucumbers, tomatoes, pepper, purslane, black olives, and fresh mint. Sprinkle over it dried mint, finely cut onions and garlic,

---

[1] Baklawa is a sweet that is traditionally cut in diamond-shaped pieces.

[2] She returns at this point to instructions about how to prepare kibbi in the form of balls. She uses the word kibbi to refer to the meat and wheat mixture prepared earlier, and also later to refer to the stuffed balls that are fried individually.

[3] The previous kibbi were spherical with a hollow core for the stuffing. These kibbi are large flat disks with a dome-like covering for the stuffing.

vinegar and oil. Finished, that's all there is to it! And, God knows, there is nothing more delicious.

—Mother, may God keep you, I want you to teach me how to make stuffed zucchini, stuffed grape leaves, stuffed eggplant, and cereal dishes.

—In October, I bring home lots of the local eggplants that are medium size—not too big or too small—about, I would say, ten kilos worth.

I fill a big pan with water, and while it is still cold I put the eggplant in it. I set it on the fire covered with a lid and wrap around it a soft cloth and an old towel so the steam doesn't escape and I leave it to boil. After awhile you take off the lid and poke the eggplant. When it becomes slightly soft—not very soft, just medium soft—you take out the eggplant with a ladle and dip them into cold water that has already been set on the side in a large container. Then put the second round of eggplant into the same boiling water and if there isn't sufficient water, add some more.

Pour water over the cooked eggplants two…three…four times until they are cold and while they are still under water cut off the stem but leave the top round. Prepare a plate of salt and grasp each eggplant in one hand while you open it with your finger in the middle and stuff it with salt. Drain the eggplant in a basket, sprinkling some salt between each layer. In other words you add about a handful of salt to help drain the water and to harden the eggplant so it won't get mushy from the cooking. When the basket is full, spread a cheesecloth over it and weigh it down with a plate and something heavy like a pestle. Put a pan under the basket, checking it now and then in order to pour off the water that has collected underneath. Leave it that way until the next day.

The next day, spread the eggplant out in a large washing pan. You should have previously prepared a stuffing of walnuts ground with fresh hot red pepper, sweet pepper, a little salt and crushed garlic. Stuff the eggplants with this mixture and wipe them clean with a fresh damp cheesecloth. Arrange the eggplants neatly in layers in a glass jar and every four layers sprinkle a little salt over them. On the second day, water will drain out of them, and on that evening, add good olive oil until they are barely covered. Be careful though, you should put a plate under the glass jar for ten days and every day look at it to see if there is oil. If the oil in the jar rises higher pour some out. The oil rises because the eggplant grows and swells. You should continue to watch the *makdus* for two or three weeks, pouring off the oil as it becomes necessary. If it becomes moldy, it's no problem—just look at it now and then. That's all there is to it—it doesn't need anything else. Taste it and see how delicious it is! And may you be healthy for many a year to come.

48

—Bless you, Mother. Now I want to learn how to make *mahshi*.

—May God save her soul, Um Jautdat taught it to me when I was still a young bride and couldn't cook. She said, "Hold the zucchini upright when you stuff it and don't shake it. Leave a small space near its top empty, and it will come our perfectly. God keep her, her cooking was delicious. My daughter, cooking must have inspiration. There are many people whose cooking you can't even put in your mouth because they have no inspiration.

So, daughter, the mahshi dish is what we cook in summer in Damascus. The vegetables are fresh and plentiful in summer. If you have invited people for dinner and want to make a lot, gather together ten zucchini, ten green squash, ten eggplants, and ten large peppers, sweet or hot.

It takes time to hollow out the vegetables, but if you put salt on the corer it will help you to accomplish the work more quickly. After you have removed the insides of the squash from both sides and peeled them with a knife, then you remove the insides from the eggplant, the zucchini, and the peppers. With a knife score the top of the pepper and press it to the inside and then lift it out. Remove the seeds and fill it with the stuffing, afterward replacing the top. To prepare the sauce, you should crush two kilos of red tomatoes and sprinkle over them salt and lemon salt while the sauce is still cold. To prepare the stuffing, take one and a half kilos of ground meat, ground fat, a kilo of rice, salt, pepper, saffron, a little coarsely ground cumin, and pinenuts. Soak the rice in hot water with a little salt, and then rinse it in cold water. Then mix the rice with the meat, fat, saffron, pepper and cumin and while holding the zucchinis upright begin to stuff them, leaving them empty to the length of a finger joint. Do the same with the eggplant, the squash and the peppers. When you have brought the sauce to a boil, adjust the seasonings and drop the zucchini, squash, eggplant and peppers into it while it continues to boil. When the mahshi becomes tender, sprinkle dry mint and garlic on the sauce. By God, no matter what anyone says, there is nothing more delicious than Damascene food. The mahshi dish shouldn't be eaten anywhere else but in Damascene homes. Of the many mahshi dishes, don't forget grape leaves (*yabraq*), collards, and cabbage rolls, any of which can be filled with vegetable or rice stuffing (*yalanji*).

—Tell me, Mother, haven't things changed a lot! No one nowadays seems to cook for their winter food that mixture of molasses and walnuts, or cereals with molasses and sugared seeds. I remember when I was young I used to go to Suq Saruja, Suq al-Atiq, Juza al-Hadba, Bab al-Jabiyya, 'Amara, and every tenth store you would find someone with a pot of cereal to sell and people eating from it. What a longing I have for those days. Mother, cook some of those cereals for us. I feel like tasting them again!

—May you bury me...since it's now the season for molasses, by God, I will cook two kinds of cereals for you, one with molasses and one with sugar. I personally like the one with molasses best. Where have you been all this time, daughter, cereal is easy to make. You need to learn it. Tomorrow I will teach you, for I would rather die than have you longing for it from another person's hand.

Take husked grain, chickpeas, white beans, and dried dark beans. I pick over them, wash them, and soak them in hot water each by itself for fifteen hours the night before. Then I get up before everyone the next morning to boil each kind of grain or bean by itself. I remove the skin of each dark bean and break it in half before I cook it. And when they are all well cooked, I prepare a big pot and put all the grains and beans in it together with the water in which they were boiled. I leave them cooking together until they thicken.

Meanwhile, I will have prepared a kilo of molasses[1] that is mixed with cold water and then heated on the fire slowly until it is completely dissolved. I pour it over the cereal and leave it boiling for a quarter of an hour until the grains and beans soak up the sweetness. When it has become thick, I take it off the fire and pour it into bowls until it cools. Over each bowl I sprinkle fennel, aniseed, and chopped walnuts. That's how you make cereal with molasses.

For the cereal with sugar, you put in sugar instead of molasses and sprinkle a few drops of flower water over it. Pour it into small dishes after it boils and thickens and leave it out to cool. Decorate the tops of the dishes with an assortment of broken walnuts, almonds, hazelnuts, pistachios, pinenuts, sweet pomegrante seeds, and grated coconut.

—Wonderful, Mother, what other kinds of Damascene food are there?

—There are *haraq isbau*,[2] *ruhu*,[3] a dish called "the Jew has travelled," *shalbatu, siti azbaqi*,[4] *fata al-maqadim*,[5] *hafati wal-qasha*,[6] roasted pieces of

---

[1] The Syrian *dibs* is a thicker version of what Americans use as molasses. It is made from raisins or St. John's pods.

[2] A black lentil dish with coriander, garlic, and toasted bread.

[3] Stew of vegetables.

[4] A stew made of burghul, eggplant, onions and tomatoes.

[5] Boiled leg of lamb with toasted Arab bread, yoghurt and garlic.

[6] Sheep stomach stuffed with meat, rice, pinenuts, and toasted pieces of Arab bread.

meat on a skewer, or sheep's lungs and livers, fried green broad beans, rice with green broad beans, broad beans cooked with meat, fried eggplant, vegetables stewed with tomato sauce, and a type of green squash cooked with tahina. There are *mafraka*[1] with zucchini, mafraka with eggs, *makmur*,[2] mafraka with beans, mafraka with eggplant, mafraka with potatoes, *basmashakat*[3] with rice, *manazala al-zahra*,[4] *fatah makdus*,[5] *rishtayya*,[6] *kanafa al-basma*,[7] *kanafa al-madluqa*, and *qataif asafiri*.[8] Also there are qataif fried in ghee with honey, *halib baluza*,[9] *hilatiyya*,[10] and then *burak*[11] with meat and burak with cheese. There are *fatah basmashkat*,[12] *labniyya* with *qishta*,[13] cereal with molasses, cereal with sugar, rice with milk, *zinkal*,[14] *'awama*,[15] *burani*,[16] *mutabal*[17] eggplant, *tasqiyya*[18] humus with ghee, *tasqiyya* humus with oil, *musbaha*,[19] *ful madamis*,[20] *kima*[21] with meat,

---

[1] Tiny dumplings made of flour and water.

[2] Meat stewed, with the cover on, slowly.

[3] A meat dish.

[4] A stew of meat and cauliflower with sauce.

[5] A layered dish of toasted bread pieces, covered with tomato sauce, stuffed small eggplants, and topped with yoghurt and garlic sauce.

[6] Sweet noodles and milk.

[7] Kanafa is a baked sweet made of vermicelli, sugar, melted butter and honey, and served on a large tray. The varieties mentioned here are stuffed with nuts, and covered with nuts on top.

[8] Thin pancakes stuffed with cream.

[9] Pudding with sweet syrup.

[10] White rice pudding with nuts on top.

[11] Burak is thin layers of pastry stuffed with other ingredients.

[12] A meat dish with broken pieces of dried bread.

[13] A rice and milk dish with cream.

[14] A sweet pastry poured in small blobs into boiling fat and then covered with honey.

[15] Small circles of dough fried like doughnuts and covered with honey.

[16] A mulukhiyya dish—a green leafy vegetable cooked with meat or chicken.

[17] A type of babaghanuj (with eggplant, tahini, lemon, garlic and salt).

[18] A mashed chickpea dish with tahina and pieces of bread soaked in the chickpea juice, lemon, and salt.

[19] Cubed potatoes cooked with meat, onion and tomatoes in the oven.

[20] A cooked bean dish with tomatoes, garlic, and onions.

[21] Truffles.

zinud al-banat,[1] *minazala bi-azwad*,[2] fried fish, broiled fish, and fish that is cooked with a ground pinenut, parsley, and lemon sauce poured over it. There is cucumber and yoghurt salad, and vinegar salad, fattush, and babaghanuj. Then there are all the kinds of *kibbi*: in yoghurt, with apricots, on a tray, fried, grilled, raw, and stuffed. There are lamb in oil, *shakriya*,[3] stuffed vegetables, and *shaikh al-mahshi*[4] in yoghurt, *yalanji*[5] in oil. And there are *muqam'a* meat,[6] *mudalala*,[7] Dauud Pasha, *asakru*,[8] *miqarata*[9] meat, meat cooked in vinegar, and *fakhda*[10] with rice. The last one we cook at the time of the feast.

Muslims in Damascus, daughter, on the 'Ashura holiday[11] and on New Year's Day of the Hijra calendar cook a white dish so the whole year will be "white" or good: for example, labaniyya, shaikh al-mahshi, shakriyya, rice in milk, cereal in milk or fresh cream. In the month of Rajab[12] they cook the "Night of God" dish, and in Sha'ban[13] *ghuraiba*,[14] and in Ramadan[15] *brazig*.[16] The Christians in Damascus also have good dishes for their feast days. At Christmas they cook chicken stuffed with rice in milk, boiled stuffed kibbi and mahashi. In the New Year, like us, they cook something white so the year will be good, labaniyya, rice in milk, mashiyya and cream. In the Feast of the Epiphany they make a mixture of molasses and

---

[1] A sweet like ladyfingers; the crisp curled pastry shell is stuffed with nuts.

[2] A thick stew of meat, eggplant, and onion.

[3] A meat and onion dish cooked in yoghurt.

[4] Vegetables such as zucchini or eggplant stuffed with meat and pinenuts in yoghurt.

[5] Grape leaves stuffed with vegetables or rice instead of meat.

[6] Meat stewed in small pieces.

[7] Similar to muqam'a meat.

[8] Meatballs in tomato sauce.

[9] A chopped meat dish.

[10] Leg of lamb, boned and stuffed with rice, minced meat and spices, and cooked in water over a low heat. The last few minutes it is browned in the oven.

[11] The holiday is on the tenth day of the Muslim month of Muharram, on the day when Hassan and Hussain were killed.

[12] Rajab is the seventh month of the Muslim year.

[13] Shaban is the eighth month of the Muslim year.

[14] Ghuraiba is a sweet.

[15] Ramadan is the ninth month of the Muslim year, when Muslims fast from sunrise to sunset.

[16] Sesame-seed and pistachio cookies.

walnuts, and *bakhat*, that is burak with meat and *arisha*. On the Feast of the Saturday before Easter they make *harira baluza*, rice with scattered molasses and walnuts and aniseed on the top of it. On the Feast of St. Barbara they make *sliqa*[1] and qataif and marmalades. On Palm Sunday they eat salted fish.

So, my daughter, you can see that Damascus food is done in the right way. Maybe it is the most delicious food in the entire world. We wear ourselves out making it, but the food is good and clean and healthy for our teeth. It is a blessing...May God keep it and not take it from us.

I left Mother in the kitchen and returned to my room to write:

> Mother is a world with no beginning and end
> Mother is a green heaven in which gazelles run, unhurried,
> Mother is a blue earth on which thick clouds gather
> Mother is wide ocean where colored fish play
> Mother is past, present and future
> Mother is time incarnate
> Mother is the blood of life flowing through my veins
> I ask for nothing more from God than her existence
> She is a blessing. May God keep her.

---

[1] Cereal cooked with sugar and covered with pomegranate seeds and nuts.

Chapter Four

You, Bridegroom, Don't Frown!

"Tickets"—invitation cards—arrived from the bridegroom's family for the men.

Two cards. I was floating on air because mother had chosen to take me to the wedding with her this time. I ironed my blue satin dress with the gathered waist and the blue ribbons to decorate my hair and was ready three hours before the appointed time.

My beautiful young mother put on a tasteful black velvet evening dress, one of the dresses of her trousseau that was the work of her dressmaker "Fahmiyya Khanum." At her neck hung a wide imitation diamond necklace and from her ears dangled a pair of long earrings made from real precious diamonds given to her as a gift from her mother—my grandmother. Stuck in her hair was a lovely fresh red rose and decorating her wrists were bracelets of jasmine buds. Her face, chest, neck, back and wrists were made up beautifully with *slismani*,[1] her eyes darkened with kohl as black as charcoal and her cheeks and lips painted lightly with red. I stood looking at my mother with love, joy and admiration. My beautiful mother...I would never see anyone more beautiful!

Eventually my father tapped at the door with quick hard taps of the knocker that we understood meant we were to open the door quickly and come out because he had come for us with a black carriage from Marje Square. Mother threw her black coat on and covered her head and face with a heavy black veil. She took my hand and we walked behind my father to the black carriage waiting at the entrance of the narrow street to take us to the bridegroom's house. I was so happy I almost wanted to kiss the driver with his red tarbush and his dear horses, one black and one white. Oh, what joy to be able to see the bride. I will never stop looking at her!

The carriage stopped at the top of the narrow street and we climbed down to walk on foot to the door of the wedding. Children of the quarter were gathered around the entrance. An old Haj sat on a rush-bottomed stool guarding the door and ordering the children to keep away. Preceding us by only a few minutes was a group of women guests with their as yet un-weaned babies. The old man started to argue with them, insisting that only those with tickets be allowed in. One of them swore she was from the bride's side of the family and if she were prevented from entering, she might

---

[1] A powder that makes the skin look clear and white.

become angry and refuse to attend the wedding at all, for which he would bear the blame!

We arrived—Mother and I—with our tickets held out in front of us. He welcomed us and made a path for us to enter without problems. Mother lifted the veil from her face and the bride's family in the entrance of a corridor brilliantly illuminated by a string of lights, greeted us their dear guests with *zagharid*[1] After exchanging congratulations and kisses, one of the women took my mother's veil and coat. With warm words of welcome she showed us to the courtyard to the place of honor in the best cane-seated chairs of the best row on the left side of the reception area. Those invited by the bridegroom sit in the left block of chairs and those invited by the bride in the right block in the most prominent area at the front as a way of honoring the bride—that is the usual way it is done.

The bride is given the highest place of honor in the reception area. She was sitting on an *aski*[2] decorated with rugs, roses, lights and large lighted posters on which in beautiful script is written "Allah," "Muhammad," "*Mashallah*,"[3] and "May the Eye of Envy be Blinded."

Not far from the platform a large basket covered in pink chiffon stood proudly, concealing layers of sugar-covered nuts, candies, chocolates in the shape of gold coins, colored-sugar toy miniatures and small imitation musical instruments all sweet to the taste. The basket waits silently for the bridegroom's arrival at which time he will turn on its lights, open it and feed the bride one of its candies. Then together they will throw handfuls of the sweets to the guests, hoping that by doing so they will spread the happy "infection" to those who have not married yet.

I sat down dazzled—mother greeted her neighbors sitting behind her, exchanging pleasantries and asking after their health and about distant family members from among our relatives. She traded comments with a nice jolly neighbor about the beauty of the bride and her adornment. She related some jokes to this group of women, and their sweet womanly laughter and the tinkling of their golden bracelets rang out across the Arabic courtyard open to the clear sky with its silver stars and came to rest in the branches of the lemon trees, the kabad, the naranj, lilac, jasmine and grape vines.

A woman asked for a glass of cold water. Another called from a window on the upper floor of the house, "Whoever has a baby wrapped in a silk coverlet with blue embroidery, come nurse him. He's about to burst from

---

[1] The trilling sound of joy.

[2] A raised platform.

[3] An expression used to confer God's blessing and protection.

crying and is going to wake the other babies." A third woman shouted angrily at her neighbor in front of her when she pushed back her chair suddenly and the leg of the chair tore a hole in the tulle of her evening dress. With the tip of an embroidered handkerchief, the bride wiped the perspiration that was forming on her brow from the heat of electric lights and pressure lamps, so her face cream wouldn't run and spoil the effect of her "toilette." The mother of the bridegroom and her daughters greeted each new group of guests in the corridor with ululations of joy and *ahlan wa sahlans*.[1] An old woman with a bright face, watching the young girls happily circling the courtyard and fountain, moved her lips silently to the accompaniment of her white hands, as she moved the beads of her Muslim rosary one by one. Despite the darkness, we recognized the faces of neighbors who were not invited on the roof of a house overlooking the courtyard, until their faces disappeared behind the white curtains of their veils.

I stared with fixed eyes at the face of the bride—the most beautiful human being in the whole world. This was the bride! How dazzling she was! How often mother would call me "Little Bride" when I would do something for her or respond quickly to her requests, and she would reward by brother with "May God bless you, Little Bridegroom" when he would fill the water jug for her from the public "fija" tap.

Being a bridegroom or a bride is the height of human glory—the end of a long road—and the supreme ideal for people who have married or those who have not married yet. Being a bride is the dream of little girls and being a bridegroom the dream of little boys. Both grow up to realize that dream.

A bride in my childish imagination was a super-human creature. She was an angel with wings that can't fly—she was not like other people— she was the center of the world—a beautiful white bird amidst a flock of black crows. A wedding to my heart, eyes and way of looking at things consisted of the bride only with everything else a shadow by comparison.

Maybe she dazzled me because of what glittered on her head, chest, neck, ears and hands in the way of real diamonds, or of what adorned her in roses, carnations and jasmine. Despite my young age, however, I sensed the underlying reality. If I analyzed what I saw the dazzle would disappear for a few minutes before it returned. The diamonds did not belong to her, they were borrowed!

Yes, you bride—I said this to her in my heart—I knew from my grandmother and my mother that most Damascene brides borrowed diamonds from the Damascene families who owned the precious old gems. Then, after

---

[1] "Hello, welcome."

the wedding was over the diamonds were returned to their owners. "I will never be convinced that all these diamonds are yours or your mother's because I do not believe that such a quantity of diamonds is owned by any one woman!" And as if the bride read my thoughts she adjusted the diamonds on her breast. I started thinking about Um Husni, a good woman who lived in Maidan at the end of the train line and my mind began to wander. She lived at the last station after a long and enjoyable ride from Marje to Maidan Fuqani. With great joy I would climb on the train with my grandmother— mother of my mother—sitting always near the window so I could enjoy looking at Jabiyya Gate, Sinaniyya, and the funeral processions heading toward the cemetery of Saghrir Gate with its marble gravestones rising above the wall along the left side of the train track. The train would stop at Shaikh Hassan Mosque and then continue its journey through Maidan quarter to the wood carvers' suq where you could find wood and marble shops, mother-of-pearl and mosaic craftsmen and all the furnishings and necessities required by brides being piled high on carts and pulled by porters: chairs, sofas, cupboards, bureaus, tables, dressing tables with mirrors, bridal clogs—all decorated with mother-of-pearl. The train would stop at Musala Gate, Shaikh Uthman where they roast legumes and nuts, at the slaughter house, then past Mujtahid,[1] Sidi, Suhaib, the Fathi Bath, the grain storehouses and Qurashi the shoemaker at the end of the line. I would jump up from my wooden seat before the train stopped, shouting at the top of my lungs, "Stop, stop, Uncle!" although of course he was going to stop anyway because we were at the end of the line. We would get off and he would turn the electric rod of the train around causing a spark to jump between the rod and its source that would frighten me. The "commissary"[2] would toot with his whistle and the train would return to Marje. What a great man he was, able to drive the train from either end! But *hamdulileah*[3] that the inspector didn't come to check all the tickets because my grandmother hadn't bought one for me!

I walked looking back at the train with my grandmother pulling me along—I was very much attached to the train and to the gentle ringing sound of its bell played by the conductor's foot in lovely soft strokes informing all the people that the train was on its way. My grandmother con-

---

[1] A mujtahid is a seeker after religious understanding through study of the Koran.
[2] The conductor.
[3] Thank God!

tinued to pull me along, "Come, walk, *'taita'*,[1] we've arrived...here is your aunt[2] Um Husni's, house...only two steps more!"

I looked at the head of the glittering bride and I remembered the face of the old woman, Um Husni, who owned a collection of real diamonds that could dazzle a person. She would lend the complete set to anyone who wanted to borrow it for the night of their daughter's wedding. Um Husni would be invited to the wedding where she would hand over the pieces to the parents of the bride on the bridal evening and she would receive them back again in the dawn of early morning and return to her house. As I remember, her collection included some unusual pieces for decorating the head, neck, chest, ears, hands, wrists and fingers. Each piece had a name that described its appearance: "lilies of birds," "comb for the head," "one hundred diamonds for the chest," "comb with eleven stars," "vine," "diamond brooch," "branch of pearls and gold jasmine flowers," "umbrella," "glittering dancing gazelle," "olive ring," "snake bracelet," and "needle." The needle was an expensive piece stuck in the bodice of the dress, with green leaves. There were also "long earrings with a spear," "earrings with a feather," "earrings with round holes like a jasmine blossom" and bracelets made of pearls, diamonds and gold.

The bridegroom is supposed to present the bride with an expensive piece of jewelry in front of all the people while she sits on the platform. This is in addition to what his father and mother and relatives give to the bride. And without doubt they have taught the bride what she must say to her bridegroom when they are alone together in their bedroom:

—I will not speak to you until you give me the price of my hair.

And she will demand the price of her long hair in the gentle enticing way they have taught her:

Open your wallet and give me the price of my hair
O feathers tickle me on my back
I am a young woman still in my ignorance
It is a long night; we can take our time.

He is supposed to present her the price of her hair in gold liras. On the morning after the wedding I have heard that they teach her to say:

---

[1] "Taita" is a familiar name children call their grandmothers. The usage here follows the pattern of adults calling children by the name that expresses their relationship to the child.

[2] Mother's sister.

58

May God make your morning happy.
You have made me meet the morning.[1]
I would take off official clothes
And dress you in your night shirt.

Despite the fact that I was very young I was like a mole, knowing all the customs of the grownups and the right things for a bridegroom to present to the bride on the morning after the wedding. It differed according to what the bridegroom prefered. Most of the time it would be a gift of expensive towels, a striped bath towel, a heavy carrying cloth embroidered with silk threads, a bath bowl, slippers, clogs, powder or rouge.

And the bride gave the bridegroom on the morning after the wedding: a pair of socks, a wallet, handkerchiefs, a length of woolen cloth, pajamas, a bathrobe or slippers.

All these beautiful images did not dispel the fear I felt for this beautiful bride. I knew the custom for the bridegroom to take some sort of strong action to show the strength of his manhood and make the bride fear and respect him from the first night. My fears were confirmed when I heard one guest whisper in the ear of her neighbor words that made my heart beat faster. I heard what she said, word for word:

—Poor thing—as soon as the bridegroom comes and goes up to the bedroom with the bride—when his eyes look into hers—he will want to slap her so that she will know that he is a man of substance and will always dominate her.

—By God, you can't tell. It depends on how clever she is. If she ascends the platform ahead of him and steps on his foot before he steps on hers she will have him in her hands from the first evening.

—May you bury me, this is a young bride, quiet and mannerly. She's not going to be able to do such a thing with this difficult bridegroom. Maybe he will overpower her from the first evening of their marriage.

—Don't worry, her mother is clever and probably has taught her everything.

—True, true! They invited me to the "Bath Evening" and "The Evenings of Decoration and Henna"[2] and we taught her ourselves what to

---

[1] This means, "You are the first one I see."

[2] These are two nights when parties are given to prepare the bride for her wedding. Henna is applied in patterns to the hands and feet to stain them a dark color. The effect is thought to be beautiful as well as soothing (henna is supposed to cool the palms and soles of the feet).

say to the bridegroom. I and the daughters of her aunt[1] and the sisters-in-law of her sister Duriyya and she will be quite equal to him and more!

—Yoo-oo, what did you teach her? Go ahead, tell me before the bridegroom comes. Yoo-oo curses,[2] why didn't they invite me to the bath. Tell me, you *did* have a good time at the bath!

—Oh how we enjoyed it and wished you were with us. God, what a wonderful bath party her family made for her. This took place one day before the bath. They invited me to the Henna Evening and hennaed the bride and young girls before my eyes.

—Tell me, how this henna is done. At the time of my wedding I didn't do the henna.

—I know, it is an old custom that doesn't exist anymore. Only a very few do it now. Two nights before my wedding we had a beautiful henna party. My grandmother[3] decorated me and taught me what to say to my bridegroom if he asked me anything. First of all my grandmother took a honey-colored candle and gum arabic and melted them together over the fire of the brazier. Then she dipped a straw in the honey-gum mixture and drew on my wrists roses, triangles, circles, amulets, three apples, and a gazelle looking over its shoulder. For every picture she told me what to say to the bridegroom if he asked "What is the name of this drawing?" I remember she taught me the designs with these words:

> The designs on your hand turn to the left.
> How happy your bridegroom yesterday and tonight.
> If he asks you about the meaning of these three flowers, tell him:
> —The three of us fell in love, I, my sister and my neighbor.
> —Embrace me so I can embrace you and if you don't I'll quarrel with you.
> —A branch of zidab[4] and my heart melts for you.
> —A cushion, my cousin.
> —Slave, slave see what your master wants; big jugs of the Nile want you.
> —He sits in front of me and I in front of him and you who look
>   like an Umayyad king with all his lamps lit, he sings to me
>   and I sing to him all night long.

God keep her and have mercy on the earth that received her. Then, my grandmother took some red henna and mixed it with cold water, and kneaded

---

[1] Mother's sister.

[2] Literally, she calls out "*arishi,*" which is a kind of cheese.

[3] Mother's mother.

[4] A plant with small delicate leaves that have a nice aroma; often women wear a small piece in their hair.

it. She painted my hand and bent down my fingers one by one, wrapping the thumb separately. Next day in the morning she removed the henna and the wax and washed my hands. Then she painted my nails with *ghushush*, arsenic and molasses, and wrapped my hand in fig leaves for about a quarter of an hour. They say that this was the design will become dark black and make the skin of the hands and wrists appear whiter. Oh, it was so beautiful it would take your breath away!

Oh, those days, you remind me of my wedding night! What a pity we were so ignorant. I remember what my mother taught me to say to the bridegroom first thing on the wedding night, and what a torture it was to learn it by heart:

> You must scale the fish
> The basis of my obligation is to you
> The hearts of the animals saw me with you
> May my bones vanish but never my love to you.

I remember they taught me to say to my bridegroom:

> My body melts whenever I think of you
> The same way that stones disintegrate on mountain tops.
> Ask someone who has experienced suffering
> And don't ask the one who hasn't suffered.
> Ask the Pleiades, or the seven stars
> You, O star of the morning, they will tell you
> about my condition.

—Fine, but you didn't tell me about the bath!

—Wait, I'm coming to that. The family of the bride rented the entire bath and invited friends, family and all the obligatory people. In my wedding we took three of the reserved basins and hung a towel at the entrance of the room to protect us from the evil eye of the other customers. At that time, we made kibbi nayya, taking ground meat and all the ingredients for the kibbi: onion pepper, salt, burghul, and salad and prepared it in the bath. Father sent us a pail of 'arqsus and ten melons that we immersed in the cool water of the fountain. We sang and danced and beat the bath cups and because I was the bride I sat at the head woman's basin. You know that no one sits there but her special customers. She washed my hair for me and treated us so nicely, "the mistress of the bath" spoiled and spoiled us! There was no one but the attendant in those days to carry cold water to the basins, and only a pipe for hot water. You know, we were all like one family enjoying ourselves immensely. After the wedding night we went to the

Ghamara Bath with the family of the bridegroom. I remember the bridegroom's family had to pay "the fulfillment" and "the soap" and the food for all the people. Oh those wonderful days, the way they expressed their happiness for me!

> Awha, mother of the bridegroom, may God repay you
> Awha, and may all happiness come your way.
> Awha, and we want your happiness to continue with the rest.[1]
> Awha, and we will come to compensate you.
> Lya lya lya lysh.
> Awha, mother of the bridegroom I am hungry
> Awha, I want roasted *sfiha*[2]
> Awha, may God keep you safe
> Awha, and your house flourishing
> Lya lya lya lysh.

—Tell me, was the bride's bath nice?

—Yi, Oh God, was it! They played the lute and danced and their voices were beautiful and everything needed was there to show hospitality: sfiha, fruit, lemonade. The young ladies marched proudly around the bath in their embroidered towels and the towels laid out to sit on were of the very highest quality. After bathing, the young girls lined up on the high area and dressed themselves in beautiful gowns, the glittering bride among them. They made a circle around the fountain for her. And they didn't let anyone pay a penny...it's a pity, too, because it cost them a lot. May God keep you, the bride was beautiful like a painted moon, young in age and it suited her. May God bring her good luck!

—Tell me, I hope they didn't forget to give her yeast for the dough to stick on the door of her mother-in-law's house to calm her anxieties and give her good luck!! God, on the night of my marriage they brought a woman to me, a good one known for getting pregnant easily and giving birth often. She was the one who presented me with the yeast dough on a green paper to stick on the door of the bridegroom's house before I was allowed to set even one foot inside so my marriage would last forever and my days would be "green" and productive. They also sprinkled salt on me to protect me from the evil eye. Really, before my bridegroom spoke one word to me, before we even went up to our bedchamber he stretched out the train of my white dress and prayed on it. And since that day, by God, all our life has been like ghee and honey!

---

[1] Her happiness will continue by marrying the rest off.

[2] A pastry with meat, spinach or cheese filling.

—Look, look, I don't know who that is who came in!

I turned my head with the two women to see who had come to interrupt the pleasant conversation and deprive me of more details. A new group of guests with their babies were there, each carrying a big bundle of clothes. They went directly up the stairs to the upper part of the house. Some entered the rooms of the first floor reserved for changing into the evening clothes they carried in the elaborate carrying cloths embroidered with silk and gold threads. The guests entered those rooms in black malayas like ghosts, and after awhile came out like beautiful Houris with gay dresses embroidered in different colored thread or gold or silver and decorated with roses and precious gems.

It was the elegant dress on the figure of a tall, fat, strikingly fair-skinned woman that began to steal the attention of the guests from the bride's beauty and white dress. Of course, the name of the seamstress was something very important in those days. One woman would have her dresses made at the "House of Farquh" and the other at the "House of Asbirdada," whom everyone knew didn't take less than 100 gold pounds. The third woman would never have her dresses made anywhere else but at Mme. Rose's in Qimariyya.

What used to astonish me most was that each young lady and each invited guest during the evening of the wedding used to change her clothes more than three or four times to various models, each a tasteful work of art. Each would go upstairs wearing one dress and come down wearing another, strutting proudly as a peacock, knowingly attracting the attention and admiration of her audience: "God willing may you never be deprived of such a fine figure." She would bring delight to the souls of the other women who commented that they hoped her husband enjoyed all that beauty. New brides who have not been married one full year yet first put on white evening dresses decorated with white roses exactly like a bride and walk around the wedding gathering like angels.

I was awakened from my sweet dreams of a world colored with beautiful clothes by the hand of a good woman, the mother of the bridegroom pushing a small packet into my lap. It was a white handkerchief containing nuts, chickpeas, Turkish delight, pistachios, almonds, hazelnuts, candy-covered nuts, and small pistachio wafers covered in sugar. A packet was offered to each invited guest for her enjoyment during that night that would extend until dawn. To my mother a packet and to me a packet. My mother swore that one was enough for the two of us and I was worried for a moment but the mother of the bridegroom, thank God, insisted that I should have my own.

What a wonderful thing it was for a child to have her own packet for herself! Oh, what a night, one of the happiest of my life!

I noticed that the breast of the beautiful sweet bride was rising and falling rapidly but I didn't understand the secret of this phenomenon. I started to ask my mother...but I was afraid she would get angry. When she decided to bring me to the wedding, she did it on condition that I would remain completely still and not run around or speak a word if I wanted to be taken with her another time. I swallowed the question although it continued to occupy my mind. What was the matter with the bride? Was she afraid, and if so, how could a person be afraid on such an entertaining evening or in such a house which to me seemed like a paradise. I remained immobile in my place though my real wish was to fly through the air and settle like a bird at the side of the bride, or sit at her feet the way the other young girls of the wedding did. I was burning with jealousy.

The bride was shy, not raising her eyes to look at the guests who were staring at her continuously. Beside her was the chair of the bridegroom awaiting the arrival of its owner. Then I heard a murmur of excitement which made all the heads turn in happy anticipation. They said that the bridegroom's people had brought a band of singers for their son's wedding but up until now no one know who the singers would be. My mother said jokingly "Maybe it's the daughters of Maknu," although she knew that the daughters of Maknu were a famous old female band which had played at the time she was a baby. A neighbor sitting beside her responded to the joke, "No, maybe it's Ramziyya al-Baqa, or Badriyya naml Badani, or Jamila al-Nukta." My mother replied nearly bursting with laughter, "Anyone except Nazmiyya al-Khanna. She would make you die! The way she plays the lute is nice but, sister, by the time she finishes a melody your heart will burst. She won't play the lute until she has eaten and you have offered her a pack of cigarettes. And then, if she likes one of your rings and you don't give it to her she gets angry and stops playing. I can't stand her!"

A third woman joined in, "Inshalla, I hope it will be Um Hilmi with Anukabrat. I like her male dress and her song '*Ya halali wa'ya mali ya rub'ay trudu 'alaya* (O Halali, O Mali, you around us, repeat after us) and the song 'Try me, I Weave and Spin.' I hope she never tires of wearing *shirwal*,[1] vest, scarf, head cloth and head band and putting on a false mustache!" A fourth woman whispered in the ear of her jolly neighbors, "By God, I don't like Um Hilmi's voice! I hope they bring Mikiyya al-Samra or Najiyya Kalash or Fahmiyya Qa'ati or Badriyya al-Naqra! I hope they get a

---

[1] Shirwal are big baggy men's pants.

singer who brings with her a band of musicians who play the *qanun*,[1] violins, drums, tambourines and castanets really loudly so we can enjoy ourselves."

Exciting news...sleep flew from my eyes. Of course the young women of the wedding must dance the circle dance with the bride around the big marble pool where the water spills out of the pipes with such a monotonous melody that it inspires sheer pleasure. The bride stood in the middle and a group of girls—more than ten, walked in step together to the music.

The songs rang out freely in the air of the wedding. The bride between the girls dressed in colorful evening dresses took awkward, stumbling steps, shyly not willing to raise her eyes from the ground. The first song for the circling began with the indistinct words *"luiha, luiha, luiha..."* expressing joy in soft tones...and as if these words "Here she is" actually pointed at the bride, the young women grasped her hand singing either "Here she is, our bride." Repeating this phrase, the group of young women began swaying from left to right in one gentle movement.

> Here she is, here she is, here she is
> Here she is, my lady, my girl, look at her.
> How many hundreds has your father taken for you.
> We were exhausted before your brother finally consented.
> God made you dear to us; may you enjoy your life.
> Lya, lya, lya lysh.[2]
>
> Here she is, my lady, my girl
> Take off this cover and throw it away
> Curse the father of the one who wove it
> And curse the father of the one who bought it for you.
> If your father's house is a veil, pull it off and
> throw it away.
> Lya, lya, lya, lysh.
>
> Rise and ascend to the high palace
> By the life of your father, the dear one.
> She made an oath she wouldn't go
> Except with a band of woman singers
> Lya, lya, lya, lysh.

And another beautiful song sung by the brides of Damascus:

---

[1] A stringed instrument resembling the zither.
[2] This line is in the high shrill ululating sound women make to express joy.

In the name of God, O beautiful one
O rose in the garden,
Plant a carnation, O bride
And the rose will shade us.

Rise up, and play with a string of pearls
Let your hair fall long and free
Let them speak and say,
O you beautiful one, you sweet one.

Rise up and play with a string of diamonds
The pearls are guarding your breasts
May God protect you from people's talk
Oh you beautiful one, you Damascene.

Rise up and play with your blouse
All bachelors are at your disposal
may God keep your bridegroom
Oh you beautiful one, you sweet one.

The young girls never tire of dancing in a circle:

Coquettishly, coquettishly
Like the steps of the gazelle
She puts on a dress and takes off a dress
Under the dress is something illuminating to me.

Coquettishly, coquettishly
Like the steps of the gazelle
She puts on a slip, and takes off a slip
Under the slip is something illuminating to me.

Coquettishly, coquettishly
Like the steps of the gazelle
She puts on pearls, and takes off pearls
Under the pearls is something illuminating to me.

Another song of brides:

O sleeping one, O sleeping one
Don't disturb the sleeping one
You are sleeping so relaxed
Your waist like a fan
O sleeping one with hennaed hands
May you have a life of pleasure
You the lover of my heart.
Had it not been for fasting and praying

66

I would have been sleeping at your breast
O sleeping one, O sleeping one
Don't disturb this sleeping one

This circling dance is inevitable at every wedding so that luck and happiness will "circle" around the bride's whole wedded life.

They returned the bride to her splendid chair on the high platform and the minutes continued to pass as though hours or alternatively the hours like minutes, I don't know which. The bridegroom remained an obscure creature, handsome, feared, beloved, and dreaded. The empty chair beside her was calling for its owner while she waited with longing, anxiety and fear the human being they had chosen for her and whom she would see and speak to for the first time that night.

We heard a clamor in the distance, shouting, the voices of men and gunshots coming from the end of the quarter. It must be the bridegroom's procession arriving from the business of dressing. The young men in a circle around the bridegroom chanted into the happy night giving the neighbors no chance to sleep.

Pray to Muhammad, the bright and fresh one
May God bless him and do well by him,
Pray to Muhammad, the bright and fresh one.

The women at the wedding responded to the men with ululating. At the main entrance from behind the door the bridegroom was received by his mother, sisters, paternal and maternal aunts and all his female relatives.

The bridegroom stepped over the threshold and into the corridor and appeared in the courtyard with his majestic height and his extreme elegance, dressed in a black suit and a wine colored tarbush and with a smile concealed under his thick mustache. The lady guests quickly pulled their veils over their faces or lifted the hems of their evening dresses to conceal their heads, chests and bare arms.

The mother of the bridegroom whispered into the ear of her son, "May you bury me, better without the tarbush, take off the tarbush! You look handsomer without it. No one wears a tarbush nowadays."

—No, I'm not going to take it off. Has honor deserted us that we should take our tarbushes off? He took two steps forward.

In the wedding hall a surprising incident took place. Laughter turned into a storm of tears that cascaded down cheeks and the ululating turned into a sharp argument between the families of the bride and groom. My heart stopped beating...and I stood on a cane chair to see find out the details of the dispute and the positions of the two sides. The bride in all her attractiveness and splendor stood on the platform trembling and waiting...and at her side were her married sister and her eldest paternal aunt...for her mother was dead.

At the end of the courtyard stood the bridegroom in dignity and silence and holding him by both arms were his mother and eldest sister, swearing with the most solemn oaths that the bridegroom would not move a step forward until the bride approached him.

On the other side the eldest sister of the bride, the tears almost choking her, swore that her sister would not descend from the platform and would not take one step until the bridegroom came to her and greeted her. Voices called out from here and there. Neither the bridegroom nor the bride had to speak because each had their advocates who spoke without even being asked to do so. The argument waxed hotter and more acrimonious and the situation became critical, each party refusing to concede a word and affirming her adherence to her position until the last!

The wedding party had almost turned into a funeral, the singing into tears, and the ululating into an exchange of curses. But by the wisdom of God, a respectable older woman with prayer beads in her hand and wearing a blue dress with a white silk garment covering her head and body stood and quietly announced a compromise. What was the solution? The bride should step forward to the middle of the courtyard and the bridegroom to the middle where they would shake hands and then he would take her hand and lead her back to the platform.

The wise suggestion of the older woman found a good response from both sides. The bride descended from the platform and her sister wiped away the tears from her cheeks. The bride reached the midpoint, shook hands with the bridegroom and he led her back to her glittering, brightly lighted throne, decked with sweet-smelling fresh flowers. He hung a precious diamond around her neck while the women clapped and young women ululated. Then his sister handed him a red carnation that he pinned to the bodice of the bride's white dress...she had plucked it out of a bunch of flowers decorating the platform. Another woman presented a white iris to the bride to put in the buttonhole of the bridegroom's suit amid sharp storms of applause. Then the bridegroom removed the transparent pink covering from the sweets and took one to feed the bride. He ate one with her and then the two of them started throwing the sweets to the guests...pieces of colored sugar, chocolate filled gold coins, and musical instruments made of candy. I myself caught a gold coin, a lute and a violin of sugar.

The crowd around the bride and groom increased. The young women rushed to the hall in two groups with, at the head of each, a woman who was clever at ululating. This time they all started the ululating with the word "awha." Then a clever woman would recite a refrain and all the young ladies would ululate in answer with the words lya, lya, lya, lysh.

Awha, don't frown, O bridegroom
Awha, untie the bundle and put on your new clothes.
Awha, your mustaches are like sweet basil
Awha, your sideburns are like narcissus
Lya, lya, lya, lysh.

Awha, there is a pomegranate at our house
Awha, sour and bittersweet
Awha, we made an oath not to promise it
Awha, until our bridegroom enters safely
Lya, lya, lya, lysh.

Awha, You[1] are the happy One
Awha, Muhammad is the Dragon
Awha, and if he doesn't say pray to the Prophet
Awha, may he lose his two eyes.
Lya, lya, lya, lysh.

Awha, 'Al'al'ali, 'Al'al'ali
Awha, O you young women get together
Awha, O you evening—lengthen
Awha, O you sun—don't rise
Lya, lya, lya, lysh.

Awha, I fortified you, Yasiin[2]
Awha, you the flowers of the orchards
Awha, you the little Koran
Awha, you over the heads of the Sultans
Lya, lya, lya, lysh.

Awha, what is this appropriate day
Awha, in which you have made all creatures happy
Awha, and the hearts of my enemies burst
Awha, when the truth was realized
Lya, lya, lya, lysh.

Awha, our houses are large

---

[1] God
[2] One of the names of the Prophet.

Awha, and the pigeons fly around in them
Awha, the mother of the bridegroom is pleased
Awha, may God make her happy
Lya, lya, lya, lysh.

Awha, O bridegroom I ask a blessing on your marriage
Awha, O bridegroom, seven blessings
Awha, inshallah, when you have a boy
Awha, your pleasure will be complete
Lya, lya, lya, lysh.

Awha, your forehead shines
Awha, your ears ring
Awha, you'll never leave here
Awha, until you feed us all that's been collected
Lya, lya, lya, lysh.

Awha, raise your head and see her
Awha, before you have done with her
Awha, if you had a girlfriend before, leave her
Awha, and don't cross the coffee shop's threshold again
Lya, lya, lya, lysh.

Awha, O all of you here
Awha, we haven't forgotten your favors
Awha, today the pleasure is here
Awha, tomorrow we hope at your house
Lya, lya, lya, lysh.

Awha, O bridegroom you one
Awha, your brother's a dragon
Awha, one blue bead
Awha, to reject the evil eye
Lya, lya, lya, lysh.

Amid the ululating that rang through the whole quarter, the bride and bridegroom ascended the stairs of the house to the bedchamber and the whispering started up among the women.

One whispered in the ear of her neighbor:

—I wish I were a tiny gnat so I could hide in the bridegroom's hair to hear what he will say to the bride.

—Yes, by God, a beautiful bride. I hope he enjoys her. Look! Look! Now they are pulling the curtains across the window so we won't see anything. Ha ha ha!

In the absence of the two stars of the wedding the atmosphere changed for the guests. The lute was tuned when the bridegroom's mother swore to one of the guests that she would play so they could enjoy her solo playing and so the young girls could dance and sing until the professional singer and her band arrived. She played for them "The Dance of My Lady" while the bridegroom's sisters pulled more than one young lady out on the dance floor. This girl refused and that hesitated pettishly but it was inevitable that each one must dance by the time they finished with her.

The one with the sweet voice was asked to sing to them "O Treasure of Damascus," and "Mijana and 'Atabaa," "O Night," and "O Dove, Fly Away." She enchanted us with her singing, forcing sighs of admiration to our lips.

O fly fly, you dove and alight in Dumar and Hama
Bring me a sign from my Love with the dark features and the beauty mark
Enough this torture, for the sake of God
I'm still a believer, but you've made me mad
In my religion love is forbidden, what a pity by God.

Fly over me dove and alight in Dumar and Hama
Bring me a sign from my Love, a cigarette and a coal of burning fire.
Enough this torture for the sake of God
I'm still a believer, but you've made me mad
In my religion love is forbidden, what a pity by God.
O bird, fly high and tell me; alight at my Love's house
Whatever they say, come tell me what happened
Enough this torture for the sake of God
I'm still a believer, but you've made me mad
In my religion love is forbidden, what a pity by God.

O bird, wild bird, alight at the house of my parents
Bring me their love and sympathy to put out the fire in my heart
Enough this torture for the sake of God
I'm still a believer, but you've made me mad
In my religion love is forbidden, what a pity by God.
Tears fall on my breasts from the day we separated, my Love
Come to me and turn to me you beauty with the mole on your cheek
Enough this torture for the sake of God
I'm still a believer, but you've made me mad
In my religion love is forbidden, what a pity by God.

Tears fall burning for I am one who loves secretly
O mama, how difficult parting is; I can't bear the parting
Enough this torture for the sake of God

I'm still a believer, but you've made me mad
In my religion love is forbidden, what a pity by God.

Tears fall; I am crying and puzzled; with whom should
I speak
I complain to my God of the longing and fire
Enough this torture for the sake of God
I'm still a believer, but you've made me mad
In my religion love is forbidden, what a pity by God.

The song ended accompanied with sighs. The woman guest tried to leave the lute but there were a thousand rejections of this idea and a thousand "By God it was wonderful" until they finally importuned her to sing the song "Hanina," which she willingly did. She strummed with the pick on the lute and the beautiful voice sang:

O Hanina,[1] O Hanina, O Hanina
What is this time that has been turned upside down by love.

You who go to the lesson with prayer beads in your hand
And return from the lesson dizzy with love
What is this affair, O "Mama",[2] may I ask you
My love, my intense love, I am for you alone
My lady, my eyes, my life
By God, I will embrace you like pearls on a necklace
remain close to my throat
O Hanina, O Hanina, O Hanina

O Hanina, O nation of Islam, where is she my lover
The wing of a bird is like the eyelash of her eye
How lucky he who smells her fragrance and embraces her
His life would lengthen by twenty years
O Hanina, O Hanina, O Hanina.

People in love should be pitied like orphans
After they become stars, they become dark
I gave them the secret of Love, but they didn't keep it
What a pity, who can keep our secret
O Hanina, O Hanina, O Hanina
What is this time that has been turned upside down by love.

---

[1] Hanina is a name that means "sympathetic."

[2] The mother asks this question.

72

Then a young lady Um Sami, happy, clever and beautiful, stood up to recite some old love sayings and dance her famous playful dance based on imitations of guests dancing: "Yurm Khadija Balmam."[1] Um Sami began the song in a natural way that didn't make the people laugh. She repeated the name of the song which means "Khadija is lost" three times as if she were looking for her and couldn't find her. She approached each one of the ladies at the party asking if she had seen Khadija. One woman, not knowing what awaited her, answered, "No, by God, I haven't seen her," and Um Sami imitated her voice and gestures, "No, by God, I haven't seen her." Then she asked a second time and a third time and a fourth time, "Did you see Khadija?" But by then the answers were brief and well planned from fear of the imitation:

—No, I swear I haven't seen her, really!

—Yesterday we saw her, No!

—No, may God help you to fine her. Weren't you with her the day before yesterday?

Um Sami imitated her, "May God help you find her. Weren't you with her the day before yesterday?" And the whole group laughed with her. There was no stopping her, Um Sami imitated each woman no matter how clever she was. For each woman there was some special gesture that would make people laugh. We encouraged Um Sami to sing more of her nice songs as she stood there ready to perform. She asked, "What song do you want? I'm ready." Shouts rang out "We want the Alphabet Song" and she began strumming the lute. The rhythmic clapping from the crowd grew louder with the opening of the strange love song and the band joined in. The first lines consisted of rhyming words with no meaning, and then the main part of the song began:

> The letter A wraps the lover in the lap[2]
> And the B, I experience the disaster of your love.
> you light of my eye
> I repulsed the Arabs, the Persians, and the Turks, my beauty
> I saw them all and no one was sweeter in my eye than you.
>
> And the T is your image, Beautiful One
> The Th means I am steadfast in my love, my tears never dry
> Tears run down my cheeks
> Pay attention to your God and see what has happened to me.

---

[1] Turkish name.

[2] In the song the names of the letters relate to the sounds of key words, though not always as initial letters.

The J, my body became thin from longing and leaving you
The H, a beautiful smiling face who plunders the girls of
Damascus
I will become like a goat and roam freely with the gazelles
For the sake of the gazelle of the countryside whose beauty is
ever present.

The Kh, you made my mind desert me
The D, you made me melt, you hard-hearted one
If you had only known—ignoring and parting, O
Forgetful One
My body feels the pain of the burning brand.

The R, your spear destroyed me, your slender figure
The Z, why are you angered. Oh, if anger had never existed
I stay awake all night because of my lover; the night has
lengthened
And sleep has left me, You Beauty, and never returned to me

The S is your secret that I'll never tell but to you
If you want me as a slave I am ready
And also if you want me as a lover for enjoyment and
happiness.

The Sh, from your head to your tail, O how you move when
you walk
The S, your refusal has made me darken
I think, my full Moon, we didn't meet your approval
I sprinkle you, my Cumin, with water

And the D your laughter has made me the color of your
knocking
The T has cured my wounds by your hands
O Sweet One, for a kiss from your lips
I wouldn't be able to swallow a sip of water.

And the Th, the gazelle escaped from me, who can return it
The 'Ayn, I am fed up with my homeland and people for this
gazelle
This gazelle put a beauty mark on his cheek
My hand raised him not to hunt him in the countryside

The Gh is angry, O Lover, make peace with me
And F, you are the only one of glory, O Lover, forgive us
And sit down to eat with us, and for God's sake, eat from our
salt
So there may be friendship between us until Judgment Day
comes.

The Q, your body has made me thin
And K stop this being away from me, I can't take it anymore
You promised you would come on Sunday
How many Sundays…one, two, one hundred Sundays; you
didn't come.

The N, cry for what has become of me
The H, it is a punishment falling in love with a dear one
I love you though I have lost my mind and my money
I have nothing left to do anything with.

The W because of your face I am incapable
The L is the thousand times I asked you not to blame
me for this chatter
She was clever to heed the advice of wise people
Never fall in love with a young man unless his intentions are
pure.

The Y, O God, be Merciful, Forgiver of all sins
Pray and greet he who brought us the passages of the Koran
And forgive all my sins that are only inventions of my mind,
starting with A.

Again the rhyming refrain was repeated and the song was finished.

The choice then fell on a tall, dark, thin, attractive woman. This young woman stood at the insistence of the jolly Um Sami whose turn had ended, to sing her famous nice Damascene song that always made people laugh because of the funny movements that accompanied it. The lute was strummed, and one chord came out wrong and out of tune. The lute's owner fixed it and then the tune was perfect. The young women recited the refrains after the dark woman in a clever chorus that was able to learn the parts quickly by heart. The drum joined in with the lute and the dark woman began:

O salted nuts, O soft nuts
See my eyes, see
See my soul, see
See how soft my movements are.

He brought me make-up wrapped in a paper
I told him my lips can't take these
He said, "Come you graceful one,"
And while I was sleeping he painted me.

He brought me some powder wrapped in paper
I told him my cheeks can't take it

75

He said, "Come you graceful one,"
And while I was sleeping he powdered me.

He brought me a slip wrapped in paper
I told him, my body can't take this thing
He said, "Come you graceful one,"
And while I was sleeping he dressed me.

He brought me a brassiere wrapped in paper
I told him my breasts couldn't take it
He said, "Come you graceful one,"
And while I was sleeping he hooked it on me.

Suddenly the clapping and singing was interrupted by loud knocking on the door, and a young woman came running into all the women of the party saying that the men wanted to take the bridegroom out for some entertainment for a short while. Several women went up to the bedroom of the bride and bridegroom and after awhile the bridegroom came down reluctantly, as if a strong force had uprooted him to accompany the young men. When the bridegroom left, the woman, "The Hair Comber," who is responsible for the bride's beauty all through the night went in to her. No one was allowed to see the bride put on or take off her clothes except this woman, even though there were many curious eyes at the door who would have liked to watch. Next the bride came down in a black velvet evening dress with a low-cut bodice revealing the whiteness of her breasts and body. The neckline was decorated with a black gilt rose and there was a long smart train that fell behind her. The long sleeves were open for the length of her arm to show the whiteness of her skin and fastened at the wrists with soft buttons. She walked to her place on the platform like a queen. An old woman murmured, "Protect her, God."

For the entertainment of the bride two young ladies, one dark and one fair, stood up and started exchanging playful accusations with one another, accompanied by the lute and drums. The accusations took the form of nice gentle songs in which one praised herself and her coloring and disparaged the other. They started the song together with this opening:

Together: Come into the shadows
I want to see you for a minute
You have no sympathy at all for me.
The dark one:
The dark one said "God is Great"
All delicacies fall to the dark skinned one
Go away, you white one, soup of soldiers

All those who love you will return to me.
The fair one:
The white one said "I am rice in milk
The colder it becomes, the more delicious
Go away, you dark one, you are like a stick
All those who love you will return to me."
The dark one:
The dark one said "I am genuinely Arab
Wherever I turn my head someone greets me
Go away, you white one, you are a foreigner
All those who love you will return to me."
The fair one:
The white one said "My eyes are big
Darkened by God and my hair is long
Go away, you dark one, whose hair is like the slave
Three hours in the bath and it won't get wet."
The dark one:
The dark one said, "I am the color of coffee
The drink of princes, mixed with art
Go away, you white one, the broom of jinns
Why should anyone love your unripe color."
Together: Come into the shadows
I want to see you for a minute
You have no sympathy at all for me.

When the song finished, the bride was laughing a little, though trying
to hide her laughter. It was as though some of her shyness had worn off and
she had found the courage to smile. With her smile she appeared even more
beautiful than before.

With the return of the bride, the group of professional singers arrived
and the female singer began to sing some old Damascene songs. Of these I
remember, "O Fish O Brown One," the words of which go this way:

O Fish, O Brown One, I hate your enemies
You play in the water, it pleases me your play
Here you are Fish, O Brown One.

The one who fishes for you is clever, and who sells you
clever
Be reassured, You Beauty, get in touch with me
Here you are, O Fish, O Brown One.

O Fish, O Dewy One, the color of silver
Life passes and you quarrel with me
Here you are, O Fish, O Brown One.

O Fish, O Red One, the color of amber

77

You go proudly, his going makes me mad
Here you are, O Fish, O Brown one.

Then the singer sang a repetition of "O Night, O Eyes," her high strong voice piercing the charming spring Damascene night:

O Lightning, greet them and tell them to be willing
My night, my night, my eyes
Hurry with the answer, O your lovers have fallen ill
My night, my night, my eyes.

It is by your eyes that I repent to God's face
For the sins, but not for love, by God
Bring the Koran for me to swear on God's words
The mouth swears but the heart says no, by God.

It was opened by the wind, I thought the Absent One
was coming
I ran happy and laughing
I took the door in my arms
Oh, it seems the wind cheated me
My lover did not come.

The enchantment of the song took the crowd by storm and the guests demanded more and more of the same enchantment. The singer was not stingy with her gifts and sang for one of the young invited brides who it seemed was pregnant in her first months and only could eat special foods because she was so nauseated. This time it wasn't a desire for a special food but rather for a special song. The singer responded to her wish and sang for her "The Beautiful Woman Craved Grapes."

O you who sell grapes
A beautiful woman craves grapes
Bring them to me, O Mama, bring them to me
He brought me diamond earrings, I hope they fit me
Take your diamonds, bring me grapes.

O you who sell grapes
A beautiful woman craves grapes
Bring them to me, O Mama, bring them to me
He brought me pearls, I hope they fit me
Take them, sell them, bring me grapes.

O you who sell grapes
A beautiful woman craves grapes
Bring them to me, O Mama, bring them to me

He brought me a gold necklace, I hope it fits me
Take it, sell it, bring me grapes.

When the bridegroom returned from the men's entertainment, the bride went up with him to the bedroom. She remained with him for a short time, and then she came down wearing a blue dress the color of the sky and with long ropes of pearls entwined in her hair. Some of the young women went to her and whispered secrets in her ear. The secrets caused her to smile shyly. I saw the bridegroom pulling aside the curtain a little so only his eyes appeared, watching the bride and the pleasure it brought to the group when she appeared again.

Then I saw across the courtyard trays of pistachio ice cream looking as though they were flying over the heads of the guests. I was pleased, for a wedding without ice cream and without colored sweets is not a wedding at all. The woman who arranged the wedding, Futika, was responsible for providing ice cream for the guests and her duty was to distribute it to everyone, big or small. If she forgot even one guest "woe be unto her," for people would never stop saying what a shame it was at that wedding that there hadn't been enough to go around.

The bride returned to her bridegroom to eat a cup of ice cream and then came back again to us, this time wearing a rose colored dress. What was left of my senses vanished with the charming sight before me. Every time she returned to us she was more beautiful and dazzling. I do remember, though, that finally she went up to the bedchamber and didn't come down again. I had heard that the bride's family had invited the midwife to be present at the wedding,[1] but I couldn't understand the secret of why she had been invited, for no one was going to suffer labor pains that night!

The lights went out in the bedroom of the bride and groom, and suddenly the ululating resumed in the courtyard and the group of dancers and singers returned. And it was as though the wedding party itself didn't want to end; a woman singer seized the lute and started singing this song, but before singing she started swaying back and forth:

I entered the garden gate
The nightingale answered me
The jasmine complained
The roses told me I could pass
O Tree of Mortality,
Why did you bear carnations?

---

[1] To confirm the bride's virginity.

79

The tree responded
My heart melts for lovers
I couldn't stand it any longer.

The dark woman sways and sways
She casts a glance, that dark one
My soul is this dark one, my eyes are this dark one
She is my life this dark one
In the light of the moon
She lit a lantern

I am a violet, I am a violet, dyed with bluing
To the young man sitting before me
You Handsome One, you've broken me like a china cup
I had the misery of loving you, May God be sympathetic
The dark one sways and sways
On whom does she cast her eye?
    My neighbor, the old woman, whispered in the ear of her
neighbor:
    —Morning is coming...I hope the bride didn't forget
what I told her to say to the bridegroom when morning came.
    —Tell me what you told her!
    —I told her to say nice things to him like:
May your morning be bright, you foreigner, you straw
of amber, you creature of God.
If in place of you they offered me a thousand or a hundred
I would never love anyone but you or want any other.

Lemon, lemon, you are sweeter than the lemon.
Your love is in my heart, you are a jewel hidden there.
And if you loved another, higher or lower
Your enemy would be the Prophet buried in the Holy Place.

I passed by the water channel side by side
I found chains of gold placed on my hands
By the life of one who taught gazelles to leap and skip
They played with my mind the way the pencil plays with this
line.

The call for morning prayer was heard and the women withdrew to the
upper floors to pray.

The light flickered and the birds began to twitter in the lemon and orange trees and magnolias perfumed the morning with the smell of paradise.
The guests started changing their clothes and donning the black robes and
thick black veils, and gathering up their evening clothes in bundles. They
wakened the little children, and picked up the tiny bodies in preparation for

their return home. The guests were surprised to find that without exception all their children had wet their beds where they slept and each woman felt ashamed in front of the hostess over her child's problem. The women until now don't know that one of the little girls woke up in the middle of the night and, discovering she had wet her bed unintentionally and not wanting her mother to know, had taken a jug of water and wet all the pants of all the children so her crime would be lost among the crimes of all the children. No child would be better than another!

Morning dawned…and the crowd grew thinner. The colored butterflies bid farewell to the cane chairs. The morning light disclosed in scandalous clarity the shells of black and white seeds and pistachios, the water spilled on the ground, and sweets crushed under chairs. The night had come to a close.

In a line the groom's mother, his sisters, his aunts, and his paternal cousins stood in the entrance hall to say goodbye to the guests. The groom's mother swore by God to some of the guests from the family of the bride and groom (in other words the necessary people) that they simply must take breakfast with them. No sooner were the other guests out the front door than the trays of *bughaja*[1] and other sweets, a hot milk and rice dish, and fresh cakes all arrived from the best sweet maker in Damascus. The groom's mother insisted we stay, but my mother apologized that she could not because she had to return to my little brothers.

All those who were invited to the wedding were also invited to be present at the congratulation of the bride on the fifth day ("in the eye of the devil")[2] and the sixth day. My mother promised her we would come on one or the other day.

My mother kissed all the women, saying goodbye warmly and sincerely, and repeating the traditional phrases:

—May what you have done be blessed. I hope it will be a marriage for life and that the oldest unmarried girls will marry too!

—Don't forget to come for the "congratulations."

—I will be honored to come.

—You will be welcome a hundred times.

—By your body and your eyes.

—Greet your husband for me and kiss the little ones.

—God bless you.

---

[1] This is a pastry stuffed with pistachios or meat.

[2] Five symbolizes the hand with its five fingers that when held up wards off the Evil Eye.

—Goodbye.

—Go in peace.

The soft cold breezes of morning penetrated my bones. I held my mother's hand, dragging my feet from sleepiness. The people of the quarter woke up with the merry voices of the women returning from the wedding unescorted in a time when women respected the domination of men over them.[1] I walked with my mother and a group of guests through the safe streets of Damascus. The beautiful guests walked with their veils partly raised from their faces, for the streets were empty and men hadn't yet left their homes for their shops or work. And then suddenly a beautiful morning dawned on a happy Damascus!

Such an evening I shall never forget! May God look kindly on those days![2]

We returned to our house carrying with us a thousand and one memories. My father was waiting for us as he had arrived with my brother only moments before us. The two of them had been invited to the "Dressing of the Groom" which continued on with a night's entertainment of singers until dawn. Father told mother and me what happened at the "Dressing" while the teapot made its rounds from glass to glass and sleep like a bird fled from our eyes.

The house of the paternal uncle of the bridegroom was where the "Dressing" took place. Naturally neither the father of the bride nor her brothers nor any of her relatives should be there. That was the way it was supposed to be.[3]

In the afternoon the bridegroom went with some of his friends to the public bath in the suq. And at about seven o'clock in the evening he went with his friends, paternal cousins and other relatives to the house for the "Dressing." There his paternal uncle presented him with a gift. His uncle's house was very large and so he was able to invite five hundred men to the party. Those invited sat on cane chairs in a spacious Arabic courtyard as the groom entered directly from the entrance to the largest hall in his uncle's house. This hall was crowded with the young men of the quarter and the young paternal cousins of the groom. The older respected people from

---

[1] In other words, it would have been better if they had been accompanied by men.

[2] Literally "May God water those days".

[3] The male members of her family should not be seen rejoicing in the fact that one of their women will be sleeping with a man of another family.

among the relatives and guests sat at the front of the raised alcove,[1] with the chanters who had been invited to read the "Birth of the Prophet"[2] beside them. The bridegroom was young, only about twenty years old. My mother interrupted to say that the bride was also young, about fifteen years old and very sweet.

My father returned to his story. The bridegroom entered the hall to get dressed and there found the white, embroidered "bundle" containing his clothes. The young men opened it and saw that everything was brand new. Before the bridegroom took off his clothes to put on the wedding clothes the young men started singing and clapping. The groom stood there ready to don his clothes, his smile of happiness tinged with shyness in the midst of all the celebrating young men:

> Pray to Muhammad, the bright and fresh one
> May God bless him and do well by him!

The sound of another group burst forth:

> What a night, what a night, from tonight he becomes a family
> The bridegroom is handsome, may he be happy
> Let him ask what he wants from us
> Handsome groom, you are dear to us
> I would give my soul and my wealth to him.

> Pray to Muhammad, the bright and fresh one

> God bless you, and do well by you.
> Take off your things and relax
> Your shirt and your hat.

> Sa'id will marry Sa'adiyya
> Our groom only marries a young one
> Our groom only marries a good, beautiful one
> Maidan and Shaghur are one[3]
> The best of human beings.

---

[1] The open courtyard often has a *liwan* which is a raised alcove set in one wall of the house and sheltered by a high arched roof.

[2] This is a reading performed on both happy and sad occasions.

[3] There are two quarters of Damascus, implying that the marriage of two residents joins the two areas.

His friends started to poke and stick him with pins but he never protested, he was so overcome with embarrassment. The barber stepped forward and combed and perfumed his hair and prepared him to appear before the guests.

The groom entered the courtyard and kissed the hands of his father and his elderly uncles. They brought a chair for him to sit beside his father and his uncle. The group of chanters recited the "Birth of the Prophet" while the young mem passed around bitter coffee, and a small boy circulated through the courtyard sprinkling flower water from a silver qumqum into the cups of those who wanted it. As the groom sat with the people, some of his cousins distributed glasses of pistachio ice cream while others in the kitchen filled the glasses from a large tin which had been brought from Bakdash's in Hamadiyya.

Really, his cousins were fine young men who made one proud! God bless them! He had four uncles and each one had ten young sons. By God, they were the finest decoration of the "Dressing." After the ice cream they distributed bags of sweets from a large straw basket for each guest. When the evening was about half over they took the bridegroom to the main wedding in his father's house where everything was glittering with lights, beautiful women, ululating, and the bride of his life. He planned to live here with her in the house of his parents.

They put the bridegroom in the middle and his father took him by one hand and his eldest brother by the other and his cousins, relatives, uncles, friends and young men of the quarter surrounded him carrying pressure lamps in their hands. Together they walked ahead of the groom through the streets with one man shooting off his gun in the quiet night and two men at the front playing with swords and shields while another shouted refrains with the whole group joining in:

> Pray to Muhammad, the bright and fresh one
> May God bless him and do well by him.
>
> Lions of the countryside stalk around
> Drink and don't be thirsty
> Drink from the well Zamzam
> Ya Islam, Ya Islam
> O Islam, I salute Peace
> For the one who stands in the Shadow of God
> The clouds obscured him and didn't include him
> Obscured Shaikh Rislan, Shaikh Rislan,
> The Protector of Damascus and its environs

Windows high above their heads opened and lattice-work shutters were raised so people could poke out their heads to watch the bridegroom and his group of celebrating men. The festive group arrived at the bridegroom's house chanting:

> Pray to Muhammad, the bright and fresh one
> May God bless him and do well by him.

Then came a banner, the banner of the bridegroom...God give him good fortune...

> The bridegroom is handsome, may he be happy
> Let him ask what he wants from us
> Handsome groom, you are dear to us
> I would give my soul and wealth to him
>
> Hurry up, my girl
> The bachelors have overtaken me
> O numerous people
> Hey, Hey
> The banner of the bride's father
> And the banners of Sa'id, Muhammad and Abdu
> May God honor them

The women were ululating from the corridor:

> Awha, Sa'id, the First one
> Awha, Muhammad, the Dragon
> Awha, the one who doesn't pray to the Prophet
> Awha, may he lose his two eyes
> Lya, Lya, Lya, Lysh

The procession of men arrived at the door:

> Eyes blackened with kohl, tall and slender, we come
> to you, God willing.

The bridegroom with his father entered the area where the women were gathered and the other men returned to the house of the "Dressing" party and remained there, enjoying themselves for the whole night and until the morning. The bridegroom stayed with his bride for only an hour before he returned to the young men to sit with them again while they sang, told jokes and entertained each other after the elderly people had left. And then for a second time the bridegroom withdrew to return to his bride.

My father heard from someone in the "Dressing" that the bride's father, while they had been bargaining over the dowry, asked the bridegroom's father to pay 100 gold English pounds, not *rashadiyyas*[1] in Ottoman coins. The groom's father replied that he was willing to do so, but added that if the bride's father asked for 100 pounds he must be ready to pay 100 pounds to match it.

The bride's father replied:

—All right, I accept 100 pounds and one for good measure!

They agreed that the *mutakhar*[2] would be one half the amount. The bride's family took the remaining cash before the ceremony in which the marriage contract was signed and with it bought mother-of-pearl inlaid couches, carpets, mattresses and quilts. Six months passed after writing the contract before they could appoint a date for the wedding and print the cards.

My mother added to what my father had said by explaining:

—There you are, sir, the parents of the bridegroom are very respectable people. They look around a long time for girls to marry their sons...scarcely leaving a door where they haven't knocked...and they hardly liked anyone they saw. This one was too dark and that one too thin and this one too tall and this one too short. They wore themselves out before finding him what he wanted.

—Why, what did the bridegroom want?

—He wanted a bride that was fair-skinned and light-haired, of medium build, not too thin or too fat. Finally they saw this girl and when they came to describe her to their son he was pleased with the description. He told them to go and ask for her hand. But he never saw her until the night of the wedding because her parents are fanatically strict about such things.

The mother of the groom is a woman who understands things well and thinks things out. All her daughters-in-law are beautiful girls. All the time she was going from house to house she could tell from one visit if the parents of the girl were good or not. She cares a lot about cleanliness so whenever people weren't looking she would turn up the edge of a carpet or a straw mat to find out if the people were clean or dirty. If she found one clog here and one there, or one slipper here and another there instead of neatly arranged when she entered a house unexpectedly she would never return to that house again, for she knew such a girl would grow up to be like her mother in a state of disorganized. If she asked for a glass of water and the girl

---

[1] Turkish gold coins.

[2] A delayed payment that must be paid the woman upon divorce or the death of her husband before the estate is settled.

brought it without a plate or it wasn't dried carefully on the outside she would say "This girl is disorganized and I'll never ask for her to become engaged to my son." From the moment she entered a house looking for a fiancee and the girl stepped forward to greet her she would kiss her to smell her breath and embrace her to see if she had body odor. And she invited many girls to the public bath to get a look at them in their natural state and would return home to describe to her son what the girl's figure was like.

After a long time they saw this particular girl and it was fate. Of course, on the first visit they didn't drink coffee[1] as is the custom. They said to the bride's sister, "We never drink coffee until we are sure of our Fate." The first time they saw her they didn't reveal what family they came from so they could make up their minds first. Then later they told them that they were people from such and such a family. After they had inquired about the family of the girl and were told that they were good people they went a second and third time and finally gave them a picture of their son and told them: "Here is our address so you can ask about us and about our son. When shall we come back to get the answer?"

After a few days they returned for their decision and the engagement took place. The men of the two families met to bargain about the dowry and at first there were differences. "This is not enough." "By God this is too expensive, 100 gold pounds on her clogs is plenty." The day they wrote the contract in the bride's father's house only the parents and close relatives were there and no one else. The groom's parents gave her a bracelet, a gold ring with diamonds, and an appliqued robe. By God, the wedding was very nice and they really spent a lot on it. Let's see tomorrow what the "congratulations" party will bring![2]

Father asked her:

—When will the "congratulations" be?

—The fifth or the sixth day.

—Is it for the women?

—Yes.

—And the seventh day?

—On the seventh day they will invite people to eat with them but only her father, paternal uncles, maternal uncles, her brothers, brothers-in-law and her paternal and maternal cousins will be there.

—Am I invited?

---

[1] Drinking coffee implies acceptance of the girl as a candidate.

[2] People usually present gifts at the congratulation party.

—No, tomorrow your son-in-law will invite you when you marry your daughter. I hope it will happen in your lifetime, husband.[1]

—May God keep you!

*　　　　*　　　　*　　　　*

Many days passed and finally the evening of evenings came. My mother dressed hurriedly and took me by the hand...sleepiness nearly overpowered me. "Where are we going, Mother?" It was a surprise...we stood in front of the house where the wedding had taken place and where I had experienced the thousand and one nights. What was this, a new wedding?

I heard the cries of women penetrating the night and saw many women dashing excitedly back and forth in confusion across the courtyard. We entered the "square" room where the women were shouting that help was needed and went from there up to a high deck where straw mats were spread on the floor and on top of them a large carpet. The walls of the room were lined with chairs decorated with mother-of-pearl, and on one side stood a large wardrobe with Egyptian mother-of-pearl and inlaid silver. Many women old and young sat around the "square" room and in the middle on two mattresses piled one on top of the other, writhing in the pains of labor, was the same beautiful bride. Her misshapen body was enough to make one weep. I pressed back against my chair near the wardrobe as if someone had slapped me out of the most beautiful dream.

The older women fingered their prayer beads and read passages from the Koran, "the Bismullah" and the "Dahwat" (Beseeching God): "Oh God, help her in her time of need and bring her through safely!" One woman said to another:

—A woman giving birth to her first child should suffer pain!

—Poor thing, The waves of pain have become very difficult for her.

—May God bring her safely through this difficult time.

—Her poor husband went out in the dark after the midwife and helped carry the midwife's chair and a lantern for her to see by.

The pains increased...one strong and one week...and her screams and cries became louder, penetrating the quiet of the night. I, the frightened child, grasped tightly to the arm of the chair crying quietly to myself. The midwife came and went, then raised the bed sheet covering the bride and

---

[1] She calls her husband literally son of my father's brother, even though he may not stand in this relationship to her. This is the preferred marriage, and it is sometimes thought that a girl should ask permission of this cousin should she want to marry someone else.

lowered it, all the time frowning. One woman whispered in the ear of another:

—Better to let her feel pain than to say about her that she is one who doesn't bear children. She will get up tomorrow and forget all about the pain.

I noticed from behind the curtain in the "square" room that her poor husband paced back and forth in the courtyard not knowing what to do. Once he heated water for the women in the kitchen...and once he handed them a bottle of oil, salt and lemon mixture but he refused his mother's entreaties to leave the house until the birth was over. They would send for him to tell him the good news she told him. Suddenly, the pregnant woman got up with her bloated belly and walked around the high bed with her two hands supporting her stomach, twisting and turning and uttering curse words as if she were an ill-mannered crazy person.

—A curse on weddings and those who get married, by God. I will never in all my life get pregnant again. Curse the fathers of weddings. Curse the fathers of all of you. I'm going to die! Please my God. I kiss your hands. Please save me. Please by your feet I...

The midwife led her back to the bed and said to her:

—God be lenient with you. Be patient. Soon you will be better. Call on God and press. Help your son! Pray to the Prophet. It is getting easier. Only a little bit more. You daughter, why don't you sit on the midwife's chair. Wouldn't it be easier for you?

—I don't want to...I don't like it...let me have the child on my bed...Oh my God, it came, came, Oh please, I beg you. O my mother, where are you?

And at dawn after the morning prayer call she gave birth safely in front of all those women who had been invited to be present at the labor: all her relatives and her husband's relatives. Anyone who was not invited to the labor would feel slighted and never set foot in the house again, as if labor and giving birth were a nice entertainment which should be attended by all parental and maternal aunts and their daughters and sisters-in-law and the sisters of the husband and the second wives!

The midwife's face relaxed and the frown disappeared as she said, "Oh God, pray to the Arab Hashemite Prophet, perfect without a defect, it's a boy!"

The poor bride smiled for the first time in 24 hours (the pains had started from the morning of the previous day). The midwife cut the cord of the navel and tied it with thread. But she remained worried until the placenta dropped, for if it stayed inside it would cause death to the person in childbirth. Silence prevailed until the placenta dropped and after it a flood of blood. I almost fainted at that sight! The ululating started again and they went to break the good news to the father that it was a boy.

—May what God has given you be blessed, father of Muhammad Samir!

The face of the mother of the groom, the mother-in-law, fell for she wanted to call the boy Abdul Ghani after his grandfather but the bride preferred the name Samir because it was modern and nice and her husband promised that she should have her wish. So his mother was overruled.

The midwife turned her attention to the baby to clean him and sprinkle drops of lemon juice in each eye and over his body. And she dusted him with, I think it was powder from the birth table, a kind of transportable table inlaid with mother-of-pearl, with many cubbyholes in which the midwife kept the necessary items for the birth: soft myrtle, salt, cumin, cotton, scissors, and the thread to tie the cord.

The neighbors woke up to the ululating and discovered that the daughter-in-law of the neighbors had given birth to a boy.

Activity started in the kitchen as the young women of the household, the daughters-in-law and the daughters, devoted their time to preparing the banquet of the "Completion of the Birth" for the guests who had spent the whole night. They moved to another hall to have their breakfast served on a large, round, brass tray inlaid with decorative patterns and placed on a low straw-bottomed stool. The women sat around the tray on which were plates of boiled white cheese, cheese in oil, cheese balls in oil with zatar[1] spice, green and black olives, large limed olives, jams of native apricots, plums, green plums, kabad, cherries, cream, honey, makhdus, cottage cheese, sesame seed sweets, molasses, tahina, milk, tea, tanur bread, stuffed pastries and fruit. When everything was prepared and nothing remained to do but to bring the milk, one of the daughters-in-law went to the kitchen, looked at the oven and gasped, then shouted at the wife of her husband's brother:

—Yi-ii, the milk has boiled over and you didn't even notice. Where is your brain? There's time enough to talk to neighbors. You can't leave me all alone with the guests waiting, you cold hearted wretch!

It was the third daughter-in-law who was responsible for preparing the tea and the tea glasses and for boiling the milk. She had forgotten everything when she heard a voice calling her from over the wall of the house. She knelt down on her knees beside the water channel flowing from their kitchen to that of the neighbor and lowered her head till it almost touched

---

[1] Thyme.

90

the surface of the water to speak through the hole in the wall to the neighbor who was shouting to her:

—Good morning, neighbor, what is all the ululating about at your house. Did the bride have her baby?

—Good morning, neighbor, yes, by God she gave birth!

—A grain of wheat or a grain of barley?[1]

—By God, a grain of wheat!

—O God. I am happy for her that she has a boy. May what you have done be blessed!

—May God bless you and bring you good.

—And you also...What's happening? Do you need help?

—May God give you good health. By God, we are preparing the banquet for the "Completion of Birth." Please come eat with us.

—Yi, inshaallah, what you have will bring you good health. Walla, my husband hasn't gone to his work yet and I can't come until he leaves, believe me!

—Take some food from us then.

—Why should I take food from you, bury me?

—I only wanted you to take this orange and apple. I'll send them to you through the water channel. Take them. Did they come?

—Yoo...bless your hands! They arrived. Thank you. Now, may you send me my myrtle,[2] my husband is calling me.

The milk and tea were poured in glasses...while the ululating of joy rose from the courtyard, sending out its intended message from the relatives of the bride and mother of the boy. It confirmed the strong differences, kept concealed, between the bride's people and the bridegroom's people. It had started when the bride overheard words she was meant to hear from the daughters of the house and her husband's brothers' wives, criticism about not becoming pregnant right away or perhaps not becoming pregnant at all if it turned out that she was barren. A sister-in-law who was jealous of the new bride praised herself as a woman who bore many children, already five of them, and she was pregnant again! There was no way to avoid such problems that result from all living together in the father-in-law's house: mother-in-law, father-in-law, sisters-in-law, and wives of husband's brothers. Every son lived with his wife and children in one room, so of course there was no way to avoid jealousy and criticism. The young

---

[1] Wheat stands for a boy, barley for a girl.

[2] Myrtle is brought to the graves of the dead, so this expression is the same as "May you bury me," a sign of endearment.

beautiful bride, the fortunate one, had entered the house only to stir up the hidden jealousies in their hearts. It seemed that the groom's mother, who was afraid she might die before she had the pleasure of seeing her youngest son have a boy was behind the whispering. It was said she wanted to make another engagement for her son if his wife didn't become pregnant. How often she would praise her other daughters-in-law who became pregnant from the first "Night of Entry," while this bride of her last son had only become pregnant after a whole month had passed! Her son said many times to her:

—Mother, it's shameful to speak like this! I am a man who will not marry more than one woman. I could never do what my uncle did and marry four women who made his life a hell. Be patient! Tomorrow she will be pregnant and God will send us boys and girls. She is still young, Mother!

—Never...she will never bear...and I will never leave her for you as long as the sky is blue.

—Mother, may God keep you. I don't want problems. I love my wife...I am very happy with her.

That was the conversation that took place between the son and his mother nine months before. The ululating announcing the birth of a son silenced the mother's conspiracies and any doubts about the ability of the bride to become pregnant. Hardly a year had passed since the wedding.

> Awha, she gave birth and is safe
> Awha, on her bed, she slept
> Awha, thanks be to you, O God
> Awha, that let no one rejoice in our misfortune.
>
> Awha, pray to Muhammad, his time and his hour
> The one who doesn't pray, may his gall bladder burst
> Lya, lya, lya, lysh.
>
> Awha, a blessing and seven
> Awha, O midwife, you deserve a woolen shawl
> And a visit to Muhammad and the Glorious K'aba
> Lya, lya, lya, lysh.
>
> Awha, we cooked milk and rice,
> Awha, the people congratulate with gold
> Awha, we congratulate with ululating
> Lya, lya, lya, lysh.

The news circulated among family and loved ones that so and so had borne a boy and the women were called for the "Congratulations" on the fifth and sixth days. I went with my mother to the same wedding house again but this time the bride wasn't there. The house was overflowing with women and young girls wearing the most beautiful clothes and decorating themselves with flowers in celebration of the coming of a boy and the good health of the mother. The "Congratulations" took place in the hall furnished with the mother-of-pearl possessions of the bride. They played the lute and danced and the young women from among the relatives and their sisters distributed large bowls of *karawya*[1] because she had borne her child during the winter months. If it had been summertime they would have passed around mulberries or *tamr hindi*[2] or pistachio ice cream. The boiled drink karawya was sweetened with coconut and contained almonds, crushed walnuts, pistachios, peanuts, hazel nuts...in all, seven kinds of nuts...a very well made karawya.

After a group of guests had finished the karawya they would go into the room of the new mother to offer their congratulations and give a present of gold to the newborn baby. The present would, be either a gold pound or a five-sided gold piece, or a half-pound piece hung on a ribbon or a pin. Each woman would pin it on the bib of the child sleeping at the side of its mother. If the newborn baby was a male the present might be a gold Koranic saying in a small box or if a girl, a thin piece of gold with *Mashallah*[3] that she could wear around her neck on a thin gold chain. Most of the gifts were gold pounds or Korans.

The new mother sat on her bed and her face shone with good health and happiness and victory. She wore her white wedding dress with the train arranged around her like a background wreath on the wall, with herself in the middle like a rose. She had put on the wedding dress so that anyone who hadn't already seen it in the wedding could see it now. Around her shoulders she wore a white fur wrap and her hair and chest were decorated with diamonds, pearls, and red carnations. The charming colors enhanced her face and brought back to me something of the memory of her beauty on the night of the wedding.

Each woman approached to kiss the boy and offer her a gift. Then, each one kissed the mother and said to her:

—May what you have received be blessed!

—God bless you!

---

[1] A thick sweet pudding, served especially to celebrate births in Damascus.

[2] A drink.

[3] God keep her.

As one group left the room another entered and at the bedroom door members of the family distributed chocolates, sugar-covered nuts and Turkish delight.

Two weeks after the "Congratulations," they held a circumcision for the boy. They invited both men and women to this party in the middle of the afternoon and while the circumciser was present the men sang:

> Pray to Muhammad, the bright and fresh one
> God bless him and do well by him.

The celebration for the circumcision continued for seven days and nights. They killed a sheep and arranged a night in which Fahmiyya, daughter of Husmi, sang and the entertainment lasted until dawn. The idea of having the operation for the boy only a few days after his birth was the father's because he didn't want his son to suffer the pains he had suffered during his circumcision when he was seven years old. They had dressed him in a long white silk dress reaching to the floor and on his head they put a tarbush decorated with pearls, diamonds and roses so he would be pleased with himself and forget the moment of pain. But he did feel the pain even in spite of the sudden shouting of the men around him:

> Pray to Muhammad, the bright and the fresh one
> May God bless him and do well by him.

The young father would never forget the way they deceived him with the festivities, and how they dressed him up in loose silk robe and a tarbush decorated with pearls and diamonds. They set him on a horse and in front of him walked a procession of his friends—students from the Koranic school repeating loudly: *salam, salam, salam, salam.*[1] The procession moved through Hamadiyya, Sanjuqdar and Marje and returned him to his house where he ate sweets with the invited guests and his student friends from school. Then they brought him into a special room where all the men gathered around him and the circumciser took a good hold of him and quickly made the operation. He screamed and wept and the sentence "May God bless him and do well by him" did not distract him from his pains. After that he spent days walking through the quarter holding his long white robe out in front of him with one hand while the heavy tarbush on his head announced to the world the coming of the newly circumcised, "Pray to Muhammad." All the glittering deceptions didn't work nor did they lessen the pain when

---

[1] Peace.

he needed to urinate. It was the memory of this pain that saved his little son from a similar memory.

Two weeks passed from the time of the birth and they made preparations for the trip to the public bath. Without exception, the "Bath of Separation" for the newly delivered woman had to take place two weeks after the birth. We were invited to be there. In this bath the new mother had to prove her strong character by tolerating the heat when she sat over the "fire" place,[1] a place where a bare foot would hardly dare tread or even touch. Black stones hot as molten metal were spread with a towel for the newly delivered woman to sit on. One of the women from among the relatives spread ointment, *shadad*, all over the body of the woman so that she would recover her strength and health. Shadad is very good, with egg in it, a curing medicine. The mixture of shadad painted on the woman was made of egg white, molasses and ginger and she sat on a mixture of egg yolks and cumin to strengthen her vein, arteries, and body and return her to the state before she gave birth. The more she was able to stand the heat the faster she would recover her strength so that she could go back to her housework and the care of her husband and son, and the care of her father- and mother-in-law's house. Before giving birth she had taken turns like all the other daughters-in-law. She was responsible on successive days of the week for cleaning the courtyard with water, the balcony, the stairs, watering the plants, dishwashing, and cooking.

I watched her with astonishment. How could she sit on the "fire" place which we children were afraid of. We would try to touch it with one toe and jump back quickly behind the fire line with our burnt toes bringing tears to our eyes. O God! Poor woman! God help her!

When she finished this hot, irrational sitting, the head woman of the bath came to bathe her herself. She washed her hair and combed and braided it in two plaits. She scrubbed her body with a lufa and soap and helped her bathe the little baby. Then she took her to the middle room where she dressed the baby and gave him to his mother to nurse from her clean breast. As he nursed the sweat poured from him because of the stifling heat in the bath while his beautiful mother's face was bursting with the pinkness of health, cleanliness, and the heat of the bath's steam. She smiled down at her son's face, glowing in a way I will never forget in all my life.

In the middle room they spread out all the food and the relatives of the newly delivered woman and all her in-laws gathered around. Their kohlrabi peels and orange peels were scattered everywhere between the feet of those

---

[1] In the bath this is the place where the water for the basins is heated.

coming and going between the outer and inner chambers. The young women turned their bathing cups upside down and spontaneously formed a musical band of singers creating an atmosphere of pleasure and enchantment when accompanied by their happy, victorious ululating.

> Awha, she gave birth and is safe
> Awha, on her bed she slept
> Awha, thanks be to you, O God
> Awha, that let no one rejoice in our misfortune

One girl started to dance to the rhythm of the beating on the cups, and clapping and sweet laughter filled the air arousing the curiosity of the other customers of the bath.

       *   *   *   *

When the boy was not even one year old, there was a knock on our door and I opened it to find a small boy carrying a big, covered china bowl. I took it from him and asked what it was. He replied:

—This is from so and so's house. They say hello and when you eat it they hope you may have good health. They wish the same for the sons of your sons.

My mother uncovered the bowl and was pleased with what she saw. She smiled and said with delight:

—Yoo-oo, thank you, his teeth have started to appear. May God keep him! Come children, come and eat sliqa. The teeth of Muhammad Samir have come out.

My brothers and I rushed to eat the sliqa, the boiled corn dish decorated with sugar, pomegranate seeds, walnuts and pistachios. It was all quickly eaten up.

Two days passed, and into the same bowl my mother poured sugared nuts which she had made for us and sent the bowl back to them with my little brother. It is a custom of the Damascenes that you should never return a plate to its owners empty. The sweetness of that boiled corn dish I can still taste in my mouth.

I began thinking about what a happy place my town was, how sensitive and spoiled it was. Celebrations of happy occasions never ended. isn't that so, Mother? It was a big question, bigger than my age. Mother sighed as she brought water up from the well and said to me as she took the pail to water the planters of flowers:

—Yes, daughter, but what have you seen in your lifetime? By God, we have had dark days in Damascus, black as charcoal, and so much heartbreak with the passing of young men and others during the days of the revolution in Damascus and in the Ghuta. By God, we were yearning for a crust of bread and we suffered a lot from Turkish rule. Never in my life will I forget how Jamal Pasha, the Murderer, hung the rebels in Marje Square while all the people cried for them. Why is it you think all our days are weddings, ululation, celebrations, and delicious food? From the time we were conscious of our surroundings we heard the sound of bullets in our ears.

Days passed...and I sent to school, and on the way I used to see the fearful Senegalese soldiers the French brought to Damascus to kill us. I walked...my canteen in one hand and my bag in the other, keeping close to the wall so as to stay far away from the eyes of the Senegalese whom my mother had warned me against.

Days and more days passed...and we went to visit the house of the bride who was no longer smiling...her husband had joined the rebels in their war against France. She cried and prayed to God night and day to bring back her husband, the head of her household and the father of her children. In her prayers she asked that he be victorious over his enemies. Her duty at that time was to cover herself with her black cloak and walk with her sister-in-law, her husband's sister, through the alleyways, hiding under her black cloak the basket of food for her fugitive husband and his group of rebel friends. Under the food in the straw basket, she smuggled weapons past the Senegalese guard without arousing a single suspicion of the guns and bullets that were there. It never occurred to him that women were helping the rebels to escape over the rooftops or that they were delivering weapons to them under the cloaks and plates of food to contribute their part to the revolution.

In 1945, Damascus celebrated the greatest wedding of all.

My mother took me and my brothers to that "wedding." The invitation was open to all the people and the wedding celebration took place in Marje Square. Torches lighted all Damascus. The guests came in carts and in cars big and small, and torches lighted up all the roofs of the city and the Manzil,[1] hotels and sidewalks, electrical poles, the gardens of Marje and the poles of the Hejaz Railway line, the iron railings of the River Barada, and all the thoroughfares and crossroads leading to Sanjuqdar and the narrow streets of Rami and Saraya and Bahsa and Suq al-Atiq. Mt. Qasyun was lit like a crown of diamonds shining on the head of the bride...the happy charming bride whose name was Damascus.

The wedding of freedom continued the whole night long in Martyrs' Square, Marje. All of Damascus was invited to the Night of Evacuation to

---

[1] An historical site.

97

celebrate until dawn with a group of singers and musicians. Among the glittering stars were Rafiq Shukri, Salwa Midhat, Sirri Tanburji, Salama al-Aghwani, Mary Jubran, Adnan Radi, Su'ad Muhammad, Najib al-Saraj, Fatat Damashq, Muhammad Muhsin, Tahsin Jabri, Mustapha Hilal, Subhi Sa'id, Fayiz al-Istiwani, Taisir 'Aql, Zaki Muhammad, Muhammad al-Nahas, Yahya al-Nahas, Muhai al-Din al-Za'im, and Muhammad al-Aql.

And the wedding of independence in Syria continued on until daybreak.

Chapter Five

Sweet *Akadinia*[1]

In our house and in front of visitors my father used to call me "Ya Hilwa," Beautiful One.[2]

I wasn't beautiful and the word was much bigger than me, like a man's shirwal worn by a child. When I was a child this word used to cleanse my soul like the April rain washes the little rosebud. I was the beautiful one! But what about the visible beauty of my younger sister which should prove that she was the beautiful one. I was the dark-skinned one and she was the fair one. They found me in a coal sack they would say jokingly in front of visitors. They found her in a yoghurt cup.

Why the "beautiful" one then? Maybe because I was the young smart one distinguished with the magnificent memory: "She knows where father's lost clogs are or where the scissors can be found. She has a special talent for cleaning up the messes of the house by returning missing things to the hand of her tidy father."

My father used to stretch out his hand to take the scissors from my little hand and by this movement of his hand he avoided a stormy quarrel, while asserting at the same time that I was the beautiful one of the house. My father rewarded me by saying "There's no one like this beautiful one."

By calling me this pet name, my father changed the concepts of beauty in my soul. Thereafter I believed that I was beautiful for my intelligence and memory even though I was less beautiful than my sisters and brothers in appearance. My name was changed on the tongues of those in the house ear to an image of beauty which would be embodied for me one day in the name of a fruit which is the most sweet and delicious of all fruits in Damascus.

In our house they tell this funny story about me. My father used to carry me in his arms and walk through Suq al-Atiq when I was only two years old. One of the akadinia sellers would call out his wares that were lined up carefully in rows in wooden boxes: "Oh beautiful akadinia," and the child that was me would answer:

—Yes, yes, yes!

---

[1] Akadinia is a sweet fruit that grows in abundance in the gardens of Damascus.

[2] The word *hilwa* in Arabic has the meaning beautiful and sweet at the same time.

The salesman called out, "Oh Beautiful," and I would answer "yes." My young father would laugh and pull me away, trying to keep me quiet by saying:

—Be quiet or you'll cause a scandal. The man is not calling you!

—But father, he *was* calling me.

This story about me stands out among my father's funny memories. The initial surprise of visitors would vanish amid waves of laughter.

The young woman in me now laughs at that bright child of my memory. I now feel that between me and the akadinia there is a nice story which gives me such a feeling of beauty and joy that it deserves to be the title for this chapter I am proud of. It wasn't really me who wrote this piece; it was written by my beloved city Damascus.

Whenever an akadinia salesman calls our "Ya Halwa," I smile. I go very often down to Suq al-Atiq or Suq al-Hal passing by the salespeople, the carts and the donkeys, swimming in the sea of the Damascene peddlers' calls. Sometimes I wake up to the voice of one of the peddlers calling out his wares as he directs his donkey through the districts of new Damascus. Then I would forget that I am here and imagine myself in our old house and our old quarter there. It infuriates me when I lean over the balcony to call a salesman and ask his price and I don't find him there. I would be sure that when his calls reached me he had been near our house, but by the time I leaned out to call him he would be at the end of the street. What's the use?! He would be riding a bicycle in compliance with the laws that prevent donkeys from going through the elegant areas of the city.

To that exemplary area of Damascus, Mazze, with its new villas I went with bated breath to see elegance, beauty and calm. Among the colorful fascinating villas on which grow vines and roses, I was atracted by an enormous white building surrounded by lush gardens. It was set in the middle of a broad green lawn like a ship or a white pampered cat on a green velvet carpet.

. —What is this they are building?

—It's a supermarket built in the modern style like the villas of the area.

I went mad. I imagined the modern operation of buying and selling when the supermarket was finished. A housewife would come with a plastic carrying basket for vegetables. She would enter the door of the magnificent building in complete silence since whispering is the language of sophisticated people. The woman would push a small metal cart with two tiers through the aisles of the supermarket choosing what she wanted from the canned meats, vegetables, fruit, ghee, cheese, butter, soap, coffee, sugar, tea, and jam. Confidence would be absolute in this sophisticated place. Nobody steals. Nobody bargains. No tomato is bigger than another. No apple is unripe, or spoiled, no unsanitary open can of ghee, no open tin of cheese, no tin of cream, no pottery bowl of yoghurt, no leather pouch of cottage cheese. On each container would be a fixed price to save the time spent bargaining by an elegant buyer and a gentleman salesperson. The woman would count the number of pieces at the end and write out the bill like someone who didn't know how to speak. The employee would play on his calculator like a dumb-mute and from behind the cash register accept the money with a stern face. There would be no conversation in that place, which was totally convenient for everyone.

Are we in Damascus or London? Are we in Damascus or Moscow? Are we in Suq al-Hal or Selfridge's, or in Gum?

The donkey no longer passes under our windows. We will not hear its voice again, that voice of the past reaching out to the present and the future. Now, we pass perilously along roads those long dead have built which we have festooned with electrical wires. The donkey is not going to pass under our window. The white-veiled, covered heads of the women will not lean out the doors and windows to bargain with the peddler who cries out about his tomatoes, potatoes, onions, and beans. The salesman will not come to us. We have to go to him. The peddler will exist no longer and his patient donkey with the heavy load will disappear. Even the interesting conversation between a man in the street selling and a woman behind a barely opened door buying will end:

—The woman: How much will you sell it for, brother?
—The seller: You want the truth, ten piasters.
—The woman: Ya, wallah! two piasters.
—The seller: What do you mean, two piasters, sister, are we selling radishes?
—The woman: Come on, it's a good price!
—The seller: Wallah, there's a big difference! Buy from someone else.
   And to his donkey: "Go on!"
—The woman: Why are you so difficult. We are your regular customers!
—The seller: Sister, it's true, and if you want you can take them for
   nothing.
—The woman: Thanks, brother, but...
—The seller: Sister, we need to earn a living, let's get on with it!
—The woman: Now, what did you say...
—The seller: God help us, seven piasters, sister.
—The woman: No deal. I don't want it (and she tries to close the door).

101

—The seller: Last price, five piasters.
—The woman: No, wallah!, Five is too much.
—The seller: Sister, look, four piasters. It's the cost price!
—The woman: Three piasters! If you like it, weigh me out half a rotl.
—The seller: Wallah, it's not fair at that price!
—The woman: Go ahead, weigh it out and we will not disagree.
—The seller: What we said was four piasters.
—The woman: Three piasters!
—The seller: It's not fair! God help us!

The donkey brays while the man puts the weights on one pan and the tomatoes on the other. The man tries to call out "red ripe tomatoes" but the donkey continues braying making the peddler even angrier so that he yells at the donkey:

—Shut up! Either I call out the wares or you do. Here's my tarbush, you can take my place!

The peddler turns back to the Damascene woman and says:
—What's your final word, sister?
—As I told you.
—I'll have to resort to God, give me your pot. Bless this beginning.[1]

She sticks her hand out the door with the pot in which the three coins are clinking and the man calls out "Ripe tomatoes."

Another woman leans out of the opposite window:
—How much are you selling them for?

I smile at the memory. The peddlers compete with each other, their voices and calls about their wares ringing in my head. I sink in the modern, red, foam-rubber chair and I close my eyes and imagine myself sitting on the wooden bench in the hallway of our house, or on the mother-of-pearl chair in the damp reception hall of the old house. I listen as if from far away to the popular symphony performed and composed by some of the good people, the poor sellers in the suqs and alleys and narrow lanes of Damascus. I listen as the playing and singing of the wares begins:

Grapes: The season is ending. Last chance! Only wood and leaves are left in the vineyards.
Zaini grapes: They are naturally grown, beautiful and ripe.
Tirmis: Tirmis, Tirmis!
Boiled chickpeas: *Bilila,*[2] *bilila,* like hazelnuts.
Dried fruits: Dried fruits, eat something sweet, Boy!

---

[1] Said for the first purchase of the day.
[2] Already done.

102

Popcorn: Fill your pockets with popcorn!
Ice Cream: Early in the morning, boys, eat ice cream.
We are famous, and you should be grateful to us.
Kerosene Stove Repairman: Fixer of the kerosene stove![1]

How can this folklore die? By God, it won't...this symphony of sound won't die because it is something genuine from our people and our culture. They will still be calling, "Akadinia, Sweet Akadania" even when the first Syrian astronaut goes up into space!

---

[1] More of the Damasene peddlers' calls can be found in Appendix A.

Chapter Six

Bottled Gas[1]

When I was young I used to care about appearances. It was important to me that we should appear better than we actually were in front of people. I put great stock in a person's origins and I liked to feel proud of anything that proved our family had a genuine past. I insisted upon looking into the family tree with all its fine members, the old Aghas.[2] I would announce to others that the men of our family were Beys and Affandis.[3]

My father fought in more than one war. He fought in the Bulgar War, the Shanq Qal'a War, and the Safar Birlik War, the first Arab Revolutionary War fought in the Hijaz. He fought as an officer in the Turkish Army high on snow-covered Turkish mountains. He walked more than ninety days through the burning sands of the Tih desert in the Hijaz. When the wars were over and my father came back to assume civilian life, I clung to the image of his military and revolutionary struggle and I would say to whomever asked me that my father was an officer.

My paternal uncle, God save his soul, they say was an officer in Yemen, which is also something to be proud of. Our paternal cousin is a famous doctor, also something to hold our heads high over.

Although the financial state of my family was one of modest poverty, I used to live like all Arabs on the past glories of the family. Proudly we pointed out the awqaf[4] left by our ancestors to the grandsons and the oldest members of our family. Our paternal aunts and cousins and my father's maternal cousins used to revel in the glories of the past in front of us youngpsters during family gatherings and I would staunchly defend this glorious past in front of strangers, even though what remained in the present was only the ruins of a family tree begining with an Agha, my first paternal grandfather.

My father who stood out as one of the nicest personalities in our large family used to boast with his paternal cousins, half joking and half serious,

---

[1] The title has a double meaning that becomes clear later on. Literally, the term refers to the canister in which gas or some other commodity is stored.

[2] Turkish title of high society in the Ottoman period.

[3] They were gentlemen.

[4] Waqf or awqaf are religious endowments—money or property—whose earnings are designated to benefit the mosque, charities, or a deceased person's descendants in perpetuity.

that they were a family of seven ministers. But he let me down one day, me the young girl growing into adolescence with mixed feelings about the pain of being poor and belonging to glorious origins.

One evening in our house we welcomed visitors who were of a higher social status than our family and more wealthy. Their visit was in itself something for us to be proud and happy about. My mother, sisters, and I didn't realize that my father avoided looking at us when he started to tell them in his nice accent and funny elegant style a very special tale about his miserable childhood. He told it as it was without making any excuses. I heard this tale as did these strangers for the first time, as if I were one of them. I sat there amazed and wrapped in silence. My mother, sisters, brothers and I looked at each other with concealed fury. We started to laugh artificially in front of the guests as if to encourage the funny parts of the shameful stories but deep inside we were burning with anger and shame. We wrung our hands in a nervous way and winked at my father. Another time we looked deeply into his eyes silently begging him to notice that we wanted him to change the subject. But of course he didn't. He didn't seem to feel that we were there at all or probably he ignored us on purpose. He went on and on telling the story while the guests sat there in suspicious silence. All of a sudden and without warning my father said to them in his simple colloquial accent:

—I was about seven years old when my father died and my mother got remarried. I have a maternal aunt who loved us very much. Every day she used to come and take me from my mother to the *kuttab*,[1] in Baltajiyya near Bab al-Jabiyya. Then one day I ran away from the kuttab and played with the children of the quarter in the alley all day. When my mother asked why I came home early I said that the shaikh had let us go. But it turned out that the shaikh had sent someone to my mother to ask why her son hadn't come to the kuttab that day. So my mother sent for her sister, my aunt, and told her that she should take me to the shaikh so he could beat me. Next day my aunt came and took me to the shaikh. She said to him, "This child ran away from the kuttab so you must beat his feet and make him sleep here tonight. Spread molasses over his ears so the rats will eat them."

The kuttab was a big school with a tomb of a *wali*[2] at one end. When I heard that I was to stay there I was scared. Was it possible that I would have to stay in the place and let the rats eat my ears? Oh, dear! I spent the whole day trying to think of how I could run away. Then something occurred to

---

[1] Koranic school.

[2] Holy man.

me. I would ask the shaikh if I could go to the bathroom. When I did he agreed but called Muḥammad and Ahmad, two boys twice as big as me, to stand guard over me. I realized there was no way out. So I went out of the kuttab with the two big boys following me. I squatted near the wall to urinate and they stood one at each side of me. I was still wondering how to run away when suddenly something occurred to me. I picked up two handfuls of dirt from near the wall, got up in a hurry and threw the dirt, one handful each into the eyes of the boys. They were blinded and couldn't see me as I ran away like the wind.

Then I thought to myself, if I go home they'll beat me and I'll definitely have to go back to the kuttab and sleep there and the rats will eat my ears. What could I do? Perhaps I should run off to my brother who was a sergeant pasha, the deputy in Duma. So I slipped on my shoes and off I went to Duma. While I was walking along someone in a carriage asked me where I was going. I answered that I was going to Duma. He said he was from Duma. I said I was going to my brother who everyone knew was the sergeant there. He said, all right, then I should come along with him and he would give me a lift. I jumped into the carriage and rode with him until we reached Duma where I went directly to my brother's house. I knocked on the door and knocked and knocked but no one answered. The neighbor came out and asked: "What do you want, boy?" I said this was my brother's house. She replied that my brother had gone to Damascus and would not be back before nightfall.

I left and walked to the Duma suq. I was starving hungry, for by then it had become afternoon. Where could I go? I couldn't beg for that would be shameful. So I wandered Duma's alleys until I saw an open door and a woman sitting behind a *tannur*[1] like a lifeguard, shoving the bread into the oven, and the fresh smell of the baking bread wafting into the air. What could I say to her? "Give me a piece" would be a shameful thing to say so I continued walking a little further. But because I was very hungry and couldn't resist the smell of the bread I soon came back and stood shyly at the door. How could I ask her to give me a piece? Since I was very hungry I finally asked her in a embarrassed way: "Please, Auntie, give me a piece of bread," but she turned out to be a crude woman, and took the shovel of the tannur and ran after me yelling, "Damn you, you infidel. You run away from the city and beg from us here!" She tried to beat me but I ran until I reached the end of the alley and she returned still swearing and yelling at me. Because I was still hungry from the smell of the bread I stood at a distance

---

[1] Bread oven.

106

like a cat peering at that door. Then, all of a sudden, this same woman came out and went to visit her neighbor in the next house. When I saw that, I took the opportunity presented to me to fly like a bird to the tannur. I looked in and found a stack of a dozen breads and I grabbed ten or so breads, put them under my arm and got ready to run. Suddenly I heard the creaking of the door and realized that she was coming back again. I was scared to death that I wouldn't get out and that she would catch me. So the only way was to retreat into one of the rooms of the house.

Where could I go? I looked around and found a *kandush* with a shelf set into the wall near it. The kandush was a big wooden one used to store wheat that was so tall it almost reached the ceiling. I climbed on the shelf and opened the kandush door, and found it half filled with wheat. So I jumped in and remained very still. The woman returned and found that ten or so of the breads were missing, "Curse your father, I will kill that boy!" She continued to curse and shout as she took up the shovel of the tannur and went out of the house and locked the door to follow me, thinking she could find and catch me in the alleys of Duma. I stayed still inside the kandush listening to her swearing and not daring to breathe. After awhile I didn't care anymore about her yelling and started to eat the bread. She came back to the house shouting, "If I see him I'll slaughter him."

Finally she finished baking the bread and closed the door of the house and went into the main room, but without any idea that I was inside the kandush. There was a small hole in the kandush through which I could see her. She took off her clothes to put on a dress with red polka dots, and then made up her face with rouge and sat on her cushions until evening came. I was dead quiet inside the kandush.

Suddenly, there was a knock on the door. She went to open it with words of welcome and a newcomer came into the sitting room. He was as tall as a tree with a thick mustache and looked very frightening to me. I thought to myself that he must be her husband. Then he took from the pockets of his shirwal pants two bottles of *'araq*[1] and put them on the floor. She went to fix a meal for them, a *mazza*[2] of pickles, olives, nuts and seeds. He wanted to get drunk. They sat there drinking for about two hours flirting with each other and then all of a sudden there was a knock on the door. She jumped up quickly and said "It must be my husband!"

---

[1] A distilled alcoholic beverage.

[2] A mazza is commonly eaten as a light meal, either in itself or as a preliminary to a heavy meal. It consists of an assortment of small dishes of various kinds.

The man didn't know what to do. He asked where he should go and she told him he should climb up on the shelf and jump into the kandush. When I heard that, my stomach sank, and I crouched in the corner of the kandush like a cat, holding the bread under my arm as if my life depended on it. He climbed up on the shelf and fell into the kandush. When he saw me he couldn't imagine if I were a jinn or a ghost or how I could have come into the kandush, so he crouched in the other corner of the kandush and we both sstared at each other, afraid to speak.

The woman tidied everything up, removed the food from sight, put on her house dress again and opened the door. Her husband asked her why she had taken so long to open the door. She said she had been waiting for him and fell asleep.

Well I don't want to make the story too long. Her husband took out a bottle of 'araq and started drinking, and she fixed food for him but this time with a frightened face. And we in the kandush still had a sinking feeling in our stomachs because her husband had a rifle and a pistol at his side and a dagger in his belt. He was notorious in Duma. While he was drinking, I don't know how it happened, but I got something in my throat and needed to cough. I tried to control myself but in vain. I coughed. The moment I coughed he heard me and asked her, "Who do you have here?" But she couldn't give him an answer. Her husband was tall, so he opened the door of the kandush and all the wheat poured out on the floor until it was up to my neck. He saw the other man and said, "What are you doing here, you dolt. You bastard! Come with me!" And he locked the door of the room and took the man with him.

He was away for about a quarter of an hour. When he came back he said to her, "When I am away you have your customers, I see," and he approached me with the dagger saying "Either you tell me what you and the man were doing here and where you are from or I will kill you." Then he pulled out the dagger which was half an arm's length. I began to scream because I was scared and because I always had been afraid when I heard a drunk man yelling in the street while I lay in my bed at home. I would cover my head and face with my bed cover. Then all of a sudden I found my mother saying "Bless you, child" and it turned out that everything that had happened to me had been a dream and I was lying safely in my bed.

The guests burst out laughing at this nice surprise and we laughed too, with relief. The end proved the innocence of my father's past. My father added, after he finished laughing heartily over the fact that he had made everyone listen for an hour to a story which had no basis in reality, that this story was one that he had memorized when he was ten years old from the famous Hakawati[1] storyteller, Abu 'Ali Anbuba[2] who used to tell funny stories at the coffee shop of the 'Amara Crossroads seventy years ago when he was in his forties. His stories were all lies that he had memorized. He could tell stories one after another without stopping.

Abu 'Ali, the storyteller, was an extremely funny man. He was short with a beard. When he would take his place at the coffee shop after supper people would gather around. He would tell his funny stories while jumping around and gesturing. The benches and chairs would be full of people, and people would be standing in the aisles. It wouldn't be an exaggeration to say that more than two hundred people would listen to the storyteller every night under the light of the pressure lamps.

My father used to tell his nice stories with laughter so hearty that it brought tears to his eyes. I am sure that he laughed just as heartily at the retelling of the story as when he heard it for the first time from the story-teller Abu 'Ali Anbuba.

People love the past and long for the days of old. They take it with them wherever they go along the path of Time. By holding to their memories they abolish the bitter reality called senility and old age. My father used to say to us, "Laugh and make your hearts happy with your laughter, children, for that is the secret of a long and contented life. Don't make yourselves miserable over worries because worries are like a long staircase that only wears you out..."

---

[1] Hawakati are traditional storytellers who entertain public gatherings in cafes or at special events.

[2] Anbuba, the name, also refers to the canister in which gas is bottled.

Chapter Seven

Those Were the People

Twenty years ago it used to rain very heavily in Damascus. The gutters would pour water down on the pedestrians and flood the narrow alleys from the walls and roofs of houses without letting up.

But let it rain! The evening party that night would be at our house and rain wouldn't stop anyone. Father had bought everything: *qanafa*,[1] *qishta*,[2] and pancakes from Bab Jabiyya, fruit and nuts from Suq al-Atiq and Suq 'Ali Pasha. My mother was busy preparing several large trays of qanafa covered with cream. She kneaded the qanafa with Hama ghee on the heat. My father did his part by putting the thin pancakes in a large dish and covering them with heavy cream while making endless funny comments that eventually would anger my mother. Throughout the preparation he would claim that he was the best and most skillful in doing these things, even more skillful than my mother:

—I did everything! All you have to do is make the sugar syrup for the little pancakes.

The qanafa pan stood on top of the wood stove and chestnuts were put to roast in the ashes. On the edge of the copper brazier, between the live coals and the hot ashes, was the coffee pot. At one end of the room on the *katabiyya*[3] were dishes of oranges, tangerines, pistachios, cashews, hazelnuts, almonds, raisins and dried dates. These were not the feast they appeared to be but only light refreshments for the guests who were coming to visit us on a rainy cold Friday evening in Damascus.

We children in a strange sort of happiness helped our father and mother without stop because the evening was to be at our house. We knew we would be able to play as long as we wanted with the children of our friends and relatives who for sure would come with their parents. No child would stay at home. Even the babies attended the parties. With his jokes and pragmatism my father had broken with tradition twenty years before and made it the custom for all the family—men, women, and children—to gather at all the meetings, visits and picnics in the Ghuta, the gardens of Dummar or on the banks of the Barada. My father also commanded that it

---

[1] A sweet made from semolina or vermicelli and cheese. Here, *qanafa* refers to the ingredients.

[2] Thick cream.

[3] Shelves built into the wall.

110

was prohibited for men and women to sit separately because we were all related. The monthly reception[1] of the women was, of course, forbidden to my father just as the coffee shop was forbidden to the women. Everyone seemed satisfied with his arrangement. He would implement his rule by letting his wife unveil at the evening parties with relatives but in the street she had to cover her face with a double black veil.

Although I was young I still remember in the minutest detail the place in Dummar we used to go every summer. More than forty or fifty of us would rent peasants' houses and spend the summer among the poplars and willows having fun in the gardens and orchards filled with pomegranates and almond trees. The sounds of our laughter would be mixed with the smells of the grill, the cooking of rice and beans, the preparation of kibbi nayya, salads, *tabuli*,[2] and the tunes of the lute. There was also the sound of the dice being rolled for backgammon, the bubbling of the water pipe, the screams of the children swimming in the Barada, women's laughter and the happy crowings of the winners of Parcheesi from their blankets spread out on the damp soil crawling with ants. Above them in one tree a lizard crawled along a branch and in another sat a cat.

Amidst all these nice scenes a small beautiful blond-haired, blue-eyed boy almost drowned, if it hadn't been for the screams of his cousin born the same year. They pulled him out of the river and the whole terrifying situation changed. Now the child had to be beaten for disobeying the rules and swimming in a deep place in the river. The men and women went back to a new game of backgammon this time with a penalty for the loser. The crying of the almost-drowned child rose higher and a beautiful child of the same age, pale-skinned with brown hair, stood laughing by a tall tree pleased to see him punished. The boy was the son of her father's sister. Why hadn't they taken her with them to swim in the Barada? Why were only boys allowed to swim in the river? His cries escalated and his mother screamed at him "If you don't stop crying, I'll break you in half." His nice, funny father threw the dice calmly, saying to his wife, "Take it easy, woman. He's only a kid. What do we have here—two sixes?"

Meanwhile, a naughty boy ran back to his family, chased by the farmer Abu Ahmad who wanted to catch and beat him with a thick pomegranate stick because he was stealing apricots before they ripened. He had also run

---

[1] Women generally let it be known that on a certain day of every month they will be at home to receive their friends in a more formal gathering than the casual drop-in visits of weekdays.

[2] Tabuli is a salad made of parsley, mint, bulgur wheat, onions and tomatoes.

through the field of fodder, thrown stones at the sheep, and ridden the farmer's donkey without permission in the direction of the train track to Zabadani. Stealthily, a group of boys jumped over the fence and a low wall to go to the amusement park next to the coffee shop of Kasr Sham'ayya without paying. A young man followed a young woman trying to frighten her with a snake that he was holding by the back of the neck. He laughed until his sides ached from seeing her frightened as a mouse.

More carriages arrived at the orchards with more visitors from Damascus, all relatives invited to Dummar to have a lunch of rice and beans, cucumber and yoghurt salad, and kibbi nayya with our large family.

A mother shouted a thousand curses at her young daughter and threatened that if she saw her talking to boys she would tear her in two. Some young girls dangled their feet in the river, washing their beautiful legs with the sweet cold water. A girl noticed the watermelon was gone and screamed "Get it, boys, find it!" The red melons and the sweet white grapes were almost frozen in the river water while waiting to be eaten for lunch. One young man stole a quick glance at his sweetheart and concealed the love in his breast, frightened of what her parents might do if they knew.

And me, what was I doing…playing, waiting for food, or jotting down these wonderful pictures for the future? I don't know…

Although I was very young at the time, I still remember one of those long-gone winter evening parties and my eyes fill with tears for the days of happiness, simplicity and a sense of security. There was a knock on the door while we were on the second floor and I ran out to the balcony in the rain to pull the rope tied to the railing that opened the door. The guests entered the wet courtyard and my mother greeted them from upstairs:

—A hundred times welcome! My mother repeated this welcome, and added: Please come upstairs.

The guests put their umbrellas in a row in the summer *liwan*, which in winter we used for storing wood. They climbed up the uncovered stone stairs, exchanging words with my mother as they came:

—My, what a rain, God keep it from the evil eye! they said as they walked from the courtyard up the stairs to the balcony and reached the winter sitting room. They took off their muddy shoes as they entered the room and walked on the carpets in their stocking feet. I still can't imagine how this humble room, the *franka*, in our small house could hold so many people.

The evening started with a parcheesi game on the carpet after all the women had exchanged courtesies and asked after each other's health. All those present formed into two teams, one against the other. Each team would shower the enemy team with exclamations of joy when they failed and offer them discouraging words or claims of their own superiority. Everyone would shriek when a woman would throw the shells and have a pair two or three times in a row. When she would get ready to throw the fourth time the other team would begin to harass her, "Dooo, Dooo, Dooo" but she would get five and not six and her team would jump for joy while the losing team would sink into despair. The prize would be an evening party or a picnic that the losing team must provide.

Then they would suggest the salad game, which is a funny family game. Everyone would have a name: this one was a tomato, this one parsley, this one oil, this one garlic, this one mint, lemon salt, cucumber, lettuce and so on. The game started with one person saying:

—We want to make a salad. There is a tomato but no oil.

In a hurry, the oil answers:

—There is oil but no salt.

The salt answers:

—There is salt but no lemon.

And the lemon would forget and have to go out of the game giving at the same time one of his possessions—a watch, a ring, a package of cigarettes, a bracelet or an earring—to the supervisor. The one who remained in the game longest without forgetting his name became the Governor who gave orders that everyone had to obey. The supervisor who had all the belongings of those who dropped out would hold them one by one under a handkerchief and ask the Governor:

—What demand do to you have for the owner of the thing in my hand? The Governor might order that he should change into a desk immediately. The guest would burst into laughter and on his hands and knees crawl into the middle of the room and change himself into a desk. Two of the humorous guests would approach him and start making an accounting on the "back" of the desk or rather the back of the person who had become the desk. They would begin a commercial transaction that had no resolution and the argument would become heated and turn into a quarrel until it became so bad that one would bang on the "desk" protesting and the other in angry return would answer with even more severe banging, while the poor desk bore their accounting with amused impatience.

I will never forget how one of the women changed into a clothes tree and a shoe rack and how a second one had to tell us a funny story, how a man had to belly dance, and how a third lady had to sing (though her voice was terrible) while another made funny comments about her:

—Wow, her voice is the one mentioned in the Koran![1]

Another had to sing like a cock calling for prayers, and another had to imitate a hen laying twenty eggs. Kak...kak...kak!

The qanafa was ready while the hen was still laying eggs and laughter brought tears to all of our eyes. They laid the table and the evening went on, as the youngsters, boys and girls, started playing "A camel was walking on the sidewalk; when I tried to force him aside, he took my scarf." The men would play backgammon, and one of the women would reach for the lute, and an old woman would take a small drum in her lap, a young girl took the castanets, and all our souls would be touched by the beat of my grandmother's dance melody, enhanced by our own rhythmic clapping. The dancing ended, and a young girl started singing like a nightingale, the song of *Ya mal al-Sham*. Enjoyment sank into our veins like sweet liquor, and the eyes of the young men lit up as they watched the girl. The evening was becoming ever nicer, the enjoyment more intense and the rain outside still heavy. A woman fingering her Koranic beads one by one said,

—God brings riches!

—God help us return to our homes!

One cunning young man insisted on mentioning the "family records," wondering out loud what the latest news was. The extended family of all the relatives kept a record in which they listed the names of the members in order by age. The eldest was always considered the candidate most deserving of leaving through the "small door," which means leaving to the other world. The latest news was that a radical reversal had taken place in the record because deaf old Abu Khalil, who was known for having his socks fall over his shoes, still remained alive though he was ninety, and Abu 'Abdu, who was the same age as Abu Khalil's children, had won and passed through the small door. At that moment gray-haired Abu Rafiq jumped forward to beg them in a manner that was half joking and half serious to relieve his mind and tell him where he stood on the list. The young men cheated, skewing the results and Abu Rafiq's face showed his horror. The young men and women burst into laughter, the men in loud masculine voices and the girls holding their sides with merriment. They laughed because they knew Abu Rafiq was a man scared of death who held onto life the way he seized any opportunity to dine on good Damascus food. At every evening party they would skew the results about his turn in the list just to see his face change with his fears of death. The old people would laugh, too: Abu 'Adnan, Um

---

[1] The Koran says that donkeys are the ones with ugly voices.

114

'Adnan, Abu Salah, Um Anwas, Um Fuad, Abu Mahmud, Abu Hassan and Um Hassan; but Abu Rafiq would never laugh.

There was a knock on the door that rainy night. A female beggar wanted charity. One of them went down to give her something, closing the door again and returning quickly to the warm party. There was another knock on the door and again it was the beggar asking charity for her father-less children. They went back and got her some food from the party. But on the third time that she knocked heavily and continuously on the door, an argument started between the beggar veiled in black and one of my maternal aunt's sons who had gone down into the rain more than once for her, while the owners of the house and the guests waited for him upstairs. Here comes the surprise! The beggar lifted the black shabby veil off her face, pushed open the door and entered, laughing heartily to the surprise of all the guests. It was Fatma, the daughter of my father's maternal aunt's daughter. She was the joyful, beautiful, smart, young girl who at every evening party came up with some new prank.

The smoke from the stove exiting through a pipe to the outside filled the air on the balcony with the smell of burning wet wood. The successful party continued on, challenging the torrents of rain outside and the fearful darkness in the narrow alleys of Damascus through which the guests would eventually have to return home with the sleepy children dragging their feet along the muddy stone streets.

Very often in the middle of our evening parties someone advanced in age and position would announce his wish to start the proverbs. Anyone who failed to think of a proverb or was slow in remembering a popular Damascene proverb when his turn came would receive a heavy blow of a cane without mercy. The older man would usually begin as follows:

> He: Here's a saying!
> Another: What is it?
> He: Today's egg is better than tomorrow's hen.

He started with himself and then each person, one by one, took a turn. By reciting a proverb each person protected himself against the punishment with the cane.

I noticed that important Damascene sayings involving the lives of women and society were the specialties of the grandmothers. Learning them and saying them in a suitable way in conversation was an art that Damascene women had cultivated very successfully. Um 'Anwar, one of the women at the party, started with a saying that is considered one of the most beautiful and important of the colloquial Damascene sayings:

115

They come and go but the keys of the hall are lost.
(Much ado about nothing)[1]

Let your money be insulted but not yourself.
(Rather than ask favors, do the thing yourself)

Having faith in men is like having faith that water will
remain in a sieve.
(Don't trust anyone)

If the camel could see its hump it would fall and break its
neck.
(Don't confront people with their shortcomings)

Despite his tatters, the garbage man pins a rose on his chest.
(Someone oblivious of his station)

The camel is lame because his lip hurts.
(Something small can affect the whole being)

A pile of stones rather than this neighbor.
(The neighbor is useless because he doesn't behave as a
neighbor should)

He asked, "What makes you go to your enemy's house?" He
answered, "My lover is inside."
(Love make one forget all else)

Open it wide with pride, or close it and hide it from others.
(Conceal what you don't want others to know)

A big house with red walls but inside something to make you
die.
(External appearances are not always accurate)

Close your door, and watch out for your neighbor.
(Be wary of outsiders.)

---

[1] Note: Explanations for the proverbs have been provided in the English text.
They did not appear, and were probably unnecessary, in the Arabic text. The
explanations have been provided by a native speaker but it is quite possible that
other native speakers might have interpreted the proverbs and sayings
differently. Only a few of the proverbs from the original text appear here. The
rest are found in Appendix B.

116

I can dig the well with two needles and sweep the pilgrim's path with two feathers, but there's no point in keeping company with animals for even two words.

(Some things can be accomplished with patience; others cannot be changed at all)

Oh God, save me from associating with animals, or I'll kill them to make a stew and not a drop of fat will ooze onto my bread.

(Said to show how impossible stupid people are)

They said to the monkey, "God wants to disfigure you." He replied, "Perhaps He will change me into a gazelle."

(Beauty is in the eye of the beholder)

And the proverbs continued until no one could think of another one.

The long evening party ended with a delightful colloquial love poem, recited as a flirtation between two of our elderly female relatives:

I wish I were a vine climbing on your house
A vine bearing beautiful red sweet grapes for you
I already miss sleeping with my head in your lap
Your lover can't stand the heat of your fire.
Apples I can't eat, because they are red like your cheeks
I cannot enter the sea, because my love left by the sea
If someone would come with the good news you are coming back
I would give them twenty pounds as a present.
Your black eyes are like an arrow on your brow
And your two lips like red agates, inviting me to kiss them
I want to rush to your house and make you lawfully mine, my love
I want to satisfy my longing to kiss you.
Your black eyes make me sing
Your black eyes make me forget mother and father
And when I'm deep in sleep
A vision of you comes to drive me crazy.

One of the visitors called out

—That's enough! Let's go. It's almost time for morning prayer.
Let's go home! What do you think, cousin, shall we go? Are you going to stay, Fuad Affandi?

And Fuad answered:

—Wallah, it's early! We're still having a good time.
—No, let's go, we'll do it another time.

117

—No, we're going too. Goodbye, May your house always be as full of joy.

—Please, come again!

—Yes, we will, we wouldn't miss the chance.

—Goodbye. Come see us, and don't just say you will, "Bury me."

—Watch out, cousin, for the bucket at the bottom of the rain spout. Come this way, along the wall.

—This alley's dark...help me carry this boy.

—Watch out, women, for the mud hole...the whole alley is full of mud.

—We're going through this way. Goodbye, let us see you, cousin. Goodnight!

Chapter Eight

My Father Told Me...

I was attending the kuttab in Baltijiyya near Bab Jabiyya. My mother registered me there when I was little. We used to sit on a cushion on the floor, and in front of us was a wooden stand on which we placed our Korans. The shaikh would sit on a pillow placed on top of a sheepskin, in front of a small platform where the children used to stand to recite their lessons.

The shaikh was very severe and, if a child had done something wrong, he would hit him over the head with a long bamboo cane. Every Thursday each child paid a pound. The children had to stay at the school from early morning until after the mid-afternoon prayer,[1] and each child had to bring his lunch with him wrapped in a piece of cloth. You could hear the voices of the children repeating after the shaikh from the end of the street:

"Alif has a lashin above. Jim has one dot under. Hah has nothing. Khah has one dot above. Dal has nothing. Thal has one dot above. Rah has nothing. Zah has one dot above. Sin has nothing. Shin has three dots above..."

When we had memorized the Sabra, the shaikh made us read a part of the 'Ama and the — Tabarak and the Rub'a Yassin.[2] Afterwards, we started to read from the Koran. When a child had memorized the whole Koran they would have a celebration, the "Khatima," and his family would be happy and invite all their neighbors, the shaikh and the children from the kuttab. Each one to his abilities. There are children who can memorize the Koran and repeat it seven times.

When I memorized the Koran my mother was very proud of me. They put me in a white silk caftan and tarbush decorated with pearls, diamonds and flowers and I went out of the kuttab with the children from Baraka Lane near Bab Sarija in a procession to Bab Jabiyya, Darwishiyya and Marje and returned to my house with the children running after, singing a song for me:

> O Lightening of Damascus
> Send my greetings to Muhammad, the best of all people.
> O, Lightning, pay him a visit and take from his light
> Spread his perfume as musk perfumes a letter

\

---

[1] About 3:30; the time varies according to the length of the day.

[2] Short selections from the Koran.

O, Moon, rise high in the night and shine; the Chosen is the
one who intercedes for us on Judgment Day
They walked the deserts and brought gifts and visited
Muhammad, the best of all people

My family served drinks and candy-covered nuts in little packets and
they gave each child from the kuttab 50 piasters. I sat in front of all the visitors in our house with my shaikh there and read a piece from Sura al-
Baqara. When I reached: "God hath set a seal on their hearts and on their
hearing" one of the children from the kuttab seized my tarbush and ran
toward my mother to take the prize.

My Mother Told Me...

My daughter, there were no schools in my day. My mother put me
with a *khuja*[1] named Taja in Baqqara Lane of Bab Musali in the Maidan
area. My teacher taught me until I memorized the Koran, God bless her
soul. The first thing she taught us was the alphabet in the Book of Sabra.[2]
She used to make us read with her, then repeat after her: "Alif has a lashin
above it. Bah has a dot below. Tah has two dots above. Thah has three dots
above. Jim has one dot under..."

Afterwards she taught us the letters with their vowel sounds and how to
sound out letters of the holy Koran, word by word. The first thing we
sounded out was the Fatha, or opening verse. "Al-hamdu..." we used to
sound it out letter by letter: Alif makes the ah sound, "l" with the sakun
stays the same, "h" with an "ah" sound makes "hah." That makes "al-hah."
Then "m" with the sakum stays "m," "al-ham." "d" with the "u" becomes
"du." "Al-hamdu." "L" with another "l" and an "h"; "l" with an "e" sound
becomes "la";"l" with a shadda becomes "ll" and "ah" becomes "llah." "H"
with an "e" sound makes "hi" "Illahi."

Our teacher taught us alif with a shadda and a double "ah" sound. When
we memorized the Sabra we learned a sentence that included all the letters of
the Arabic alphabet. And she taught us, too, the words for father, mother,
brother, uncle, grandfather, mouth, palm, core, shadow and rival.[3]
Afterward, she had us read part of the 'Ama and Tabaraka, the Qadaama'a,
and the Ziyarat.

---

[1] A woman teacher who takes children into her home for lessons.

[2] This book is often called the alphabet book.

[3] All simple words of few letters that help a child learn the alphabet.

After we memorized all that, we moved to the Holy Koran. By the time I was eight or nine years old I had memorized it all. I studied in my khuja's school, and taught there too. We used to go here to school from early morning until the afternoon prayer. I would take my food with me and share it with my girl friends. They wouldn't let us leave until late in the afternoon.

God rest her soul, she was patient and good, not like the teacher in Zaquq in the other quarter. It was like a prison there and she didn't even teach the children to read well. Even though I am grown up I still love my teacher and whenever I pass through Maidan I look at the quarter and pray for her soul. I still remember how she sent me a boy to teach because I was such a good student. He was one of the four impossible things of the world to try to teach. Even now my heart aches to think that he absorbed nothing. When I tried to teach him to read he learned absolutely nothing until I got very tired of him. I told the story to my mother who had no children but me and spoiled me and she went to the teacher to complain, "What are you trying to do to my daughter?" So the teacher sent him to another girl to learn. By God, in all my life I haven't seen a boy like that one. His name was Salim, I can still remember.

I still remember how we used to sing to our teacher in the late afternoon, begging her to let us go home. We would chant, "Teacher, let us go home, it's time for us to go. The sun has started to set and our hearts are failing." Then we would beg her by the life of Sidi Khalid to let us go home. Finally, our teacher would let us leave two by two. We would put on our clogs and leave to our houses, happy to be free!

God bless those days. Learning at that time had a value. After I memorized the Koran, I started reading on my own, books about the prophets and Kalila and Dimna,[1] Abu Zaid al-Muhalhal,[2] Zir Salim and al-Manfaluti, al-Malak Dahir, One Thousand and One Nights, and Qais and Laila. I used to borrow so many books from my aunt's husband Abu Jafar and my other aunt's husband, may they rest in peace. And all that goes back to my teacher, Taja, who taught me to read and made me read everything. God bless her soul. Oh daughter, our days have passed and learning has changed. Now it is your turn. God bless you and help you and give you the fortune of finding satisfaction.

---

[1] These are animal stories.

[2] Abu Zaid is the great romantic hero of narrative poems all over the Middle East.

Chapter Nine

At the Doctor's

"At the Doctor's" was a radio play written in Damascene colloquial Arabic by the late artist and folktale teller Hikmat Muhsin. All Damascenes laughed when they heard it, for it was one of many of his works begun many years before which comically criticized the faults of old Damascene society. At the same time it recorded much of popular Damascene heritage so it would not be lost in the new waves of modernism that seemed to engulf beautiful images of our society, hiding them in the folds of time with all their faults and merits. The young people of this generation don't realize the danger there is in giving up those old traditions, customs and genuine values.

The producer of the play for Syrian radio was the artist Taissir al-Sa'idi, one of Hikmat Munsin's loyal friends and students. A number of the best actors from Hikmat Muhsin's group, beloved by Damascenes since they started working together after the 1948 Palestine War, had parts in the work. Hikmat Muhsin performed the role of Abu Rushdi, Taissir the role of the doctor, Abdul Salam Abu al-Shamat the role of Abu Ibrahim, Fahd Ki'ikati the role of Abu Fahmi, Anwar al-Baba the role of Um Kamal,[1] Taibu al-Sidawi the role of the peasant and Huda Sidqi the role of the nurse. This is the play word for word:

We are now in the clinic of a Damascene dentist.

Peasant: Sir, I told him, may God prolong his life, I don't have the two and a half pounds to pay for the medicine so please lower the price a little out of generosity to God and Muhammad his Prophet.

Doctor: Um...m.

Peasant: Tell me either that you'll pay the two and half pounds or I'll...

Doctor: I understand. You meant he wouldn't accept less than that from you and you didn't have two and a half pounds.

Peasant: Yes, in the name of God. I've come to God and to you, sir, so that you'd give me medicine which is less expensive.

Doctor: I wrote you a prescription for the medicine that you need, so what's all this about you have and you don't have? You don't even have enough in your pocket to buy medicine to keep you healthy?

---

[1] A male plays this famous female role.

Peasant: O Sidi, in the name of God and Mohammad the Prophet of God, I don't have the money. Am I not a creature of God, man?

Abu Ibrahim: (Off stage and far away) Sir, I feel my tooth there and my jaw is numb.

Doctor: (To peasant) O.K, O.K. So you're saying you don't have the price of the medicine.

Peasant: No, in the name of God, Sir, may God prolong your life. Help me out. I'm a poor man.

Doctor: O.K. then, I'm going to write you out a prescription for a medicine you can get at the free municipality pharmacy.

Peasant: What was that, sir?

Doctor: I'm telling you, I'm going to find you a medicine you can get free.

Peasant: Get my medicine for free, Sir! May God prolong your life. From where, Sir?

Doctor: From the municipality's pharmacy. Don't you know the municipality's pharmacy?

Peasant: Not yet, sir.

Abu Ibrahim: (From closer) Sir, my jaw is anesthetized and my face is numb.

Doctor: (To patient) O.K. one minute. Here is another prescription. Do you understand how to use the medicine?

Peasant: Yes sir, every two hours I gargle with water.

Doctor: Right, and while gargling you paint your gums with medicine from this little bottle with a piece of cotton.

Peasant: Paint what, sir?

Doctor: I mean paint the gums!

Peasant: Ha...yes, yes, yes, sir!

Doctor: Goodbye.

Patient: Goodbye, may God keep you, sir (Getting farther away)

Abu Ibrahim: My jaw is numb.

Doctor: O.K., I'm coming...'Afifi!

Nurse: Yes, doctor.

Doctor: Prepare the anesthesia. (Turning to Abu Ibrahim) You're telling me your jaw's numb?

Abu Irbahim: (From close) And I can't feel my face anymore at all.

Nurse: Here you are, doctor. (Sound effects of putting down surgical instruments.)

Abu Ibrahim: Is this anesthesia so strong that it does all this, sir?

Doctor: Of course, open your mouth so I can see.

Abu Ibrahim: But doctor, I'm afraid it will hurt.

Doctor: But didn't we anesthetize you? Why are you afraid? Open your mouth.

Abu Ibrahim: Sir, I'm afraid it will hurt when you pull the tooth.

Doctor: Don't be afraid, don't be afraid! You won't feel a thing, open your mouth.

Abu Ibrahim: Sidi, God...

Doctor: Ho, ho...what are you, a boy? Open your mouth.

Abu Ibrahim: Uh...

Doctor: Open it some more. Why are you afraid? Why are you so tense?

Abu Ibrahim: I'm not afr... Ah...Ah.

Doctor: Some more.

Abu Ibrahim: Ah. Ah...

Doctor: Some more, some more!

Abu Ibrahim: Ow...ow...ow...

Doctor: Right, some more, some more. Don't be afraid.

Abu Ibrahim: Ow, Ow. My jaw's falling apart.

Doctor: Well, she has to get the pliers in your mouth. Right, very good. There you go.

Abu Ibrahim: (In pain) Aw...aw...aw.

Doctor: There you are, it's out.

Abu Ibrahim: What, what, did you pull it, sir

Doctor: Of course, don't you see how big its root is?

Abu Ibrahim: Bless your hands, Doctor.

Doctor: Swish some water in your mouth and then you can talk. (The sound of the pliers being dropped on the table.) Take these instruments and sterilize them, 'Afifi.

Nurse: Yes, Doctor. (Sound effects of instruments being gathered while the talk continues)

Abu Ibrahim: Let me tell you, doctor, now I must really have been imagining things. I was so worried about pulling this tooth.

Doctor: Of course. It's the imagination that is more real than the pain itself.

Abu Ibrahim: Bless your hands. To tell the truth, by God, you do have quick hands.

Doctor: May God keep you. Don't forget to gargle every now and then.

Abu Ibrahim: Whatever you say, sir. May God keep you for us. (Getting farther away) Goodbye, doctor.

Doctor: Goodbye...'Afifi!

Nurse: (From far away) Yes.

Doctor: Take a look in the waiting room and see who's next and bring him in. (He starts humming to himself) La...la...la...

Abu Fahmi: (From far away and getting closer) Aw...aw...my jaw, my tooth. Greetings, sir!

Doctor: Greetings.

Abu Fahimi: Ow...In the name of God, let me kiss your hand. My tooth, my tooth.

Doctor: And why is your face wrapped up in twenty layers of gauze?

Abu Fahmi: It's just bandaged, sir.

Doctor: (Laughing) Why is your face so wrapped up that we only see your eyes?

Abu Fahmi: Sir, I piled on the starched layers so my tooth would be well protected.

Doctor: O.K., sit right down on this chair.

Abu Fahmi: Ow...In the name of God, Doctor, help me out, I kiss your hand.

Doctor: Unwrap this bandage so I can see what's inside.

Abu Fahmi: Ow, my jaw. Oh, my jugular vein. Ow...

Doctor: Help him, 'Afifi, get this blanket off his face.

Nurse: Here, let me do it, sir.

Abu Fahmi: Hey...Hey...in the name of God, you're tearing the skin off my face. Take it easy!

Nurse: Don't worry. The starch from the gauze has dried on your cheek.

Abu Fahmi: Aw...Aw...By God, I can feel the base of my skull being torn off.

Doctor: Enough, already! Are you a little boy?

Abu Fahmi: In the name of God, I haven't been able to sleep for eight days from the pain. Trust me, doctor!

Doctor: Why have you left yourself all this time without medical attention?

Abu Fahmi: Who told you I left myself without medical attention? By God, there isn't a barber in the quarter I didn't show my tooth to.

Doctor: Uf...What does a barber have to do with an inflammation in the jaw?

Abu Fahmi: Why, is my jaw inflamed, sir?

Doctor: Of course, can't you see how your face is like a drum? Which barber did this to you?

Abu Fahmi: One of the barbers in the neighborhood.

Doctor: Didn't you know before now that there are doctors and specialists in this world? You should have seen a doctor before letting it get like this.

Abu Fahmi: I know, sir, but I said to myself, why should I put all my life savings into a tooth cavity which isn't worth it in any case.

Doctor: Just so you don't pay a small amount you let your jaw get inflamed and poison your blood, you dumbbell?

Abu Fahmi: I'm going to die, sir?

Doctor: Well, if you hadn't come now and I hadn't seen you, in two days your jaw would have had gangrene and poisoned your blood and you would have died.

Abu Fahmi: W...W...What are you saying, doctor?

Doctor: But, of course, can't you see how your cheek has turned blue?

Abu Fahmi: In the name of God, with all the bandaging I put on I haven't seen my face in a week.

Doctor: Open your mouth so I can see.

Abu Fahmi: Sir, I'm unable to open it. I can feel the nerve pulling from my eardrum to the bottom of my jaw.

Doctor: Open your mouth as much as you can so I can see what the barber has done to you from the inside.

Abu Fahmi: Aw...Aw...

Doctor: Open some more, some more.

Abu Fahmi: Ah...Ah...

Doctor: What's wrong with you? Open some more.

Abu Fahmi: Huh...Ah...

Doctor: My man, just let me get a mirror in your mouth to take a look.

Abu Fahmi: Ah...

Doctor: Shut your little museum there...enough.

Abu Fahmi: Um...Ow...So what did you see, Doctor?

Doctor: What did I see? I see that the barber has broken your jaw.

Abu Fahmi: No! Why...?

Doctor: It's all because when your honor was in pain you ran to the barber as if you had been around for a hundred years.

Abu Fahmi: Sir, I said to myself why should I put all that money into a doctor. The barber is my neighbor and he will pull out my tooth for half a pound.

Doctor: Which is more important—your health and your life, or your money, you dumbbell?

Abu Fahmi: When a man's molasses is water,[1] what is he going to do with himself?

Doctor: Don't you know that the Ministry of Health has clinics in every neighborhood so that disadvantaged people like you can get free medical help?

Abu Fahmi: By God, I didn't know such things existed, sir.

Doctor: In any case, your condition needs hospital attention for an immediate operation.

Abu Fahmi: No, what are you saying, Doctor? Please, I have young children. I can't leave my work and stay at the hospital. May God prolong your life!

Doctor: Is it better to sleep a few days in the hospital and get your health back, or sleep in the cemetery?

Abu Fahmi: Oh, what a pity this has happened to you, Abu Fahmi. Ah...ow...my jaw...aw...

Doctor: Please go out into the waiting room until the ambulance comes to take you.

Abu Fahmi: Ow, the seeds of my jaw. Doctor, can I go say goodbye to my family and come back?

Doctor: Why do you let your imagination run away with you? When they give you penicillin and medicine the danger will pass. You'll be fine. Ya, 'Afifi!

Nurse: (From far away) Yes, Doctor.

Doctor: Make a phone call to the center to send an ambulance. (Turning to Abu Fahmi) And where are you going?

Abu Fahmi: (From a short distance) Didn't you tell me to wait outside in the waiting room, sir?

Doctor: Come, before you leave give me the name and address of the barber.

Abu Fahmi: (Coming nearer) Why, sir, do you want to have your tooth pulled, too?

Doctor: (Laughing) No, but we want to turn him over to the court to take care of him.

Abu Fahmi: Sir, may God prolong your life, it's not his fault!

Doctor: How can it not be his fault? Did you ask him to break your jaw?

Abu Fahmi: No, sir. Isn't he offering to pull out a tooth for half a pound?

---

[1] An expression meaning he is poor.

Doctor: Yes, and so...?

Abu Fahmi: Well, I made a deal with him to pull out two teeth for three-quarters of a pound.

Doctor: Why, were both teeth bothering you?

Abu Fahmi: No, sir, only one was bothering me, but I figured three-quarters of a pound for two teeth was a good deal and I said to myself, you might as well pull them both out.

Doctor: (Laughing) Uh...What a strange mentality. Anyway, go out and wait for the ambulance.

Abu Fahmi: Whatever you say, sir. (Farther away) Ow, my teeth, the seeds of my jaw.

Doctor: 'Afifi...

Nurse: (From far away) Yes, doctor.

Doctor: See who is in the waiting room and tell them to come in. (Starts humming)

Um Kamal: (From far away, coming closer) Oh, the roof of my mouth. Aw...Aw...my gums...ow...ow... Hello, my son.

Doctor: Hello to you. What is it, Haji?[1]

Um Kamal: May God keep you in good health, may you bury me, my gums have turned against me and I can feel everything tearing apart inside. God keep you from such pain...Aw...Aw...

Doctor: No problem, no problem, Sit down in this chair. Hold her hand, 'Afifi.

Um Kamal: Yo-o May God be pleased with you and lead you...Ow...Hmm...

Nurse: Lean back, auntie.[2]

Um Kamal: Yo-o May God be pleased with you and send you a husband.

The nurse laughs.

Doctor: So what's happened to you, Haji?

Um Kamal: Bury me! The roof of my mouth, my jaw, my gums, the bones in my face, my tonsils...

Doctor: (Interrupting her) O.K., be patient. Open your mouth so I can see.

Um Kamal opens her mouth for him to see.

Doctor: Open wider, I can't see a thing!

---

[1] Title of address to an older woman. Literally means pilgrim.

[2] Another polite term of address to an older woman, here the term for aunt used is mother's sister.

Um Kamal: Uh...Uh...

Doctor: Some more, Haji, some more.

Um Kamal: The skin of my face will burst.

Doctor: Don't worry. Open, open!

Um Kamal: Huh...

Doctor: My good woman, why are you so afraid? Open wide so I can see the roof of your mouth.

Um Kamal: Uh...you want me to open more than this? You can see my intestines, not just the roof of my mouth. (She opens her mouth). Uh...Uh...

Doctor: Well, well, is this a bridge I see in your mouth?

Um Kamal: What else can it be? Do you think I have furniture in there?

Doctor: (Laughing) Well, since you don't have any teeth and you have a bridge, what's hurting you? What are you complaining about?

Um Kamal: Bury me? I bought it ready-made.

Doctor: Umph! Who buys a ready-made set of teeth?

Um Kamal: Bury me. I found it cheap.

Doctor: What a novelty! Don't you know that you shouldn't put someone else's set of teeth in your own mouth?

Um Kamal: Yo...Why shouldn't I, sonny? I never heard as far as teeth are concerned that things should or shouldn't be done.

Doctor: It has nothing to do with teeth but medically and scientifically it shouldn't be done. Don't you know that there are germs and contagious diseases in this world?

Um Kamal: Yo...Say God is one![1]

Doctor: So then how did you get it installed in your mouth?

Um Kamal: Bury me, before putting it in I washed it with soap and red bath powder and I said seven prayers over it and then I put it in my mouth.

Doctor: (Laughing) What a novelty! Whoever led you here was wrong, aunt. Anyway, sets of teeth cannot be enlarged or made smaller. You ought to see a doctor who will make one to fit you exactly. Then your jaw won't get inflamed and your mouth won't bother you any more.

Um Kamal: Bury me. If a camel costs a piaster and I haven't a piaster what can I do?

Doctor: At this point I'll send you to the University where they'll make one for you free.

---

[1] By this expression she hopes to ward off evil.

Um Kamal: Yo! May God give you happiness for giving me this information. May God give you such good news!

Doctor: Any time, Haji.

Um Kamal: Yo...May God take you by the hand, you and every good man.

Doctor: And now I'll write you a letter of introduction to take to the University so they will take care of you.

Um Kamal: Go with God. May he take care of you and every decent boy who cares for the poor.

Doctor: Wait outside in the waiting room. I'll send you the letter with the girl.

Um Kamal: Bury me, I'll wait outside. Goodbye, sonny.

Doctor: Goodbye. 'Afifi!

Nurse: (From far off) Yes, doctor.

Doctor: See who is outside in the waiting room and send them in. (He starts humming again)

Abu Rushdi: (Coming nearer) Aw...Aw...my tooth! Hello, Doctor.

Doctor: (From the other room) Hello to you. Have a seat.

Abu Rushdi: O.K. Aw, my tooth. My God, my God, such pain! Aw...Aw...it pains as if I have a sword in my tooth.

Doctor: (Again, from other room) What do you say, uncle?[1]

Abu Rushdi: What, sir?

Doctor: Relax, I just want to write this letter for the woman outside. Why all this carrying on?

Abu Rushdi: Would I do it if my tooth didn't hurt, son?

Doctor: Keep your voice down. You're not a child!

Abu Rushdi: O.K. I'll shut up...Aw...Aw...Aw...my tooth!

Doctor: Ho, ho, already again. Aren't you going to let me write these two lines?

Abu Rushdi: O.K. I'll be quiet...Aw...Aw...my jaw!

Doctor: Enough with you!

Abu Rushdi: O.K. I'll shut up...aw...aw...aw...

Doctor: (Coming nearer) Ho, ho, so I'll stop writing. What's wrong with you?

Abu Rushdi: My tooth, God keep such pains away from you. It kept me up all night, may God be my witness.

Doctor: Open your mouth so I can see.

---

[1] Polite form of address for an older man; the term used here is literally father's brother.

130

Abu Rushdi: Huh. (Opens his mouth)

Doctor: Umph. Close your mouth.

Abu Rushdi: So, Doctor, what do you see?

Doctor: I saw the Castle Yaldiz.[1] What do you think I saw? Give me those pliers, 'Afifi!

---

[1] Yaldiz is a castle in Turkey that is referred to when someone wants to remark on the size and extravagance of something.

Chapter Ten

"May You Live What is Left of His Life"[1]

In return for life is death.

It is pointless…this death…

I hate death. I fear death. Nothing defeats me but death.

I flee from the death of others. Since I was a little child and until I reached adulthood I always avoided my obligations toward the parents of those who died. When one of my neighbors died, I escaped from the house so I wouldn't have to hear the crying and wailing of women in windows and on balconies, nor the heartbreaking words of farewell spoken to the deceased as he left the house, never to return. The words leaving the lips of his mother or wife, "Go in peace…," nearly killed me. What peace did they mean? These words fell like a dagger in the hearts of us still living while the dead one could not hear, feel, see or remember anyone and would never respond to their words, "May the peace of God be with you."

The husband of one of our dearest friends died. A beautiful, smart, kindly, young woman suddenly lost her handsome, beloved, esteemed husband who loved her, spoiled her, and gave her all that a young woman could want. He left her behind with two children, not to return.

Damascus was shaken as if by an earthquake. The man was one of the best young men in the city in his manner, position, and education…and now he was gone, God be merciful to him.

It was imperative to stand with other friends beside a bereaved friend.

Me…!!?

My God, how could I enter that once happy home that now had lost all happiness forever? The name of the man was still written over the doorbell…! He was the one who used to open the door for his guests with a welcoming smile…and now…? In the wine-colored sitting room all had changed. Where were the burgundy colored curtains and where were the glittering chandeliers? Nothing…cane-bottomed chairs now stood side by side against the four walls of the room, and at the end was the young widow, draped in black and crying continuously and passionately, while over her head hung a portrait of her husband who smiled with mockery at life, a life that in a wink of an eye could be so easily snuffed out by death.

Was death stronger than…?!

Her youngest child jumped up, asking:

---

[1] An expression used when offering condolences.

—Where is my father? ...When is Father coming back, Mother?

No...life is stronger. The child is strongest.

We shouldn't avoid performing our social duties in the case of death. But I was removed from Damascene tradition as far as death was concerned.

Before I went to the condolence, I asked an older relative of ours about the proper way to behave. She began my instruction by saying:

—Daughter, there are many Damascene customs and traditions associated with death that you should know about and respect. If the deceased is a family man then the tragedy is very great...even more so when he is a young family man. In such cases his relatives, his wife's relatives and all his friends and neighbors ought to go to his home immediately after the publication of the obituary.

When the deceased leaves his home the men escort him to the Umayyad Mosque or any other mosque to say prayers for him, and then men take him for burial at al-Diahdah or Bab al-Saghir. There at the burial ground his family members form a line to accept people's condolences.

The man offering condolences says:

—God has truly enlarged your debt.

The family member replies:

—God appreciates your concern, your deeds, and your sympathy.

Then, one of the relatives at the funeral invites all those present to a meal at the house of the deceased and they all drive there in a funeral procession. Of course one of the women relatives would have already invited the women, who came to the house upon hearing the news, to have a meal with her—lunch or dinner, depending on the time of the funeral.

The dinner after the funeral usually consists of a simple main dish like "zi, which is prepared with layers of pastry stuffed with rice, meat, pistachios and pine nuts, with a side dish of yoghurt. Damascene pastries and fruits are also served. When the deceased comes from a wealthy family the dinner table is usually laden with Damascene style meats and vegetables. Each house offers what is appropriate to their economic level. At the end all are served a cup of bitter coffee.

Then, the female relatives spend the night at the deceased person's house. In the old days it was the custom for the men to pay their respects on the following morning at the burial ground, where they would erect a tent above the grave site, and have the Koran read by a shaikh while bitter coffee was passed around to all the guests. But times have changed now and men pay their respects to the deceased's family on the same day as the funeral in the evening between sunset and dinner time. This visit is called a *timsayya* or evening visit, and a *subhiyya* is a morning visit. Usually, however, right after burial one of the relatives will call out "The morning visit will be forgiven, brothers!" meaning that visitors will be welcome on the evening of that same day.

Condolences are accepted separately and with different traditions by the men and the women of the family. In the case of the former, the family of the deceased sit in a row near the door in order to see all those coming and going, and every time a mourner comes in they stand up and welcome him, shaking his hand and then leading him to sit alongside the rest of the mourners while the shaikh reads from the Koran. Every time a group of mourners comes, another group leaves. Passing the parents on the way out, they shake their hands exclaiming, "May God compensate you for your loss" to which the family member responds "God thank you for what you have done." They must accept condolences on three consecutive evenings.

As for the women relatives, one of them volunteers to get in touch with the closest of the female relatives, calling them to the deceased person's house to stand in the room in which they accept condolences, the 'asriyya. Thus, all the aunts, parents-in-law, nieces, sisters-in-law, daughters-in-law, and all the closest female relatives come to the house as soon as possible. The older women, of course, are the ones who actually stand in the 'asriyya accepting condolences. This act is one way of showing how the deceased person stood with his relatives and the respect they owe him. Sometimes about ten women stand in the 'asriyya and at other times maybe even forty-five women, naturally depending on the deceased person's place in the hearts and minds of his friends and relatives.

The 'asriyya itself is usually draped with white or gray curtains or even black ones. The faithful, however, tend not to use black draperies. The entrance to the 'asriyya is simply draped with a curtain to avoid having a door that is either wide open or shut. Inside, chairs are lined up against the walls and the deceased's wife sits in the middle of the row facing the entrance to the room, wearing black with a black scarf on her head while her daughters sit beside her. The rest of the relatives standing in the 'asriyya wear grey or navy blue while covering their heads with white georgette and silently reciting prayers for the deceased. Traditionally they should silently repeat "God is One" from the Koran 100,000 times. Each woman holds special prayer beads with one hundred beads and repeats the prayer a thousand time at each bead. By the end of the 'asriyya at least ten women should have said the prayers for the deceased.

In the room itself the drapes are usually pulled shut to darken the place. To the right of the room three chairs are placed for those mourners who are not related. They are allowed to come in three at a time. Three women enter in the order of their ages, the eldest first and the youngest seated nearest to the door. Upon their entrance the relatives stand up silently in recognition, then all take their seats together. Each of the three mourners says the prayer mentioned above three times. When their prayers are finished the women depart again in descending order of age.

Meanwhile the shaikh is in the next room reading from the Koran. This 'asriyya ritual continues for three days and the first Thursday following the death. Some people turn over their rugs and mirrors and cover their furniture, including closets and chandeliers, with white or gray material for a whole year but these traditions have diminished with time because now we believe real sadness is found in the heart and not in appearances. But traditional dress has remained the same with the deceased's wife wearing black along with her unmarried daughters, while the married ones wear navy or gray and relatives wear navy, blue or gray. In the wife's case, she wears black for a whole year or until one of her relatives gets her to change first to navy, then gray, then blue, then white and finally to any color.

Condolences are accepted by the women on the same day of the death, but with very little talking allowed. Thereafter condolences are accepted on the same day of the week as the death, every week until forty days have passed and in some houses until a year has passed. By contrast the tent put up at the grave site by the men remains there until the first Thursday following the death and on the days of the two Muslim holidays, 'Id al-Fitr and 'Id al-Adha, when mourners are welcomed at the house or burial grounds. Finally the grave site should be visited seasonally and on religious holidays.

When forty days have passed and the one-year anniversary of the death comes, a dinner is given for the shaikhs and for the poor by the parents of the deceased. Money is also given to the poor in the name of the deceased person's soul.

After the husband's death a wife goes into seclusion for four months and ten days[1] during which she should not see or hear a single man and vice versa.

In olden times the customs of mourning were much more complicated. They would take apart their beds and sleep on mattresses laid out on the floor and eat on the floor, while the deceased's wife slept on a bare mattress. She wouldn't wash for prayers from the water jug because its waters were not sanctified and she didn't comb her hair with a comb made from fish bone because that was tainted. She didn't eat from a fork or a spoon and

---

[1] This is the 'idda period, the purpose of which is to assure the paternal parentage of a child.

didn't drink from a glass but from a bowl. She didn't dry her hands with a towel or sit on a chair but on a cushion. The deceased's clothing was given to the poor and the assistants of the pallbearers, but of course all this has ceased today and funerals have changed with the times. The coffin is now transported in a car and flowers are carried on the cars of the mourners who follow in the procession.

Things have changed a lot in our city, daughter, but it would be shameful to ignore the original tradition of taking condolences in the 'asriyya. Daughter, we should recognize the proper respect due people and should help them out in times of trouble and sadness so they will know how we feel and so that they will come to us when we're in the same position. What are people made for but to help each other?

And from that day on I have dark clothes for all seasons along with gray or blue head coverings and scarves so I will be ready to perform my duties toward those I love when they lose a loved one. Damascus is a city that venerates the dead so why shouldn't I do what Damascus expects!

But I still fear death.

I am not afraid of dying myself but I am afraid of losing those whom I love and I ask nothing of God but to let me die before all of those I love.

Selfish! No matter, let them suffer more than I. I wish to die while my precious loved ones live on!

Chapter Eleven

Images:
1: Karakuz and 'Aiwaz

In the coffee house of the Juzza bath in Suq Saruja on the low straw stools I used to listen with the rest of the children during my childhood to this conversation between Karakuz and 'Aiwaz done by the voice of the popular anonymous artist Karakuzati:

'Aiwaz: Brother, tell me what you and I are going to do without any work? Tomorrow, if there is a robbery in town they will blame us.

Karakuz: Well, there isn't any work. What can we do?

'Aiwaz: Karakuz, you just don't like work. You are a man used to being lazy.

Karakuz: Find me a job and I'll work.

'Aiwaz: Why don't we work as money changers?

Karakuz: So they'll call us Jews for sale?

'Aiwaz: Well, why don't we take up your father's profession? Go inside and ask your mother what he did and we'll do that.

Karakuz: Mama, what did Dad do for work?

Um Karakuz: Oh, thank God, my son has finally come to his senses. God's mercy has descended on his head and he will become rich and will have money to spend. Lya, lya, lya, lysh!

Karakuz: O.K., but what did Dad do?

Um Karakuz: Your Dad clipped dogs.

Karakuz: What do you mean?

Um Karakuz: He used to buy bread for ten piasters and gather the dogs to cut their hair and sell the lot for five piasters.

Karakuz: Do you hear? That's what my Dad used to do.

'Aiwaz: That's not a real job. God shorten your life, you and this job.

Karakuz: Then what do you want us to do?

'Aiwaz: Why don't we become beggars?

Karakuz: Who's going to give money to us? It would be the same as if they tied us to a walnut tree and we had to pull it out by its roots.

'Aiwaz: Oh, yeah. You think I would beg just like that? I have an axe so we can cut off your hands and a sledgehammer to break your legs, and an ice pick to poke out your eyes. That's how I will take you around to beg.

Karakuz: Get out of here, you and your jokes!

'Aiwaz starts singing:

Kazal Kazal, Dar
How wonderful the riches
Our world is strange
Bash Bash, Ya Bash Bash

Karakuz: Let's get moving to the Umayyad Mosque, you Bash Bash.

'Aiwaz: (At the Umayyad Mosque) Asking for the sake of God and his goodness and his bounty. Fill my bowl with five pound notes. It's not a lot to ask, Oh God.

Karakuz: By God, his mind has gone. What is this Bash Bash, are you out of your mind?

'Aiwaz: If I knew you were such a low person I wouldn't have come begging with you. Do you want me to start begging for 50,000 pound notes all at once?

Karakuz: No, but you can't believe you'll get all the money in the world at one time. Walk up those steps, I think I see a charitable face.

'Aiwaz: I'm going to knock at this door.

Karakuz: Knock and maybe God will give us a reward.

Woman: Who is it?

'Aiwaz: What do you mean, who is it? Curse the father who brought you to this neighborhood. (Turning to Karakuz) You see that, she dares to ask who it is?

Karakuz: What do you expect her to ask?

'Aiwaz: Don't you know that Karakuz and 'Aiwaz have come upon hard times and have nothing left to their name. Give us whatever you have, a couch, rug, mattresses. Whatever?

Woman: My husband is in Istanbul.

'Aiwaz: Well, wire him.

Woman: I'm divorced, divorced!

Karakuz: I trust you've ended your 'idda?![1]

2: Sugar and Tobacco

A friendly old Damascene man said to me:

—Daughter, in Damascus there are a lot of good people worthy of being called human beings. We had some good days when we were young but now that we are old those good days have passed away.

---

[1] The period after her divorce or the death of her husband in which a woman can't marry.

138

For awhile, when I was young in the days of the Turkish rule I was an officer in the Turkish army. Ottoman Turkey had forbidden trade in sugar and tobacco and anyone caught smuggling these items was punished by death.

Once I passed by my uncle's place in Suq Ali Basha and he said to me, "Nephew, bless you, I want you to walk behind this child at a distance until he takes this box of tobacco to a merchant in Bizuriyya." I replied, "Whatever you say, uncle, let's go, boy." We walked and walked until we reached Suq Midhat Pasha and just when we were about to come to Bizuriyya, I was surprised to see people running and Turkish soldiers chasing them. I took into consideration the fact that we were carrying a box of tobacco and, afraid they might catch us, told the boy to turn back quickly. At the Bizuriyya crossing I saw a big crowd coming from a funeral bearing a coffin. The mourners started running away as did the pallbearers and their assistants. People were running everywhere. The world was turned upside down with the deceased's parents crying and the Turkish soldiers insisting that the coffin be opened. The parents swore they couldn't open the coffin. One Turkish soldier stepped forward and said:

—Just explain to me then how ten funerals can come out of the same house in one day. I can't figure that out!

Apparently the funeral procession had come out of a small lane where there was only one door and from that one door had come the ten funerals in one day, thereby attracting the attention of the Turkish soldiers.

—I want to open the coffin!

—No, you cannot!

—I will break it open!

Finally they broke the coffin open and found it filled with cubes of sugar being smuggled between various houses. They were taking it to the burial ground where it was hidden in a certain cave until it was taken out and distributed.

—This story, daughter, is a funny one but at the same time it shows you how the invaders were never able to control Damascus.

There are a lot of good stories in which we were the heroes when we were young. There was an old tradition in Damascus if a poor man or woman died and the parents were unable to pay the expenses of the funeral, the best young men of Damascus would carry a bar of soap in one hand and a scale in the other and go from shop to shop taking what the shopkeeper in his heart was able to give. The scale and the soap meant without need for explanation that there was a poor person whose funeral expenses had to be covered so he or she could be taken to the Dihdah or Bab al-Saghir cemetery. This shows you the goodness of Damascus. Occasionally when we were out of pocket and didn't have enough money to go and get drunk, a few of us young mem used to take the scale and the soap and go to collect money for the poor woman whose mane we couldn't mention. We would have a wonderful evening laughing and talking and asking mercy for the poor woman...Such were the boyish prank of young men.

Other times we would take the scale around to shops to collect money for a poor woman at the bakery who had no money to buy bread. Of course there was no penniless woman at the bakery. We used to try that trick to get money to buy meat pies at the bakery so we could have a good picnic by the river Barada...of course, at the expense of the bountiful shopkeepers.

Young men! May God bless them and those days, daughter!

I know a nice story about a Damascene called Abu Ahmad. Abu Ahmad set out once with a bedouin for a trip in the desert. On the way, they became thirsty and stopped at a water well by the side of which stood a pretty young girl filling up her bucket. The bedouin asked, "Hello, will you give us some water to drink, daughter?" She replied, "Help yourself," and she brought up the bucket from the well and gave it to the bedouin to drink. Then she said, "If you would please tell me your name so I can wish you good health." He said to her, "My name is in the beauty of your face." So she said, "May you drink in good health, Muhsin"[1] She took the bucket and drank from it. He said to her, "If only I knew your name to wish you good health." She replies, "What your hand can hold." He answered, "To your good health, Khazna!"[2] Then Abu Ahmad walked up and took the bucket, drank from it, put it down again and said with a loud voice, "Thanks be to God." The bedouin woman said to him, "If only I knew your name to wish you good health." Abu Ahmad turned to her and said in his Damascene accent, "Listen, I'll have nothing to do with this nonsense. My name is Abu Ahmad!!"[3]

3: Between One Damascene and Another

One of my neighbors called Abu Ahmad said:

Abu Ahmad: We needed a few school bags for the kids, Shawkat! How many did we need?

Shawkat: A few school bags.

---

[1] She uses a masculine name that means handsome.

[2] Her name means storehouse.

[3] This story reveals the pragmatic, no-nonsense nature of the Damascene.

Abu Ahmad: We took the kids and went down to Suq al-Khuja. Where did we go?

Shawkat: To Suq al-Khuja.

Abu Ahmad: We bought three school bags. What did we buy?

Shawkat: Three school bags.

Abu Ahmad: Afterwards, we went to Suq Qarwan. Where did we go?

Shawkat: We went to Suq Qarwan, sidi.

Abu Ahmad: They were auctioning off a carpet. What were they auctioning?

Shawkat: A carpet.

Abu Ahmad: They reached five thousand. What did they reach?

Shawkat: Five thousand.

Abu Ahmad: Then we heard the call to afternoon prayer. What was it?

Shawkat: The call to afternoon prayer.

Abu Ahmad: So we took the kids and went down to the Umayyad Mosque for the afternoon prayer. What did we pray?

Shawkat: The afternoon prayer, sidi.

Abu Ahmad: Then we left through Bab al-Bizuriyya. From where did we leave?

Shawkat: Bab al-Bizuriyya.

Abu Ahmad: From there, we went to Suq Midhat Pasha. So where did we go?

Shawkat: To Dummar.

Abu Ahmad: So you are not understanding a word I'm saying. Aren't you following me?

Shawkat: No, I left you a long time ago in Suq al-Khuja!

Chapter Twelve

'Antar, the Bravest of the Horsemen

The famous Damascene storyteller Abu Kasim used to tell the stories of 'Antar and 'Abla[1] in the cafe at the Bab Sarija crossing. One day, he happened to be telling the story of one of 'Antar's battles where he fought and fought, only to end up being taken prisoner. "Then they jailed 'Antar...Oh, yes..." And Abu Kasim left him in jail and broke off the story. He left the cafe, and with him the audience.

Among this audience there was a man who loved these stories and was a fervent supporter of 'Antar. He went home and had his dinner. When bedtime came his wife told him to go up to bed but he replied that since 'Antar was in prison he wouldn't be able to get any sleep. So he got up and took his gun and went straight away to Abu Kasim's house and knocked at his door. It was past midnight. Abu Kasim opened the door, "What is it? Is there anything I can do for you?" The man said, "How can you in all your goodness go to sleep while 'Antar is in prison? By God, if you don't get him out tonight I will slit you open with a knife. You must get him out even if you don't want to so he can go back to 'Abla."

The story teller knew this man was a rascal and was afraid of him. He asked him to come into his house and brought out the story of 'Antar, and read to him until 'Antar was out of prison with his honor intact. Then our friend's heart was at ease and he was able to sleep peacefully. But the story of how 'Antar got out of prison that Abu Kasim read, God bless his soul, after he had been awakened and all hope of sleeping again was gone, is a long one:

My dear sirs, when Abu Duh had inspected the guards of the army and had started on his way he began to think about marrying his cousin[2] Halima. He went happily along singing:

> Oh Time, forever you will regret it
> If you give me no hope about those I love
> Love must go on uninterrupted
> I thank you for your generosity
> Which gave me more time before my soul died

---

[1] These are the most famous of the Syrian epic stories. 'Antar is the black hero and 'Abla his fair cousin.

[2] His paternal cousin.

Halima told me she was indifferent to me
And told me to leave gentlemen's daughters alone
Her harshness has hurt me; she has fought with me
And not listened to those who rebuke her
In a little while I will reward her for her trouble
And she'll find her house a pile of rubble.

He rode on, his spirits rising in anticipation, crossing plains and mountains until he neared Damascus and there was no more than a day or two remaining to reach that city. He called out to his men, "I have decided to undertake a matter which there is a good chance I can accomplish if you agree to help me." His men asked what he had in mind. He replied that they would take the Dailam[1] and the non-Arab foreigners that they had with them and tie them to their horses, and send along to accompany them, one thousand Arab knights. "We will go in front of these knights with another one thousand knights carrying banners and crosses. We will approach the town with the last thousand dressed as prisoners, so that if my uncle is nearby, he won't be able to miss seeing us and will come to ask what happened to us and our soldiers. Then I will talk to him about subjects that interest him to distract him until fifty of you take over the town. That will make it easy for me to cut off the head of my uncle's deputy and poke our swords into his friends until we've killed everyone from the town."

The listeners said, "By God, Abu Duh, you are right and what you have said is easily comprehended by anyone of intelligence. If any of this news should reach your uncle it would destroy him. His soldiers, who are as many as the leaves on the trees, but whom we know from what we hear to be dispersed and ready to desert, if they should hear about this they will come after us and defend the town. At the same time, our friends will be encouraged to capture the town, so Damascus will be destroyed and its soldiers killed."

The men set the plan in motion and tied one thousand horsemen dressed as prisoners to their horses, and they all rode until they reached Damascus and news of them reached Hamid Bin Hafiz, who was the successor to Harith al-Ghasani, Caliph of Damascus. Hamid bin Hafiz had 300 knights who accompanied him as he rode out to inquire about the news he had received. He saw Abu Duh's men coming from everywhere and on closer inspection noticed the banners, crosses, and prisoners being driven along in a demeaning way. Hamid Bin Hafiz exclaimed, "What glory this is for the Arabs, they have broken the resistance of the Iraqi soldiers and brought them

---

[1] A tribal name.

to us in chains." Then he looked at the leader of the Arabs and recognized Abu Duh. "May God increase your rewards and my kindness, Oh Abu Duh!" Abu Duh called back, "Rejoice, Hamid, rejoice in victory and riches. My uncle's army has fulfilled our hopes and broken King Kisra's army, sending many of its soldiers to their death. He followed them to their lands and seized them. I've returned this way to show you the prisoners and hand them over to you. They include many foreigners and heroes of Dailam. I have also been instructed to round up all the men of Damascus and send them to my uncle in Iraq so he can invade and take over the countries of the fire-worshipers. I need the men because they are of more use to us in the case of a siege than are our knights on horseback.

Abu Duh then took Hamid aside to distract him with plans for attack until the men he had previously selected had finished taking over strategic locations in the capital. Once he was sure his men were in charge, he pulled his sword out and sent Hamid's head flying, while the men who had escorted Hamid were taken care of by Abu Duh's knights who maimed and brutalized them until none of the three hundred were left.

By this time the sun had risen and as Abu Duh rode into the city, he could feel victory in his bones. After he had killed Hamid, he commanded his men to untie the bogus prisoners so they could all ride together into Damascus, attacking and instilling fear in all they met in the name of Kisra. Upon hearing this the knights, followed by the Arabs, pulled out their swords and began slaughtering the people of Damascus. People screamed and blood ran in the streets as the men fought hand-to-hand. The victory finally fell to the Iraqis since most of the civilians took to their heels while the rest either hid or shifted their allegiances to the winning side. The fighting went on and the women screamed out of fear for their children and their houses. The trumpets which the people had brought out earlier to celebrate the victory and the capture of the prisoners now disappeared in their fear of the foreigners and Arabs who didn't spare anyone from the blade of the sword.

Abu Duh was also making sure he spared no one because he was a man of principle who had decided to capture and take his love Halima for himself. He rode through the neighborhoods announcing to the people of Damascus, "Go back to your homes and escape this catastrophe which has come upon you. I have surrendered your city to King Kisra, King of the Persians and foreigners, because of what my uncle has done to me, robbing me of my right.[1] Tomorrow Kisra's army of Pharisees will be at your door and you will have no other choice but to drop your arms and beg for mercy. If you do not I will make slaves of your women and children and do to you what I have just done to your soldiers at the gates, for my uncle is vanquished and those left living of his men have been taken prisoner. From today you have become the subjects of Kisra, King of Iraq and Khurassan, ruler of all there is to see and all countries. So take precautions instead of crying over fate. Don't fight the one who has servants and power unless you want to have your families taken as slaves."

And Abu Duh went on in this way until he overcame all the obstacles that blocked his path and all the civilians dropped their weapons and no longer possessed the determination to resist, instead begging for mercy. They returned to their homes, shut the doors and hid there. No sooner had evening passed and morning come than Abu Duh led his men, the one thousand knights, through the city to the castle. By this time, Halima had learned of what happened and, along with her entourage, was wailing and tearing at her hair knowing that her cousin had done all this for her sake. She fell into despair, let down her hair, beat her breasts and mourned for her father who had been killed. In fact, her condition was so bad that she was almost as close to being dead as her father. She called all her female cousins together, saying to them in fear and despair, "In the name of Jesus, I must kill myself so my cousin cannot humiliate me and my people." She seized one of her father's swords and held it to her breast.

At this sight her mother struck her and tore at her clothing to bring her back to reason. Holding her in her arms, her mother said, "Daughter, if your cousin offers to marry you, you must say 'I don't want to marry any man but want to remain as I am, pure and faithful, until I meet Jesus, son of Mary.' What could be better than that, daughter? I beg that you be patient and listen to what I have to say and see whether or not it is for your own good. After that you can plan and do what you want."

Halima, who by then was even deeper in tears and despair, begged her mother, "Say what you will, Mother, so I can listen and act accordingly. Oh, what a fate he will meet, that sinful cousin, or my name isn't Halima. I will keep his evil being away from me to avoid sin; he had better not come near me."

Her mother replied, "Daughter, the right thing to do would be to have all the women, daughters, wives, neighbors and midwives in the castle let

---

[1] As her cousin, son of her father's brother, he has the right by Muslim custom to marry her. However, later Halima rejects this right for other reasons.

their hair down[1] and walk in crying to the prisoners of war. Each should go to one of the men begging for their help and explaining the catastrophes that have befallen us. Then promise them their freedom and safe return to their people loaded with presents and gifts if they will help us ward off our attackers. If they agree we will ask them to take an oath of good faith and loyalty. Then we will give them arms to fight. If they save us they will have their freedom, horses, and gifts and if they are killed we will kill ourselves but at least we will have tried to save ourselves. I have often heard your father tell of how powerful and brave our prisoners are, unchallenged in fighting and trustworthy in keeping their word. So since we are both near death, letting them free at this point would probably leave us better off than keeping them in prison."

When Halima heard this, her heart was eased and she accepted her mother's advice out of fear and guilt. She gathered all the women, teenagers, wives and servants, and told them of her mother's plan. They agreed to go along with it and let down their hair, all of them as pretty as the moon and fairies. Halima then took them to the cell where 'Antar Bin Shaddad and his worthy friends and other prisoners were held. Having heard the trumpets and the screaming and fighting in the streets, the prisoners were aware that something had happened and they all rose up when the women entered, crying and approached them. 'Antar Bin Shaddad who was very protective of women was extremely moved when he saw Halima and her entourage. He begged them to cover their faces, stop their crying and tell him what had happened and why they were in such disarray. Halima recounted the events from beginning to end that led Abu Duh into the city and how his men had killed so many people. She also told him that she was the reason for all this, not that she would have consented to be his wife under any circumstance, for she was his cousin and marriage between cousins was forbidden in Christianity. Baptized people who did such an act were abhorred by their religion. The women then explained how they would free and reward them if they fought the attackers.

'Antar replied, "Ladies and servants, your coming here in this condition has made me forget the pains of imprisonment I have been suffering. The immensity of your suffering makes me sorry to see you this way. I will go along with your plan, not to gain gifts and presents because the generous do not ask for a reward when they give from themselves, nor do they point a finger at fate for what happens to them. They gladly accept all the good that

---

[1] A sign of mourning.

comes to them because God is good and anything he does cannot be anything but good."

The women were astonished by such talk and readily put matters in the hands of 'Antar. He then put Halima's mind at rest by promising her victory. He ordered the women to unlock his chains and shackles and they did this, not only for him but for his son, Maissara, and his brother, Mazin, and all the prisoners, of whom there was not one who did not promise to try and maim and kill her cousin with every effort in his power. Thus, the women's crying lessened as did their fear and they spent the rest of the night until morning bringing arms, weapons and swords for 'Antar and his friends and taking off the chains that bound the men.

By this time Abu Duh and his men, Arabs, foreigners and heroes of Dailam alike had invaded the town and started to chop off heads left and right as the screaming increased and the battle waged on. 'Antar and his friends at this point dressed themselves in armor and took their swords in their hands. They warned the inhabitants of the castle, "Don't scream or wail, let them all enter the castle and you will see what will befall them!" Meanwhile, the boys and servants readied horses for 'Antar and his men but they refused them, saying they could not take them until they killed all the attackers and were able to leave in peace.

No sooner had they finished saying this than the Pharisees knocked down the doors and came running in, sweeping up all the valuables along the way and shouting and yelling. In the lead was Abu Duh who was also shouting, "Halima, this is the day you will be taken into slavery and humiliated and given a taste of true suffering!"

Meanwhile, 'Antar held his men back until the enemy was in the courtyard of the castle. Then he called his son Maissara, his brother Mazin, 'Urwa Ibn al-Ward, his paternal cousin 'Amr, his father Shaddad and the rest of the men to seize weapons and fall upon the enemy, hitting them with a ferocity more powerful than lightning falling upon mountain tops. The first to die was Abu Duh who had planned all this treachery. It was Maissara who engaged him and recognized him when he called out, "I am the victim of love for Halima and the man who was made ill by the sight of her eyes." When Maissara heard this he was sure it was the leader of the opposition forces and thus he struck him a blow with all his might that caused his head to fall from his shoulders. As for 'Antar, he was taking care of the foreigners and scattering their skulls in all directions. Mazin and 'Urwa at the same time were taking care of the heroes of Dailam, and them following the rest of the enemy into the streets, killing them as they caught up to them and striking fear into the hearts of the enemy and joy in the hearts of the people

147

of Damascus. No sooner did the enemy enter the castle to fight than their heads rolled on the ground. The people cried, heads flew and women screamed but this time they knew that the enemy was destroyed. Halima knew that her cousin, Abu Duh, had been killed and she rejoiced. The Pharisees, the Dailam and the Iraqis continued to enter the castle and the Bani 'Abs, ('Antar's group) continued to wipe them out until dawn came and the sun rose. Those that were left of the attackers fled or begged for mercy while people of the city flung abuses at them from every side.

None of the people had any doubts about the state of affairs since the leaders of the defending force had proclaimed victory from the top of the castle and told of the release of the prisoners of war. When the people of the city heard this, they hunted down and stoned the remnants of Kisra's army to their hearts' content, until none of them were left in one piece. It was a terrifying day!

'Antar and his friends mounted their horses and followed the remaining Pharisees out of the city, striking them with their swords so the blood flowed from their wounds. They didn't cease until they were all dead and lying on the plains. 'Antar then turned back to the city and 'Urwa Ibn al-Ward approached him to ask, "Oh Father of Knights, what are you planning to do? Let us escape from our enemies!" 'Antar answered, "No, by God, we will not deceive the women who released us from our chains and shackles or let Halima say that we have broken our oath. We will return to the city and see whether the gates are open. If they are we shall go in and deal with matters until the responsible authorities return. Otherwise if the doors are closed we will ask for Asma, wife of Majid, and return with her to the Hijaz[1] and people will have nothing to hold against us."

Harith[2] had brought Asma to the castle to visit his parents and his daughter and ordered them to treat her royally because of her beauty, kindness and intelligence. He also had rebuked Maissara and Mazin on her behalf many times while they were in prison. Mazin apologized for what they had done, and Maissara explained how he loved her and that was the reason for his behavior toward her. So 'Antar, who was sympathetic to all young lovers, forgave him.[3]

Meanwhile, 'Urwa Ibn al-Ward had agreed to return to the city with 'Antar, following his example of truthfulness and loyalty to his word. Such was the case also of all the rest of the Bani Abs who realized that without

---

[1] In what is now Saudi Arabia.

[2] See earlier in the story. Harith had been the previous Caliph of Damascus.

[3] It is not clear exactly what the behavior is that they are discussing.

her they would not return safely on their long road home. Maissara, however, proposed to his uncle Mazin that they ride on and not return to the city with the rest of the men because he feared being taken prisoner again. But Mazin replied, "What happened in the past is enough and I will never follow your advice again. I have never seen good come of it. It is our ignorance that landed us in prison in the first place and if it weren't for 'Antar, my brother, we would both be dead by now. So let us follow his lead since, in any case, he will not accept any more deceitfulness from us."

With this they reached the gates of the city and found them wide open, and people calling to them from the tops of the walls. Priests and monks welcomed them and walked with them, reciting from the Bible until they reached the castle. Halima met them at the door, surrounded with her entourage. She was dressed proudly in the garments of royalty and greeted them with great happiness and rejoicing. She said to 'Antar, "Oh Father of Knights, today you are the leaders in the city because you have saved us all with your swords. If it weren't for you our houses would have been destroyed and our women taken in slavery. I ask you to stay on in this house as guests until Father[1] Salim returns and rewards you for your brave deeds and begs your forgiveness for what time and imprisonment have shown you. 'Antar answered, "Oh most free of the Arabs, from the moment we returned to the city we have come in good faith and not to ask for rewards or money. We are here only. Do with us what you please. The slave cannot do other than his master's will." When Halima heard this she was amazed but knew that what he said was from honesty and not in an attempt to deceive. So she ordered her servants to take 'Antar and his men into the quarters she had prepared for them and to remain at their service day and night. She then sent messengers after the Father to tell him of what had happened. 'Antar and his men lived in luxury, grateful for their safe deliverance from having been prisoners waiting for their death to suddenly becoming like kings ruling over their own enemies in a royal fashion.

The storyteller Abu Kassim said as he yawned, "Here I bid you farewell." Our friend sighed and bid the storyteller goodnight and returned to his house for a restful night's sleep.

"One should not belittle the importance of 'Antar's release!"

---

[1] Priest.

Chapter Thirteen

What a Magnificent Place this 'Azm Palace is!

I told the cab driver, "Here, right here please. Thank you!" And I got out in the middle of Suq Bizuriyya. The smells of incense, ropes, soaps, perfumes, coffee, ghee, tea, cumin, ginseng, flour, rice, oil, rose jam, flower water, zatar,[1] walnuts, bags of burlap, wax, salted nuts and dried fruits envelop the heads and souls of the passers-by, tourists and sellers, and their walls, ceilings, shops and khans. In this way, you are welcomed by the smell of Damascus, the smell of Suq Bizuriyya, that is, when you are heading toward the 'Azm Palace from Suq al-Silah which ends at the old jewelers' suq overlooking one of the doors of the Umayyad Mosque. The same is also true if you are coming from the Qimariyya or from Suq Midhat Basha or the new Hariqa district or from Bab Sharqi.

I can smell Damascus in the Bizuriyya and the scent of that old historic city overwhelms me. I smell Damascus when I come out of the desert and into oases shaded by white poplars and willows in Hama, Dummar, Shadrawan and the Rubwa.

Here I am again at the main door of the 'Azm Palace. I enter into the most beautiful Arabic palace in Damascus, if not in all the Arab East. In the palace library which has been turned into a museum of folkloric artifacts I read the story of the Palace. The story starts, "Once upon a time in the olden days..."

The 'Azm Palace, or house of the 'Azm family, is situated in the center of old Damascus, near the Umayyad Mosque at the beginning of Suq Bizuriyya. The site of the present-day palace is within the area that used to be the Roman Temple of Jupiter. The only remaining walls of the temple are found at the gate separating Suq al-Harir from Suq al-Khayattin, and it is said that the house of the Umayyad Caliph Maawiya bin Abi-Sufiyan was in this same spot or near it or perhaps even a part of it, but no one has looked into it thoroughly. It is known, however, from historical sources that it was the house of Prince Dankiz at one time. Excavations that were made in one corner of the palace have revealed a tomb made from marble mosaic that had the coat of arms of prince Dankiz. It was called the "house of gold" when the prince lived there, though before he moved in, it was called the "house of money" (the mint) because it was the place where they

---

[1] Sweet thyme.

printed money. Prince Dankiz was the one who built the Dankiz Mosque on Nasr Street.

In 1749 A.D., or 1163 of the Hijra calendar, the house was taken over by the Governor of Damascus, As'ad Basha al-'Azm, the Wali of Damascus and Prince of the Pilgrimage who was an enthusiastic builder of monuments. He left behind important historical constructions in Hama and Damascus and remodeled this palace for himself in the Arabic fashion that was popular at the time. As'ad Basha brought together the greatest artists, builders, carpenters and painters and confiscated a great deal of wood, construction material, reliefs and columns from other houses and historical monuments in Damascus for use in his house. The work in the palace was finished in three years and was considered the model of beauty, harmony and ornamentation. As'ad Basha spent day and night overseeing its construction and the people of Damascus contributed large quantities of materials: wood, marble and valuable stone, all of which was recorded in detail by Shaikh Ahmad al Bidiri al-Halaq in his diary. He was a clever Damascene barber who used to record everything that happened in Damascus day by day. He related many of the daily events in the time of As'ad Basha al-'Azm including many humorous exaggerated stories about building the palace that were told to him by customers who frequented his shop. Because of his daily contact with people and his love of popular Arabic poetry and writing, Shaikh Bidiri was able to record these events in colloquial Damascene Arabic. He often added rhymed couplets, as for example in the story of Fathi Daftari who insulted the wife of Suliman Basha and was finally killed by him when he caught him:

> Oh what happened to Fathi when he took over the accounts
> Time cheated him, and his happiness over the house left him
> His wheel of fortune revolved round and round
> He never thought time would cheat him.

Turkish rule was all the same with ministers and walis alike using the same means of control. The populace groaned under an inflation caused by the rich: the merchants, the walis, the rulers, their armies, mercenaries and janissaries who all fought among themselves, tearing down quarters of the city one after another and pillaging, burning and attacking the property and lives of the people. One day they would work on Maidan, the next on Suq Saruja and then in Qanawat. In describing those days, Bidiri the Barber said:

> Inflation was high everywhere, especially where food
> was concerned, because of the lack of controls. In the absence

151

of government inspection, merchants could sell at any price they wanted. Lamb was scarce, and so butchers started to sell buffalo, camel and goat meat. A rotl (3.2 kilos) of Damascus meat sold for thirty masriyyas[1] and a rotl plus two wagiyyas of ghee was sold for one piaster. With the coming of Ramadan, prices went up even for vegetables. Before Ramadan we would pay one masriyya for one hundred zucchini, whereas during Ramadan four or five cost one masriyya and every two rotls of eggplant which would cost one masriyya before would cost two masriyya. Meat was nowhere to be found and all this because government personnel didn't carry out their inspections as they should.

Bidiri wrote about daily life in Damascus 205 years ago. In discussing the 'Azm Palace he wrote about the owner Prince As'ad Basha al-'Azm:

For the house he cut down twelve thousand pieces of wood in addition to those pieces sent to him by the gentry of the cities and he hired the best carpenters and masters in the craft, plus painters, for working with the wood. Wherever he needed tile, marble, or pieces like columns or fountain structures his practice was to send someone after them and only offer a fraction of the price.

Bidiri continued on, describing the houses and Suqs ravaged by the Prince to get his materials:

He would say, "Bring me marble and cedar and do your best work in ornamenting, building and inlaying it with gold and silver." Every time he heard of an antiquity or a rare work of marble or porcelain he would send someone to get it, with or without the consent of the owner.

The structure was completed in 1749 A.D. As'ad Basha lived in the house only fourteen years.

Who was this man who was owner of such a great palace? He was As'ad Basha Ibn Ismail, the Minister. He was born in Ma'ara Nawman in 1117 of the Hijra calendar. He took over for his father in Ma'ara and Hama and was later punished and then freed with his father. After that he spent some time with his uncle Suliman al-Wazir in Tripoli, Lebanon. He and his uncle were later rewarded by the Ottoman Empire with the Kingdom of Hama and its surroundings, each getting half. He took over the administra-

---

[1] Coins—literally, "an Egyptian."

tion and ruled well, building khans, baths, gardens and houses which had no equal in all the lands of Greater Syria. In Muhammad Raghab al-Tabakh's book about the aristocracy he says in his third volume on page 334:

> And the state rewarded him with two tukhs[1] of the Roman ranks[2] and he then became an assistant to the Amir of Pilgrimage, Ali Basha al-Wazir. In 1153 H. after his return he became Wali of Sidon until later when, after becoming impatient with the post for many reasons, he was relieved of his duties at his own request and sent back to Hama in 1154 H. There he spent large sums of money giving the town his own personal stamp under the supervision of his Grand Wazir, Bakr Basha.

In the *Daily Book of Bidiri the Barber*, page 35, one finds:

> Suliman Basha from the state of Damascus, appointed in his place his nephew As'ad Basha al 'Azm to replace him. Before that time he was the ruler of Hama, and then he became the Wali of Damascus for fourteen consecutive years from 1156 H. to 1170 H. which made him the longest-ruling Wali. As'ad Basha was given the state of Damascus during a difficult period and he proved a great administrator, receiving much praise in comparison to his predecessors.

Mikhail Brik al-Damashqi in his book said:

> He was killed in Siwas Turkey after having his luggage, money and jewelry confiscated.

Professor Ahmad 'Azzat Abd al-Karim who published Bidiri the Barber's work said:

> The stories about the circumstances of As'ad Basha's death were numerous but I think the real reason was that he let himself be driven to his end in the same way many of the Ottoman Walis did. For the short time they ruled they collected and piled up money thinking it would keep them safe from the Sultan and other potential problems. They did not consider the consequences or possible death such actions might bring.

---

[1] A tukh ia a tail of a horse attached to a pole in the manner of a banner.

[2] The Romani region, a name the Turks gave to the area between the Balkans and the Black Sea, was a state of 24 sanjuks.

As'ad Basha had two children: 'Asma', a daughter and Qublan, a son. 'Asma' was married to her cousin[1] Mustafa bin Faris; Qublan neither married nor had children. As'ad Basha lived together with all his family members and the members of the family of Ibrahim Basha al-'Azm, his great-grandfather. The house remained in the possession of the 'Azms until 1920 when those in the family who inherited it sold more than half to the French Institute. In 1945 the Syrian Government took over this part and then confiscated the rest. In 1953 after having been a center for the study of Middle Eastern Art, it became a folkloric museum for the display of artifacts and local handicrafts. The Palace occupies a piece of land that is 5,500 square meters. It was built in the Damascene style which prevailed in Syria throughout the Twelfth Century Hijra, which is equivalent to the eighteenth century A.D. It should be noted that the outside gives no clue to the richness of the interior and the outside door, despite its relative grandeur, has only modest ornamentation. The door leads to a central hall which connects the two parts of the palace: the *salamlik*, or the outer section, and the *haramlik*, or the inner section. The main entrance leads from the right to the salamlik which is designed to receive male visitors only. It is arranged as an Eastern courtyard where rooms surround a central open area in the middle of which is a large rectangular fountain surrounded by citrus trees and grape arbors. There is also a staircase going up to the top floor which is reserved for the overnight housing of guests.

The haramlik section is attached to the main entrance by three successive doors which lead to the grand courtyard centered in the middle of the prettiest and richest of the palace rooms. This vast courtyard with its fountains and shade trees is reserved for the family so they may enjoy the fresh air, especially the women, for society at that time looked down upon women leaving their houses except in very special or emergency cases. The haramlik courtyard is rectangular in shape, laid out from east to west, and overlooked by the main wings of the building which are made up of six parts, two sections along either side of the two long sides of the rectangle to the right as you enter the courtyard, and the first section divided into three parts that form the Latin letter "T" overlooking the garden in the back. One of the special features of this first part is that you reach it by a double staircase with high rectangular windows and curved double arches forming a beautiful whole.

---

[1] Paternal cousin.

154

The second part, still on the right side of the courtyard, has an *iwan*[1] set in its central wall, flanked on the left and right by two small rooms. The final rear section of the building contains the palace baths, which are a smaller version of Damascene public baths. They were sufficient for the residents of the palace and included the outer, middle and inner sections plus four small compartments and a storage room. From the right-hand room of the second part there is a staircase going up to the *qasr*. This was the room in which the Basha used to sleep with a fireplace in the Turkish fashion with colored marble and inside a coal grate and chimney to allow the smoke to escape. The qasr is considered one of the prettiest rooms in the house because of its harmony in design, and the colors and the ornamentation of the cedar furnishings.

The second section of the house, though the facade lacks balance as far as the numbers of windows, openings and lines are concerned, still forms a pleasing whole, restful to the eye and, like the rest of the building, is a model of creativity. It reflects the genius of the master Damascene engineer and the imaginative builder who had a natural appreciation for things aesthetic. These two parts form the main facade for the large open courtyard.

The facing facade, the north one, is also made up of two parts, one of which consists of five arches supported by four columns, some made of granite and the others of marble. The arches are decorated with vari-colored geometric designs. The iwan formed by these arches has two raised areas, one on the left and one on the right and on each level is a triple-layered fountain with water that flows beautifully over its tiers. On the flat area between the two raised areas is a single-tiered fountain inset with colored mosaic. Overlooking this hall are three rooms with large main windows, circular skylights to let in the sun and "moonlights" to allow the moon's rays to enter the rooms. This facade, along with its background in which you can see the 'Issa minarets of the Umayyad Mosque and the cedar trees of the palace, forms a beautiful view. This hall is designed for sunny winter days. The section which completes the northern facade is simple, with half its wall completely plain and the other half containing one room which, along with its ornamentation of ceiling and windows, is considered to be one of the treasures of the palace.

The eastern section overlooking the haramlik connects the northern and southern parts of the palace. It looks as if it consists of two stories because of rows of high and low windows which are separated by a wooden overhang protecting people who enter from the rain and dividing an otherwise unbro-

---

[1] A large alcove for sitting.

ken facade. Inside there are three great halls, the walls of which have been decorated with wood painted in gold and colors and with lines of poetry from famous poems like "Barada" by al-Bussairi, and other anonymous Damascene poets.

I stand reading poems written with gold wash in praise of the palace and its master:

> People stand and gaze on the beautiful creation built by the Prince
> A house whose history will remain through eternity
> Built by As'ad Basha al-Wazir; a house of good cheer
> With an inspired name, built with the blessing of the Almighty,
> The sun in the middle of its celestial sphere, shines with no equal
> May happiness be always present in the season of happy beddings
> Served by Glory and sheltering Honor,
> It is the most entertaining companion, O Lucky One.
> Venerated in the bosom of pride.
> may the Lord God of Heaven help you and
> May you live forever guardian of the heavens,
> Eternally kept in the care of the Enlightening Book.

The western part which overlooks the haramlik includes a part forming a large hall and the rest forms a courtyard shaded with a trellis of local roses and violets that serves as the main entrance. The haramlik's courtyard leads to a smaller one which is called the kitchen courtyard. The latter contains a rectangular fountain and a few fruit trees. The kitchen is located there with all its utensils and platters plus a special area in which sweets are made. Finally there are the servants' and concubines' quarters and a well for water.

At the entrance to the haramlik courtyard you are welcomed by a star-shaped fountain with sixteen angles and water gushing forth at a rhythmic, mind-soothing pace. Next to it is a rectangular area divided down the middle by a water course which reflects the cedar and citrus trees and roses planted in this small garden. Attached to the garden is a rectangular fountain laid out at ground level from north to south and touching the center point below an arch that supports the front of the large open summer sitting room. The arch with all its ornamentation and designs, along with those on the ceiling of the sitting room, are reflected in the clear water of the pool. The location of the fountain allows visitors sitting on the stone benches surrounding it to sip their tea in the shade of jasmine bushes climbing trellises east to north and forming a special jasmine corner so beloved by all Damascenes.

The courtyard itself measures forty-five and a half meters in length and twenty-six meters in width. It is full of flowers and fruit trees and planters from which vines can climb the walls of the house supported by traditional trellises. These wonderful trees and shrubs of the palace are the resting places and shelters for birds returning from the day's journeys to sing an evening symphony before their night's sleep.

In the evening the palace used to be lit with glass lanterns half filled with sweet oil containing wicks in their centers. These lights were hung between the arches by metal chains. Those lanterns that used kerosene were placed in their proper holders in each room, the hallways and the courtyards. Should it rain, large lamps covered with glass were used instead.

The palace contains sixteen great halls, nineteen rooms on the first floor, nine on the second floor, three open sitting areas, one hallway with five arches, four storage rooms for wood and other supplies, four large fountains fed with water from the Qanawat River (one of the branches or the Barada River), nineteen basins with taps, three water wells which are still in use today, five staircases leading from the large halls to the second floor and small hallways leading from each bedroom to one of the main stairways. Sometimes the bedrooms have windows which overlook the large halls below. There is also a prayer room attached to the second section of the house and a garage for carriages that has now been turned into a storage area. Standing apart from the main palace was a stable for horses which is now used for commercial establishments.

The part of the palace I like best is the haramlik. There a person can feel relaxed and secure in the magnificent richness of an Arabic art that takes its inspiration from Islam. The building, like the religion, is open to God and men, putting them in touch one with the other.

The master Damascene artists who constructed all the parts of the palace from blueprints of its ornamentation and designs, are themselves no less rich nor less original for they too are in touch with eternity. This was what I felt during my visit to the 'Azm Palace, one of the most famous landmarks of Damascus. I left repeating to myself in my heart and to anyone I came across:

What a magnificent place this 'Azm Palace is!

157

Chapter Fourteen

The Flock Keeper

—Be quiet a minute, Abu 'Azzu! Today I caught a bird that will really blow your mind. He was an *ablaq*[1] with rings as big as a *majidi*[2] coin. They said it was a "Sikh."[3] His eyes were as big as charcoal, sitting there just like a rooster.

—Well, show him to us! Take him out from under your shirt.

—Here, take a good look!

—Oh, he's very short and has small wings!

—What do you mean? What do you know about it? Take a good look! Really, what's the matter with you? Are you new at this business?

—Me, new at this business?

Hey, hey! Take it easy, man. We'll get Abu Stif to judge since he's the eldest. What do you say, Abu Stif?

He's right, Abu Hamid he's quite short and has small wings.

—Well, whatever you say, Abu Stif. You are our teacher.

—By God, today I sent mine after Abu Sakhr's. He and I crashed to the ground struggling this way and that for about two hours. He fought like a lion so I attacked him, twisting him back and forth for about a quarter of an hour until finally I finished him off by breaking his back. I turned him upside down and he slipped away into a corner. I turned him over again and put him in a sack. I twisted him and pulled at him and finished him off, and then I released the bag.

—Uncle Abu Hamid, it's as if you were talking to me in Turkish. I don't understand a word you're saying! What do all those words you were using mean?[4]

—"*Karashtilak*," to crash someone, means to send my pigeons to mix with his pigeons and "*libistu*" means I send my pigeons after a bird that was going to light on my roof so as to bring him down. "*Masah*" means the whole flock landed on the roof, but if the one who is the object of our attention doesn't land with the flock, we would say it has "*zahal*," escaped. A

---

[1] *Ablaq* means piebald.

[2] A Turkish coin minted during the reign of Sultan Abdal Majid.

[3] A "Sikh" is considered one of the best kinds of pigeons; it has a particularly long and pointed beak.

[4] He is using the specialized words of the flock keeper's trade which have double meanings in Arabic.

"*barmi*" is the circle the pigeons make around the prey and "*shanshal*" means that the prey came down but didn't stay.

—Uncle Abu Hamid, they say that pigeon keepers are not trustworthy so no one will marry a daughter to them. Is that true?

—Son, it is practically true. For the pigeon keeper, his birds are more precious than human beings and the act of controlling the pigeons takes all of the keeper's time. I know a certain pigeon keeper who divorced his wife three times because of his birds. When his wife used to tell him it was either her or the birds in their house he would always say "the birds." One time a pigeon keeper went on pilgrimage to Mecca and left behind fifty gold pieces with his pigeon-keeper neighbor for safekeeping. After he returned from the pilgrimage he came back and took his money. A week later they were "mixing" their pigeons and the neighbor brought down one of the pilgrim's birds. The pilgrim went to him and said "Give me back the black and white one!" The neighbor replied "Which black and white one?" The pilgrim answered, "The one I saw you catch." The neighbor answered, "By God, you didn't see anything and I didn't take anything." From this story you can see, son, how the pigeon keeper lied to keep the bird but returned the gold since the bird was more valuable to him than gold.

My son, we pigeon keepers have our own secret way so we won't have to swear a false oath. For example, I have a number of wooden crates, each named after a quarter of Damascus. For example, one is called 'Amara, another Suq Saruja, another Bab Sarija, another Suwiqa and another Muhajjarin. If I catch one of my neighbor's birds while I am hunting with him there is no possibility of compromise between us. If I take his bird I keep it; if he takes my bird he keeps it. If he should come to claim it I put my hand on the crate in which the bird is and swear I don't have the bird. I say it is in Muhajjarin which is the name I secretly gave to the crate where he is hidden. What do you expect, son! These birds are expensive. If a pigeon keeper was on the roof training his pigeons and his wife called him he wouldn't leave them even if his favorite person in the world came to visit him. By God, one time in Bab al-Jabiyya on Burghul Street a policeman attempted to confiscate some pigeons in accordance with a new ordinance banning pigeon keeping. All he succeeded in doing was starting a revolution in that quarter. Another time about three or four people died as a result of the birds in Dummar and Duma!

—Why was there an ordinance banning pigeon keeping?

—Because of the way the pigeon keepers behave at times. A pigeon keeper's neighbors are constantly complaining about him, especially the women who are bothered by having a man on the roof looking down on them. To tell you the truth though, a pigeon keeper never looks at a woman for to him every pigeon is worth as much as fifty women. Also, the neighbors are bothered by the mess the birds make and feathers they drop in the summer. Another thing that bothers them is the potato skins and lemon peels that the pigeon keeper throws at the birds to train them but which sometimes land on the balconies that the neighbors have spent all day cleaning. They claim that the pigeon keepers use stones in their training that break windows but a pigeon keeper would never throw a stone at a pigeon for fear he might kill it.

—Why does a pigeon keeper whistle?

—So he can keep other birds away. If a neighbor's prey comes near and attempts to land, the pigeon keeper wants to scare him off so he won't land at the neighbor's. But if the pigeon keeper wants to make the birds land and they won't he strikes a tin can with a whip making a noise that scares them and brings them straight down to the roofs.

—When do you train the pigeons, Uncle Abu Hamid?

—Morning and evening. The new bird in a flock is trained after sunset so that it is too dark and he is too hungry to fly away.

—How does the flock return after it flies off?

—The female pigeon calls them back. The flocks they use have all male birds. If a male pigeon sees a female pigeon from five thousand meters away he comes down for her sake. The farther away a bird goes and still returns the better the reputation of the owner. People will speak of how far their birds fly.

—What do the birds eat?

—Yellow and red corn in winter and white corn in summer. We feed the young bird barley so he'll grow strong and the weak bird *qumbiz*.[1] When the cost of feed rises the profit in the bird goes down. Birds are cheaper in the summer because their wings are clipped and they moult. For that reason we don't start the real training, the "*kish*," until the first of September and we stop around the first of May or the beginning of summer.

—How is the kish done?

—The female pigeons' wings are cut so they can't fly away in pairs. We keep the males away from the females so that when they fly away we can wave a female pigeon at them and they will come back. The pigeon keeper works with a stick that has a black or red flag tied at the end to wave the birds back. Sometimes it can happen that my flock gets mixed up with

---

[1] Small seeds given to birds but also eaten by people.

160

my neighbor's and it comes back with a new member, or missing a member or just the same as before.

—Where do you buy your birds?

—From Janabaza in Khan al-Batikh, or from the Sunday market in the Jewish quarter, or from Shaikh Hassan in the Maidan Quarter of Damascus.

—How do you pigeon keepers deal with one another?

—Humpf! I can tell you, it's either accord, buying or hunting!

—I don't understand!

—Accord means my neighbor and I have an agreement to treat each other equally. If I catch one of his birds I'll return it and the same if he catches one of mine. Accord is necessary between close neighbors so we can return each other's birds and give them a beating so they won't make the same mistake again.

—Beat them?

—Yes, beat them. There is a special way to beat them so they won't do the same thing again. One way to beat them is with a tara which is a stick made of flexible wood with a net on one end. I let the bird fly away twice and both time catch him in the tara. Or I grasp the bird and pierce the flesh above his beak with one of his feathers or a pin and I send him back to his owner with the feather in his flesh so the owner knows I caught, beat and returned him. Or sometimes I rub his feet against the wall until a thin layer of skin rubs off and he is disabled for four or five days before I return him to his owner. Or we pluck his feathers around the anus. Of course in this matter of accord there is money, ranging from one to three pounds for each bird returned. There can be a free accord if the pigeon keepers are very good friends.

—What about hunting?

—Uh...huh, hunting means war! There is no understanding with money nor is there any compromise. If my neighbor and I are in a state of hunting with each other and a bird of his fell into my hands I wouldn't return him for even ten times his price. I might even kill him and I wouldn't return him no matter who intervenes. Why, you ask? Usually because he's a show-off and I don't want to bother with him.

—What about buying?

—Buying means that our treatment of each other is related to the value of the birds...Where's the tea, don't you see we have guests?...Well, anyway, son, what I mean is that if there is no formal relationship between myself and the owner of the bird concerned a dear friend of mine might intervene on his behalf saying, "Dear Abu Stif we'd like this bird back, may God bless you!" So I answer that anything he says goes and then usually the bird's owner will pay me the price of the bird or even more than its price in return. If I don't care about the money I don't take it, for the sake of my friend.

—From what I can see, Uncle Mustafa,[1] this job can bring in quite a bit of money, wouldn't you say?

—Son, in the past, professional flock keepers used to live from their birds but all that changed when the order came out banning the keeping of pigeons in 1938. Nowadays it's no more than a side job or a hobby. If you take a look at the sky of Damascus you will see more than one pretty flock flying around. As I say, flock keeping is a hobby like drawing, dancing and music are with young people these days, no more nor less. To know each other and how to deal with offers depended a lot on the flock keeper's personality and values. Once I caught a certain type of pigeon belonging to a rich flock keeper from the upper classes and a friend of mine came to me to intervene on the man's behalf. He asked if I had a certain bird belonging to so and so. I told him I did. He said the owner wanted him back and would give any amount in return. God forbid that I should take a penny! I returned the bird to the friend, who returned it to the owner but the owner refused to take the bird until I came in person and received a present of two birds of his choice in return. Of course, I didn't go because I was too embarrassed.

—Uncle, are the roofs of the new buildings in Damascus better for flock keeping than those of the old houses in the traditional quarters of the city?

—Son, these new high buildings have really hurt the old Damascene houses, but to tell you the truth the flock keeper is always looking for a higher roof.

—You didn't tell me how you catch a new bird with your birds.

—If I see a new bird flying with my usual flock I would wave to the birds with the female so they would circle above the roof a few times in an attempt to land. But I would wave them away a few times until I was sure that once they had landed they would be too tired to fly away again. And, of course, the new bird lands with them.

—How do you raise pigeons?

—Each flock keeper has his own way of raising birds. You know when the female bird lays eggs that she will incubate the eggs during the evening and the father will incubate them at night. You know also that the chick will first be fed by its mother, then it will eat dirt and finally it will be

---

[1] Up until now, Uncle Mustafa has been addressed by the name "Abu Stif" which is a commonly accepted nickname for Mustafa.

ready to eat corn and grain. I swear to you, son, that once a very strange thing happened. Would you believe that with pigeons there are stepmothers? You probably don't believe it. Well, listen to this story. Once a mother pigeon of mine took off and never came back because she became so frustrated raising her babies. Their poor loving father took care of them night and day. A neighboring female saw him and started hanging around him until he was persuaded to marry her. After marrying him she walked in on his children and in front of their father, out of jealousy, she cracked their skulls open with her beak because they weren't her children and she wasn't about to raise anyone else's children. Would anyone believe this story? I could tell you many more stories like it.

—Now I want to know something about the kinds of birds.

—Right. I'll let you talk with Uncle Biru, because he is the expert in bird identification.

—You don't mind do you, Uncle Biru?

—No, I don't mind at all. Welcome to our little evening group. Your generation should learn all it can about these old Damascene traditions. Now where can I start? You have three kinds of birds: homing pigeons, flocking pigeons and domestic pigeons. You should know that the most important features of a pigeon are its feet, its cheeks and its feathers. The number of feathers in each wing should be ten, eight or nine, or eight on one wing and ten on the other and if the bird has less than this number of feathers he would be called "loose" or "difficult." The birds are usually decorated with a nose ring, leg cymbals and bracelets set with semi-precious stones and made from wax, plastic, nylon or buffalo horn. They put blush on the cheeks of the female bird to make her look prettier so the males will land more quickly. An especially pampered bird would be decorated with pearls and colored beads on its shoulders or might have a necklace of metal decorated with pearls. In other words in the olden days a bird and its accessories might cost as much as three or more gold pounds.

—Wow! How I wish I could see those birds.

—Before we do that tomorrow, let me list the names of the birds, their kinds and their characteristics. First, you have the Baghdadi in black, white or blue. You have a bastard Baghdadi with a Baghdadi father and a mother of another type. You also have the blue-grey Rihani, and the Sharabi of the same color. Then there is a sugar white bird with yellow silver tint, and the Rocker which is either plain white or plain black and is known to rock all the time. Then there's the Austrian which is yellow with a white head and white cheeks. The Austrian can also be plain white with furlike fringe around his head. Then there is the Ra'ufi which is a solid color resembling the blue Umayyad, or the red Makawi that is solid red or comes in solid white or black. The Makawi is noted for long feathers that cover its claws and make up its crest. Then there is the Miswad whose body is either black, red or yellow with white wings. There is also the black and white Ablaq which, of course, is better than the Miswad since it has a white spot on each cheek and is generally bigger. Then there is the Ablaq bi Halsa whose color is lead grey with white wings or the Ablaq bi Khadra which is plain grey with white wings or finally the red Ablaq. Of course, there are different types of red, black and blue pigeons, though the red ones usually have white on the tips of their wings and tails. Then you have the Shakhshirili in black, red or blue, which usually comes in small size with good cheeks, a spot on his head and two white fish-shaped spots on his belly. Then there is the Barbarissi; one is red and another yellow. The Barbarissi is usually all white with yellow shoulders for the red bird and vice versa for the yellow one. Then there is the Buni which is all white with black wings that have the correct number of feathers, good cheeks, and a white spot on his head. You also have the Takilji in black, red or yellow with a white tail and crest of his own color. There is the Halabi which is a picture-perfect replica of the Takilji in flight but can be differentiated by eyes and beak. The Halabi usually comes in red, black or yellow. You have the small Nuri in black or blue with a tail that is usually white. Then there is the Buz which is white with two black lines on each shoulder and a black fringe on his tail. There is also the ʿAmri Ahlas whose shoulders are partially black and the ʿAmri Akhdar which is a whitish grey. Also, son, there is the white Bilindi, the red one, the black one and the plain one. He has a crown and crest shaped like the head of a hammer and is known for his large eyes which are one of the beauty marks of a bird. Then you have the Qawiz that is white with a black tail and the Istanbuli that is grey with a blue tail lightly spotted with black. He has two grey lines on each shoulder slightly darker than his own color. Then there is the Baladi which is of large size, uniform color, and without a crest. The Baladi comes in red, yellow, blue or black. There is also a patchwork colored bird which takes his colors from both his parents if they happen to be different types.

Then there is the Munamar whose father is red and whose mother is yellow and which comes in a color that is neither one nor the other but somewhere in between. There is the huge Abrash which is normally black or blue but he might come in white. The black Abrash is really white with a black tail and the blue one is white with a blue tail. His feathers are usually crinkled and his cheeks either black or blue. He also has an imprint on his head.

The Mifatal is plain white with back feathers that are twisted, but otherwise he has no differentiating marks. The Dubani and the Kashmiri have feathers of alternating color, red and white, or red and black. The Karkati is all grey except for the fact that the grey on his neck is of a lighter shade and he doesn't have a crest. The Qurunfuli is all black with red shoulders. The Arjani is all black with two brown stripes on his shoulders. Sometimes he comes in blue. The Nahasi is blue with brown splashes on his back, and the Baqjunsi is all grey with good cheeks, an imprint on his head and a back that is usually of a dark grey closer to black. The Inglizi is blue with long ragged feathers covering his feet and a crest on his head. The Buluni is of a single color and differentiated by its tail. He also has good cheeks and an imprint. There are also Bulunis in yellow, red and black. The Buluni in yellow is all white with a yellow tail, a yellow imprint and yellow cheeks. He's a very beautiful and rare bird. Also beautiful and rare is the Birmali which is black with white spots on his back or one that is blue-grey with tiny white spots on his back. Finally, there is the Austrian and the Tuffahi which are all white with apple-colored shoulders, a ring and an imprint.

—Amazing, Uncle Biru, you are an encyclopedia of pigeons. Now I would like to become a pigeon keeper because they seem to be true artists.

—Why, what's your job now, son?

—I'm a journalist.

—May God be with you. They say literature and journalism have become respectable professions, is that true?

—Yes, really they are, uncle. Now I must say goodbye. Our date is for tomorrow morning on Uncle Biru's roof, where he will show me his beautiful birds and teach me how to become a pigeon keeper.

—We will be expecting you!

Chapter Fifteen

Safar Birlik[1]
The Balkan War

My father, Fahmi Bin Mustafa Agha al-Terjeman, recounted this story of his life to me in his unaffected Damascene accent:

We used to live in the Alish house. I was five years old when my father died. Before my mother he had been married ten times but only had children by three of his wives. My mother, 'Aisha Ramadan daughter of Sa'id Agha Ramadan, bore him Muhiba, Murad and myself, Fahmi.

Before my mother he married Khaldiyya who bore him a daughter, Badriyya, and before Khaldiyya he was married to a Circassian who bore him my brother Subhi. Subhi is the father of Shufki who is the mother of 'Adnan.

After my father died I was orphaned.[2] My brother Subhi worked in Homs as a Bash Shawish[3] who conscripted people into the army. He asked my mother to send me and my brother Murad to him in Homs but she sent only Murad and kept me and my sister Muhiba with her. My mother married a rich elderly man and I stayed with her until I was grown up. That's when I learned the silk trade. How, you ask?

My brother Murad returned from Homs after having learned the silk trade. He advised me to take up the trade in Damascus since it was good work with a chance for advancement. In the silk business there is a subdivision called *misdi* (fibers). My brother brought me to a misdi master who started me out at ten piasters when I began work at about ten or twelve years of age. I learned the trade and became a skilled craftsman and my pay went up to one-half majidi every day. I worked for Halbawi in Kharab, and afterwards with Master Sawaf in Qimariyya. The misdi's job, daughter, is to spool the thread. I could do about twenty-five spools a day, after which they would be ready to go to the dyeworks where they colored the thread, re-spooled it and made it into skeins of silk.

---

[1] Literally translated this phrase means "travel by land" but the phrase as it stands is the way older Syrians refer to the Balkan War. In colloquial usage it means also, "to go off and never come back again" which is what happened to many young men who were conscripted into the Ottoman armies.

[2] Orphaned here means only that he lost one parent.

[3] A low level officer in the Turkish army.

I kept working in the silk trade until I was about twenty years old. We used to be paid by the number of rotls. Our house was in the Bahsa area at the time and we would work from sunup until sundown. At sunset exactly we used to have our dinner which we shared with the spoolers. Afterwards they would come over and help us skein...that's a real job, my daughter. First, they had to import the braided silk from Europe and then take it to houses in the countryside where they would spread it out and separate the coarse threads from the fine threads. After that they would make the skeins with the help of two pieces of bamboo. The skeins would then be brought to the misdi master. He would give them to his workers to spread out again, dampen them with water and reel them around thin metal skewers which would then be sent up to us and we would make them into skeins again. We'd send them on to the master who would separate the thick skeins from the thin skeins and then send them to the Jewish dyeworks. The most popular colors were green, black and purple. By that time the raw silk had become fine-dyed silk which was cut into lengths of thread, connected again and respooled on wood and then sprayed with a grease that comes from boiled lambs' heads until it was soft and pliable. Each spool would then be made into skeins that were delivered back to the master. One would be black, another red. They would be hung side by side for five or six days until they straightened out. From there the silk would go to the carding works where it was combed out. One worker would sit in front and another behind and together they would spread the silk out flat and comb it. From there it went back again to the misdi master who handed it on to the weaver. The weaving usually was done in large workshops which held about fifty looms. Each worker would take a skein and work with the shuttle and foot pedals, watching the frames go up and down until he had finished a large piece of striped material. The material was then cut by the masters into seven or nine lengths of about seventy centimeters[1] each. They were usually sent to Egypt where because of their high quality they could command a price of five English pounds. The Egyptian lengths were usually wider and of a heavier weight.

Before packaging, however, there was another process the material had to go through first. When the weaver finished with it, it was taken to the master to rid it of the lamb's grease and the grime of the looms. It went to a special bath where it was washed and returned to its natural softness. Next it went to a machine where it was stretched from beginning to end and then ironed. After that it went to the banger who slapped it on wood until it

---

[1] This is the length of the measure called *idra*.

shone and finally it was re-ironed and packed for sale. Among the packaged products there were different qualities, ranging from poor to better quality.

Each craft, daughter, had a master and a whole hierarchy of workers but all the craftsmen worked under the supervision of the master. For the silk trade there were twenty subdivisions and almost half of the city's population was involved in the trade somehow.

When I was nearly twenty years old it was suddenly time for military service. First they wanted to take my brother Murad who was five years older than me but it turned out that he was considered the provider[1] of the family and so they took me instead.

Every year they convened a council which decided by lottery who of the twenty years olds would be drafted. Then in each quarter there was a military committee which would round up the recruits. They sent a soldier to the shaikh of our quarter who had all the birth registrations. I was not yet old enough so they sent for my brother and asked him to bring me along. I went with him to the military committee. We entered a large hall where there were many people, notebooks and a commandant. My brother Subhi was already an officer and since they had proved Murad was the provider for my mother they sent me out. They told me, "You're not eighteen, you're twenty," using the Turkish word for twenty. So I became a soldier two years ahead of time.

I went through the process of induction and became an honorable officer doing the same kind of job my brother did, recruiting, thanks to Yahya Bey Sidqi, who worked in the War Office and whose mother was Nafuz Terjeman, a relative. What he did for me was give me the exam to become an officer. This position is not appointed, does not get an additional salary and is called the rank of Bash Shawish Scribe.

I forgot to tell you that when I was working in the silk trade, I also used to take lessons in Suq al-Tiban[2] in Bizuriyya near the Bizuriyya bath. I learned reading and writing at the school of Shaikh Kamal al-Qassab, a politician who taught Turkish and Arabic. I learned all the Turkish grammar rules over a period of two years and was appointed a special tutor by Shaikh Kamal. I went to this school because I found myself unable to read or write in a job that needed reading and mathematics. Each craftsman had to write on the piece of material how many lengths it contained and how many layers. In addition he had to know math in order to figure out how much he

---

[1] Not all male children are conscripted. One is left to provide for the family.
[2] The fodder suq.

ought to be paid by the end of the day for the number of rolls he had produced.

I was about fifteen years old at the time. I was learning Turkish, and I can still remember some of the Turkish words: a window is *banjara*, a door is *kabu*, a pencil is *qalam* and a table is *masa*. We also learned writing. We would do our calligraphy with thick pens, writing the letters either singly or connected in one piece. Later on we wrote with regular pens. Each one of us had a lined work book, Ottoman style, which showed the way to write letters in the beginning, middle and end positions. They also had us memorize the *lamiyya*[1] of Ibn al-Wardi, from which I remember the following lines:

> Forget the songs and ballads of love
> Declare you will renounce them
> Avoid those who tease you about it
> Keep the memories of your youth
> Because the days of your youth are as a setting star.

They taught us songs and stories, math, division, multiplication, addition and subtraction and we memorized the Koran.

I became a Bash Shawish in the Reserve, that is, I worked on the council that recruited soldiers. My company was located in Qanawat and nearby was the military advisor's company and also his house. His company took care of the War Office.

The Wali lived near Marje Square. When they recruited me the advisor was the Tatar Uthman Pasha. I stayed in the company for the one month in which the council met and then a month later independence was declared—freedom, justice and equality! The coup d'etat was led by Anwar Pasha, Niyazi and Mahmud Shukat Pasha, against Abd al-Hamid. As a result all the Bash Shawishes were recruited to the new army and we became soldiers once again. But then they cancelled the order and sent us to the telegraph company office in Salhiya at the site of today's Officers' Club. The telegraph company was a four-year mission with Arab and Turkish officers. I learned how to use the telegraph and the walkie-talkie, using lamplight by night and sunlight by day. We also learned how to use the electric telegraph. They wrote on our ID cards that we would be finished with military service four years after starting with the company so you can be sure we kept those cards in a very safe place. There were about two hundred of us working with the company. During the time we were learning how to use the telegraph,

---

[1] This poem ends each line with the lam or "l" sound in Arabic.

169

how to file and writing we were surprised one day to learn we had to turn in our ID cards. The Balkan War had started.

Yes, indeed. We got all packed up and had the company ready to leave when the revolution took place and thereafter every day was taken up with learning how to use arms and the telegraphic equipment. We were taught how to use rifles Turkish style. In Turkish *arimarsh* means forward march. *Saghadun* means march to the right. *Suladun* means march to the left. *Ghiriadun* means march to the rear. *Dur* means stop. Then we were taught to use the rifles. *Salahimza* means rifles up. Peace *dur*—no more peace, war had begun!

We would drill daily at the fort until it was time for us to go out to the fields to spend the remainder of the day working with the telegraph. The company with its two hundred men completed the preparation of its equipment, carriages, machinery, telephones and wires and was sent off to Aleppo by train. The train was supposed to stop in Aleppo and not continue on the Kalaq Bughazi. We stayed ten days in Aleppo with our carriages, mules and horses and then set off on the road to Alexandretta and Antioch. Each night we spent in a different village and one night we stayed in a place that was completely deserted. When we woke up early the next morning we found ourselves bitten from head to toe by bugs which had attacked us during the night without our being conscious of them, we were so tired.

We also had a cook who travelled with us—actually, a whole kitchen and staff. My, how we used to eat—vegetables, eggplants, tomatoes, green peppers, onions and pieces of meat made into a stew and distributed so there was one bowl for every ten people. The bread was made by the soldiers themselves with each sub-company allotted its own flour.

We arrived in Alexandretta and set up the company. We stayed there for about a week and then went down to the sea with Arab Unit Twenty-Seven, numbering about ten thousand men, and boarded a ship, the Iqdanz, to cross to the Dardanelles. We disembarked along with our company in the town of Maidus and in the snow and rain set up our tents. From there the company marched on to Gallipoli on a peninsula that was one of the states of Turkey. We stayed in Maidus for a few days to divide up the company so as to ensure good communications between stations.

Why? I was chosen by the head of the company along with twelve others and we with our equipment, telephones and walkie-talkies were shipped off in a steam boat and advised to bring back a few "heads." We sailed up to Gallipoli and found the coast full of Muslim refugees who had fled Bulgaria and Greece. Meanwhile the Bulgarians had marched on from Edirna and pursued our army until they reached Gallipoli where the population was divided

170

half and half between Christians and Muslims. The Christians had conspired with the Bulgarians and slaughtered and demeaned the Muslims. Hearing this, people fled to Gallipoli.

We crossed over to the commandant's station and stayed for a few days while we wrote our report. Then we carried our equipment back down to the coast. We didn't know where we were going as we trudged along in the mud. When we met groups of refugees and they asked us where we were going, we'd say we had an order from the commandant. They would reply that our army had been defeated and that the Bulgarians were waiting at the tip of the peninsula while 'Abbas Pasha's army was retreating. I didn't know what to do. I had an order to see the General and so I had to go.

We arrived at a village named Bolayir not far from the sea. There again we saw floods of refugees and retreating soldiers. I asked where the general was but no one knew. Then I saw a colonel on horseback who was very clearly retreating. I thought I might as well ask him where the General was so I saluted and said to him in Turkish, "Bak Affandi, I have a message from the commandant for the General that I must deliver." He replied that 'Abbas Pasha was then in the village of Bolayir. When I started again to say "Bak Affandi" in Turkish he answered me in Arabic and so I knew he was an Arab. I showed him the message. He told me to turn back and climb the mountain where I would find the rest of the army waiting anxiously for the arrival of the Bulgarians. We climbed the mountain and found a fortress-like structure there that was actually a small house with a number of cannons protruding from it. So that was their fortification! Oh, well! The Turkish army followed us up the mountain and set up their tents alongside ours and we waited. I wasn't going to risk myself and my company just to deliver the message. Why should I do it just because he was commander!

What we wanted most at the time was food. We tried to enter company headquarters but were forbidden to do so by a few Turkish soldiers. So we had to stay out, along with the other soldiers and the equipment in the rain. Suddenly I saw a general passing by and I ran up to him, begging him to tell me where I should deliver my message. He said to deliver it to 'Abbas Pasha who was in the headquarters and told me to go on in. Right away I went in and found an old man with white hair who asked if I belonged to the telegraph company. I replied that I did. So he called over the general who had showed me in and ordered him to set up a tent for my company and my equipment.

Far away on the peaks of the mountains we could see the Bulgarians so I prepared the walkie-talkies, keeping one myself and sending the other off to the tanks. I would call the tanks and order them to shoot at such and such a place on the Bulgarian encampments and at such and such a distance. Then we would just sit there and watch with our binoculars to see where the shells landed. That was our work.

Then 'Abbas Pasha came over and said that since I understood how to use walkie-talkies, I should do down to the beach, and with a few other men, take some dynamite across to the Bulgarian side in a boat and plant it in a fortress where the Bulgarian leaders were staying. There was always a small building at each encampment where the chiefs-of-staff stayed.

So we went down to the beach, taking the equipment for blowing up the fortress with us. We took off in a steamboat at nightfall, cruising along the shore until we reached the Bulgarian lines. We stole into their encampment, hiding behind trees until we could see the fortress guarded by a sentry. We waited until he moved to the other side of the building and then we inched along on our bellies until we reached the wall of the building. There we dug a hole while we talked in whispers. We placed the dynamite in the hole and covered it with dirt and then slowly retreated, dragging the fuse back with us while praying that the sentry would not return and see us. We went straight down to the boat. The whole affair took us two and half hours. Once on the boat, we ignited the fuse and a grand explosion could be heard through the fields and across the valleys. No sooner did we hear the explosion than we were on our way just as firing started between the mountaintops across the sea. But fortunately we returned safely to camp.

Abbas Pasha called me to him and said, "You are a very brave soldier," and gave me a decoration and a letter of commendation for completing the mission.

We went back to sitting in our tents in Bolayir for another ten days with the Dushman only four hours away. Daughter, Dushman is the name we give to the Bulgarians and the Greeks. So we set up a front. They had come from Edirne (Adrianople) ten days earlier and arrived at the peninsula of Gallipoli to blockade the access of Istanbul, Chanakkale and the straits of Bugaz. What a tiresome affair! Everyone on the same peninsula with explosives and weapons, yet each blocking the other's way with tanks and boats.

—What kinds of boats, Father?

—Steamboats were used to blockade the waterways so no one could get through. We then set up stations from and around Bolayir with a distance of about an hour between each so we could send reports of the movements of the Bulgarian army.

Once again I was called by 'Abbas Pasha. He told me to get myself ready for a six-hour walk to the town of Qawaqli to set up a telegraph station that would keep us in touch over that distance. From Qawaqli we set up several stations.

To sum it all up, we spent six months in an Arab company while another company, the Martab Company, was being set up. Each of these companies numbered twelve thousand soldiers. We were visited by Anwar Pasha, head of the War Office and Chief of Staff, and Mahmud Shukat Pasha, the Minister of War. They visited all the stations, inspected both companies and distributed wages to the soldiers. The enlisted men got one majidi, commissioned officers got one and one-half majidis, *shawish* officers two majidis, and *bash shawish* two and a half majidis. I was a bash shawish, that is, leader of the telegraph company.

We were given an order to attack the Bulgarians. Both companies set themselves up with a cavalry in front, followed by the infantry and then by the cannon. We marched on and on as though in a parade, day and night. To everyone's dismay we were drenched from rain without a single roof anywhere to protect us. The rain didn't stop once with all those poor soldiers on their way to war.

The Bulgarians saw us advancing and started shelling us. They sent out bombers that dropped bombs capable of digging holes as big as packing crates. Yes, daughter, during that time they had airplanes! Our men kept climbing on despite the shelling, and as we got closer the cannon became more ineffectual. When that happened the enemy opened up with gunfire until we reached their encampments at the end of the day. That was when they fled and we were able to take over the whole top of the mountain. Oh, yes! They fled leaving their cannons. But our soldiers were so lacking in discipline that everything got out of hand and our generals couldn't even find their own men among the dead, there were so many. We were unable to take our cannons up the mountain because it was so steep and the mud was so deep. But instead of making use of the Bulgarian equipment our soldiers, in the flush of victory, pushed everything down into the valley. What we didn't know was that Diyus, the Bulgarian leader, had prepared a new force for a return attack.

Meanwhile our soldiers were occupied with catching chickens. Rather than preparing weapons and cannons they were eating chickens! The Bulgarians by then had returned again along with their shells and they began their assault. It was so deadly that from the twenty-four thousand soldiers we began with, we only returned with two hundred. They were lying everywhere on the ground. The two hundred surviving soldiers reached Bolayir in an effort to join the refugees fleeing toward Gallipoli. But Zaki Bey al-'Adma, who was in charge under 'Abbas Pasha in Bolayir, threatened to shoot anyone who deserted. The soldiers were forced to make a human chain across the water to the peninsula of Gallipoli. We spent that night in great anxiety. We were with the two hundred survivors but hoped to be able to get in touch with Istanbul by the next day. All night we tried to contact Anwar Pasha and Mahmud Shawkat Pasha to tell them of the army's defeat. The next morning while we were sitting around we saw about forty steam-boats that had arrived overnight from Istanbul. The soldiers remained for one week to ward off the Bulgarians and reinforce the surviving two hundred soldiers. The Bulgarians were frightened off and didn't reappear. So once again the tents were set up on the peninsula with about twenty-seven companies assembled, and the army took over the mountainsides and fields facing the Dushman.

The Bulgarians sent out planes to reconnoiter and found us set up on their land. We were there for six months in the tents in those fields, getting ready for a new attack. We spent the time in the tents under the rain and snow. The cold was so penetrating that you would freeze if you spent more than fifteen minutes out in the open so our watches were set for only fifteen minutes each. Finally the snow melted and summer was on its way. We were ordered to begin our attack. By then all our tents were destroyed and we were in a pitiful state. We thought this was it and we would be finished. There were enough of us, twenty-seven companies in all—altogether fifty thousand soldiers. Our leader was 'Abbas and most of the staff were Arab soldiers, among them Arab Pashas like Salim Bey al-Jaziri'i Miralai who was the leader of the company belonging to the War Office. There were also Riza Bey al-Kilani, who was deputy to the Chief of Staff, and Zaki Bey al'Adma, who led four thousand men.

To make a long story short we walked along the coast and up and over mountains, sending scouts ahead of us to check on the enemy whom we discovered had fled. We kept after them spending the nights in villages where Christians had slaughtered Muslims and forced the others to flee. Now with our advance, refugees were able to return to their villages. The Muslims were very supportive, catching every Bulgarian soldier they could and killing and burning him. Our General, however, ordered them not to burn any more people or villages.

In this way we continued on for ten more days until we reached Edirne. At Edirne, our twenty-seven companies took over the front and recruited four thousand Kurds and a group of Arabs who had come from the Hijaz by order of Prince Faisal, but unfortunately they were at the head of the army and all died. The Kurds went on to open Sofia, the capital of Bulgaria, but the English blocked their way and ordered them to stop. So we stopped and stayed in Edirne for another six months and while we were there a truce was declared. At the end of six months we started our assault up again but the Bulgarians by then had taken over Edirne. The populace was sympathetic to them because they were clean and imposed law and order and provided services for the people. It was often said about the Bulgarians that they were a very orderly people. So, in short, when the British declared a truce we were stuck for six months under the snow. May God never burden anyone with a snow such as we saw. Finally they signed a truce and a bridge was built between Bulgaria and Edirne. The Bulgarians were given an area called Klissa Knissa which means the area of forty churches. In the beginning the Turks had wanted the area but the British maneuvered so the Bulgarians got it, and the truce was signed.

Our district headquarters was the Damascus Telegraph so they told us we were disbanded and put us all on boats along with the rest of the company and sent us on our way back. There were seven thousand of us authorized to take our leave papers and be on our way so there wouldn't be any disputes among us. We voyaged on the sea for sixteen days until we reached the port of Beirut. A group of doctors was sent down to examine all of us on board the ship. They filed a report that there was cholera on board and declared the ship unfit to dock. We were told to go on to Haifa, where we could spend the quarantine period. By that time after spending sixteen days on that ship, we were fed up, not to mention the added burden of treating the sick. There is no God but God, may he have mercy on us. The faucets were broken from too many people fighting over turns to drink. The food was limited to pressed dates and *buqsamat*, a round dry cake issued to us which was available in great quantities, enough so that each of us could eat his fill. All we did was cook and eat. The soldiers who were no longer receiving their salaries had to pay for their food out of their private funds.

We spent that first night at the port of Beirut but by the time we got up in the morning to set out for Haifa we discovered that everyone except for the telegraph unit had deserted the ship. They had used floats on board to flee under cover of night.

Thus it was decided that our telegraph unit should be sent to set up the Turkish headquarters in Beirut. A special train equipped to carry soldiers, cattle and machinery was sent to pick us up. Travelling one night near Sirghaya in mountainous terrain, I suddenly heard a crash and the shattering of glass. What was it? Apparently the locomotive and three cars had gone off the track. The cause of the accident was a rock that had rolled off the mountain and had fallen unnoticed in the path of the train. It broke twenty rails of the track, causing the accident with the locomotive and the three cars. It was so cold up there. We spent the whole cold night there until they were able to send us a train in the morning from the other direction to take us on to Damascus. Another train was sent from Beirut to transport the horses and equipment back to Beirut until the track was cleared and the train could continue on to Damascus.

Once in Damascus, leaves were reissued to all of us and each of us took off to his own hometown or village. Even those of us whose leaves had expired were issued new ones.

I had not been in Damascus for more that six months when the First World War was declared. Orders were issued that anyone who didn't report within twenty-four hours would be sentenced to death. On orders I was sent back to my old telegraph unit which had been increased in numbers from one hundred fifty to one thousand men. Our offices were in Salhiyya, in what is now the Officers' Club. We stayed there for three months and in the meantime the brigades at headquarters were slaughtering lambs and drying out the meat in order to send rations out to the soldiers on the front.

During my six months in Damascus I had gone back to my old job in the silk trade, indeed I had! And while I worked I lived with my mother and stepfather in Baltajiyya near Bab Jabiyya in the house of Abu al-Shammat. Our landlord was a merchant who sold salted nuts, peanuts and almonds and had two sons working for him. His shop was in the Shaghur area, but he was originally from the Bab al-Salam area. We paid him one gold coin rent each month. After a short time, the government announced job openings in the police for those with telephone and telegraph experience. Surely after six years in the telegraph unit I had enough knowledge and experience. I was capable of hooking up lines and of working with walkie-talkies, electric telegraphs and telephones.

I presented my army credentials to the police and applied as a veteran of the Balkan War, the Druze Mountain War and the Karak fighting, with the last two occurring before the first. In the Druze Mountain War, fighting had started when Sami Pasha and three battalions were sent to punish a group that showed disobedience to the Turkish rulers. In the end Sami Pasha hung the elders of the community and took over the area. In the meantime the Arabs who had been ordered to enlist in the army by the Turks attacked the Turks at Karak and killed a few Pashas, including Abd al-Rahman Pasha. They killed all of them, in fact, except Ayubi Pasha who fled disguised as a Bedouin with the help of some of the local merchants. The battalion leader at that time was al-Kahali. An order was issued for our unit to connect the telegraph station of Qatrana with that of Karak but by the time the team had gone from Qatrana to Karak it was completely destroyed. The inhabitants along with the local governors were trapped in a fortress surrounded by angry Bedouins. The Arabs had burned down the town of Karak itself and taken the women hostage. In this way the Karak conflict ended and we were sent back to Damascus.

Chapter Sixteen

World War I

Just six months after the Balkan War, they announced the beginning of World War I.

Before that I had tried to go back to my old job with the police! When the government announced that there were openings in the police force I applied. The commissioner at that time was Aziz Bey, a Turk. They asked for my birth certificate. I was born in 306 of the Roman calendar. At the time the conscription council was drafting all those born in the year 303, and for some reason they had me down as being born in 303, so I was drafted. They didn't know they had made a mistake. When I got my draft papers I thought because the Turkish dates were similar to Arabic that I could change them. I crossed out the 303 and went to the census bureau to request a correction. I presented all my papers to the police commissioner. he stared at my draft notice and said, "This paper looks as if someone has been meddling with it. You have ten days to bring me a new one." I had thought no one would notice it since it was from the military. But that was the way it was, so I had a new set of papers made and this time the date on them was 306. I went back to the commissioner and he asked to see the old copy. He said the one which had been crossed out looked suspicious and he put me under arrest. Then he sent me and my papers to court, that is, after they had locked me up overnight. I cursed that job and the day I applied for it. I had some relatives at the courthouse who helped me out to a certain extent. My cousin, Assad Bey put in a good word for me. At the trial I told the judge the full story and he suspended all charges and let me go. I told him that I had gone to see my friend Kamal Bey at the census bureau to set things straight and he had told me to cross it out! Apparently, Kamal was known for his nefarious ways and had taken off for Egypt. At any rate, the judge saw no reason for a trial and I was cleared. I was completely disgusted with the whole system by that time and wanted only to forget the police force and that job so I went back to my old work weaving silk.

But when they declared World War I, I was called back into the service. I registered with the same telegraph communications unit I had been with before. Once again they were handing out the ration of three loaves of bread per man and food was served at the unit to whomever wanted it although you were allowed to go home for meals if you chose. The government also started sending us quantities of butter, lamb and dried dates which we were to prepare and package.

During that war the Germans and Turks became allies. The British had asked the Turks to remain neutral and even offered them money to do so. But the Turks decided to fight alongside Germany. They started bringing camels in from the desert so they could use them in the war effort.

To make a long story short, we started into Palestine through Nazareth, Haifa, over Mount Carmel and Tell Shammam. It was from there that the Arab Unit was sent to the war. Other units soon followed us to Palestine, and full mobilization of the army was finally underway. We marched through the Sinai desert of Egypt in the hope of taking some of the pressure off Bughaz. Shanq al-Qala was under attack by units of British tanks and their allies. The major objective, though, was reaching Egypt. We marched on to Bir al-Saba'a and from there to the trenches of 'Auja, which was the beginning of the arid lands. After that it was through desert sands, walking an average of eighteen hours a day. We camped out at night and started again early every morning. Accompanying us was another force made up of one thousand men who were led by a German officer. They were responsible for digging wells and providing water for the soldiers en route. They set up water reservoirs at various stops where soldiers would receive their rationed shares. Water was distributed to each soldier once a day by weight, along with dried dates and bread. Whoever had a canteen was allowed an extra ration of water. So it went. We would send out the camels to the stations and they would load them up with supplies and send them back to us. If I remember correctly each camel was able to carry back eight large tins of water.

Our division was made up of some twenty to twenty-seven thousand men. Our leader was Dali Fuad and his rank was Major General. He was to lead us on this expedition covering an area of half the desert as far as Isma'iliyya. Other divisions covered the areas left and right of us. The desert itself could be crossed in a period of twenty-four hours with the march along the length of the canal taking about the same amount of time. The whole area was divided among a number of divisions, one on the right, one on the left and a third division, ours, in charge of the area in the middle of the desert. Before leaving Damascus we had made large flat-bottomed metal boats, each more than twenty-five meters long. We also made carriages on which to transport them. All in all, there were thirty-five of those carriages which we all, soldiers, camels and cattle, helped to move, though to tell the truth the cattle were more of a hindrance than a help. As far as the camels were concerned, there seemed to be enough of them to cover the territory end to end...altogether a hundred thousand...more than there were soldiers. On the salt lake we practiced making bridges with the boats.

The German commander's job was a separate one where he had to go ahead of us and complete his work with one thousand men. The army would take two days off at a time to rest and give his division enough time for the preparation of the water supply. Our travels continued in this way with wells dug and the soldiers reorganized after each stop to pull the metal boats on their carriages over boards so the wheels wouldn't sink in the soft sands.

For sixty days we walked eighteen hours each day, woke up with or even before the sun and lived on our rations of bread, dates and brackish water. It seemed as though this desert was an endless ocean with not even a single island. Finally, after we had crossed halfway over the desert we came to the only mountain in the whole desert, Jifjafa Mountain. I and ten soldiers from my division were ordered to set up a telegraph station for the army on the mountain. In this division we were given work to do that would require twenty-four hours in a day to accomplish what they needed in the way of round-the-clock communications networks. We stayed at the first station thirty days until the entire army had crossed the area. We then moved on to Mahdaz which was the last stop before the canal, just ten hours short of it. There we were able to make telegraphic contact with the main division of the army. We moved again until we were at a point only three hours away from the canal. There we set up another communications station to contact the division which had not yet caught up to us and inform them about the water supply, which in this case was plentiful. The availability of water encouraged Jamal Pasha the Great to visit us and have his three tents set up by the side of the canal to watch the army settle in. Eventually Jamal Pasha left and we kept up with the army until we reached the canal.

The soldiers positioned themselves among the dunes in preparation for advancing on the canal and there we stayed for three days. On the third day, the soldiers were ordered to leave their positions after dark and proceed to the canal with their equipment where they were to make a bridge out of iron and wood. We arrived at the canal late at night, moving quietly with no smoking or talking allowed. No one was to make a single sound walking across the sand. A German came along. We were to lower two of the metal boats in the water. The German took one to the other bank and returned after about an hour. He picked up the second one filled with soldiers and also took it across to the other side. As each boat was filled he would drop the soldiers on the other side of the canal. In this way, by taking the full boats over and returning empty he took two hundred and fifty of the soldiers to stand guard around the work site to prevent anyone from interfering.

Meanwhile, I had dug a trench and installed another communications line to keep in touch with headquarters. Once the canal was cleared and work on the passage completed, I was told to call Damascus and inform them of that fact. When Damascus received the news they were ecstatic. But just as our sixth boat was crossing the canal, we were overwhelmed by a burst of gunfire—more than a thousand machine guns, it seemed. The bullets were all over, hitting and exploding in the water and making the water of the canal churn like a kettle of boiling water The boats were hit and started sinking and most of our men could not shoot back although those who could did. Those who could swim saved themselves but those who could not drowned and went down with the boats. The German who was a very good swimmer made it back to the shore. A message we received from our attackers gave us the choice of returning to our original positions before daylight or being completely overrun. We began running faster than we had ever run before. By the time we reached the top of the hill the sun had risen and we could make out seven armored ships crossing the canal and pointing their guns toward us. Above us planes began bombarding us, along with the ships from the water. Each armored ship held about thirty-five guns, each about as big as me. They would point the guns at us and fire but the shots didn't always go off. So there we sat under all this shelling. I set up my equipment and made contact with the troops behind us to apprise them of the situation while the guns at the canal continued all the while dropping shells on us.

That day, when the light appeared we just sat there. I had thought armies on their own would make some kind of movement. But the dunes stretched out in front of us, one after another, without a single movement visible anywhere. It turned out that the army upon arriving at that spot had sent word back to headquarters and were awaiting instructions! We, too, were waiting for a soldier to come to us with instructions about what to do next. All day I sat around and no one showed up. It turned out, as we found out by the end of the day, that the army had gone on ahead and the messenger they had sent to us lost his way and decided to turn back and catch up with the troops. There were ten of us with our equipment and three camels who made contact with those to the rear. It was from them that we learned of the idiot who was sent after us and never made it and of the army having moved on.

I sent some of our men to bring us water but they took off and never came back. We were left without food or water until nightfall. Again, I watched the horizons looking for someone coming our way. Nothing! As it grew colder we dug a hole in the sand and started a fire. I ordered one of the men to go back to the canal and fill containers full of water for us. The rest of the men went to sleep while I stayed on guard waiting for the water.

While I was sitting by the fire with my gun in front of me I suddenly noticed two figures in the distance, appearing and then disappearing and reappearing again from behind the dunes but coming always in our direction. What in the world could this be! As I jumped to my feet they appeared again on the rise of the nearest sand dune.

They were bedouin clad in wide-sleeved robes resembling those of the Egyptians. They greeted us and said they hoped all was well and that our army was victorious. Boasting a little, I told them that the army was in Egypt. One replied, "May God make you victorious." Come to find out these sons of guns were spies! I asked what had brought them there and they answered that they had buried some boxed of dates up in the hills but when they returned to get them they had found them missing. "Where are you from?" I asked. "From the north," they replied. Just before leaving they asked me for some cigarettes, but I told them I didn't have any. As they started off I realized they would be heading toward As'ad who was grazing our three camels. Although they would be able to see him he would not be able to see them. "My God," I thought, "they will steal our camels." So I jumped to my feet, gun in hand, but they were already out of sight. I shot seven bullets in their direction hoping, if nothing else, to scare them off. When As'ad came back I asked if he had met up with anyone. He said he had seen two men with guns. Apparently before coming to our camp they had buried their guns in the sand.

Nightfall was upon us and the air was becoming colder. We started a new fire with some wood and cardboard boxes we had on hand. As we were getting warm by the fire a light went on in the communications post. The man on duty told me to get over there because there was a message coming in. I picked up the receiver and asked who was calling. A voice replied, "It's Ahmad." The only Ahmad I knew was with the troops and could not possibly be at the nearest communications post which was eight hours to the rear. "Don't kid me" I said, "You can't be Ahmad, who are you?" Well, it *was* Ahmad! "What are you doing back there?" I asked. He said, "Don't you know? The army has retreated back to the permanent communications post. We sent you word yesterday at sunset. Didn't you get it? I've just received a telegraph from the commandant ordering you to return here with all your equipment." "Fine," I said, "Keep your searchlight on so we will be able to find you." The first thing that occurred to me was that we might be attacked by the spies, now that the main part of the army had pulled back, leaving only the ten of us communications specialists behind.

When the army had retreated, they had lost their way in the dark and were unable to reach their destination until late the next morning. The soldiers were totally worn out, half dead, in fact.

How was I going to get my men safely back? The army, as big as it was and with all its guides, had managed to get lost! As'ad said that he knew a shortcut through the desert and he would guide us. All we had to do, he said, was to go along the canal and from there follow the usual trail the camels take. "We have guns," he said, "and not even a tornado could erase our tracks." I told him we should just take the usual route. As'ad assured me that by following his way we would reach our destination in just two hours. "But, As'ad, we might get lost," I reasoned. No, he replied, for he was a son of the land. So we put our faith in God and prepared the camels. Together we were ten men with three hundred bullets each. We had hardly any bread loaves left. I put out the fire by smothering it with the cooking tin and ordered the men to begin the march. At that point they all of a sudden became above all this and the poor camels were loaded with what would usually have required ten camels to carry. We gave As'ad the go-ahead and put ourselves in the hands of God. We climbed one dune after another. We would ask As'ad, "Where is that road?" and he would reply, "It should be coming up right ahead." "Where ahead?" we wanted to know. Finally, he admitted he was lost. When he said that, all I wanted to do was pull out my gun and shoot him! This huge desert was no place to get lost or to play games. The last group lost in the desert had had more than two hundred and seventy camels, soldiers, officers, and their equipment. They were never found...all buried by a sandstorm someplace.

I said to As'ad, "Damn you, how are we ever going to get anywhere? If we had taken the other route we would have arrived by now." We kept on walking until the first camel collapsed. Though we urged him on he would not budge. So we took the load off him and divided it between the two other camels. A few miles later, the second camel collapsed so we unloaded him and put everything on the back of the third camel who was the frailest and rangiest of all three camels. "Tshu, Tshu..." he was up on his feet in a couple of seconds, it must have been with the help of God. We did have to steady him to make the first few steps. So far, so good, but we still had no idea what path to follow. On we walked getting more lost with every step. Across the canal we could see the enemy searchlights so we stayed away from the canal to avoid running the risk of falling into the hands of the enemy. I had no idea what to do. Each of us had his heart in his hands, praying and fearing that we would be dead by the next day. Just as I thought all hope was lost, from the top of the dune we were climbing, I spotted the road. Ten souls were restored to life! I ordered the men to let the camel rest. We had some bread crumbs left which we put in water and fed to the camel. He rested and we caught our breath at the same time. It was now two o'clock in the morning but I was no longer worried. Despite our hunger we began singing old folk songs. Finally we got the camel to stand up again and by God he did it even with that huge load on his back. We continued along the road. The further we walked, the further away from the canal we seemed to be getting. All along the way we could hear the sounds of starving camels which had collapsed and were abandoned in the desert. It was one of the most horrible nights of my life. We kept walking until morning. At daybreak the army spotted us and sent out soldiers in our direction in case we were the enemy. They stopped and questioned us and wouldn't believe we were the communications officers until one of the meteorologists flashed a light in our faces and recognized us. We walked into camp and found soldiers lying everywhere. "We just arrived," they said, "because we were lost in the desert for two days with the guides!"

The commander asked for me. I went to see him. He looked me over and then asked how we'd reached camp and what took us so long. I answered that the reason we were so late was that we hadn't received word of the move. How did we find our way? God led us here, I told him, and related our adventures. He thanked God and exclaimed over how a whole army could get lost in the desert.

Next the commander praised me for saving my men and equipment, and made me a cup of tea worth at least a gold pound to me at that moment and gave me along with it some pastries from Damascus. I told him how it was the camel, God bless him, who was most responsible for our safe arrival and that I felt the animal should be rewarded in some way. Right away orders were given that the camel should be painted with tar[1] and given as much food as he could eat. (Here, my father's throat became choked with tears of joy for the memories of the commander's kindness to the brave, sickly camel...and tears now fill my eyes and obstruct my pen...I will always weep when I read my father's words about the camel.)

Really the commander was so courteous to us all the way back to Sab'a. We walked on, sleeping nights and getting up at dawn. There was no more water...food, they needed food...they wanted meat...they began eating the camels alive, taking chunks from the poor creatures' thighs and leaving them writhing on the ground. We ate camel meat and it tasted good. We would barbecue it over the fire and eat it, bite by bite. After a few days we

---

[1] Remedy for irritated skin.

arrived at the trenches of 'Auja. My beard, like those of the crooks of 'Ajlun, had about reached my belt. What an awful state we were in. Near the trenches were a few wells and the first thing the men did was head for the wells where they could drink to their hearts' content. I found an old tent lying there which I fixed up and then I heated two tins of water, gave myself a haircut and shaved the hair on my chest to get rid of the lice we were infested with, God help us! I've never had a better bath than the one I took that day. It felt so good I slept for fifteen hours there in that tent.

We stayed there for about a week. The soldiers rested. All of a sudden one day we were surprised by a burst of bullets. Quickly everyone grabbed their guns. The first thought that occurred to us all was that the enemy was upon us. As it turned out one of our own men had shot off a bullet by mistake and in their fright and surprise the others began shooting their guns. We then returned to Bir al-Sab'a. 'Auja had been a city as big as Damascus but now there was hardly a trace of it left. From Bir al-Sab'a we continued on to Nazareth.

We stayed in Nazareth for a year assuming the responsibility for communications between Nazareth and Mount Carmel. I erected a post on Mount Carmel in the Convent of Mahraqa. From there we kept in touch with the forces on the beach guarding the sea approaches. Actually they were policemen and their main fear was the French battleships which from a distance could send out planes that would bomb the army on the beaches, on Mount Carmel and in Nazareth. To keep track of the battleships they sent a division high up on the mountain where they would observe the beach, the plain of Ibn 'Amar and even Nazareth.

We would pass on orders from the commander on the coast to Nazareth, and orders coming from Nazareth we would pass on to Mount Carmel. There was a bakery outside the convent and we expelled all the monks. I was ordered to take over the convent and treat the monks as though they were the French enemy. We entered the convent and found woolen bedding, ammunition, wine, a whole store of tomato juice and walnuts. Back in the mountains they had fields of potatoes, chickens, ducks, and all sorts of birds. We ate and made merry and stayed there for about a year and a half while a number of posts were set up between us and Damascus.

Later on we received orders to move to Nazareth. The night we arrived in Nazareth the army was ordered to mobilize and march to Bir al-Sab'a. The army was put under the leadership of 'Asmat Ainunu. On the Gaza front, at the coast, the commander was the German Funkers Pasha who was in charge of all the armies in Palestine. We were at Bir al-Sab'a with Ainunu. The British had concentrated thirty-five of their battleships on the Gaza coast, planning to land their troops and take over the mainland. We had seven strong fortifications along that route and from where we were located we could see the shining sea...and also the shining guns! We would see these guns start shooting ...pow...pow...pow...pow...on the Gaza front; night and day they shot at us and finally their troops landed. During all this time the planes were bombarding us from above. What was the result? Though we thought we had a strong front the British were stronger. They had the guns and planes on their side. They took over five of our seven fortifications and we were left with only two.

Our troops were starving once again. One of the Turkish troops attacked a British soldier one night and killed him. He stole the clothing and food he had on him he was so crazed by his hunger. From this one man the frenzy passed on to the other troops. That night twelve thousand British troops were slaughtered. The Turkish army was barefoot while the British were well clad. The British had all their clothing stolen and were left naked in the fields. The Turkish soldiers wanted food and warmth and they found it with the British troops who carried rations of meat, nuts and bread. The planes came out the next day and found the dead lying on the coast. They, the British, wrote to Funkers Pasha as follows: "If we had known about the condition of your troops we would have sent you food and clothing rather than have you strip the dead." They threatened revenge but first wanted time to remove the dead which we gave them. In truth, it can be said that if it weren't for that one hungry soldier Palestine would have been long lost. In short, British health officials made it to the coast and removed their dead, clearing the front.

Then that front quieted down and the war moved elsewhere. At that point it became our duty only to hold Sab'a. The British also stopped fighting, and busied one hundred thousand Egyptian workers with the construction of two railway lines between Egypt and the Gaza front, one going and one coming. Alongside the tracks they installed water pipelines coming from the Nile. They spent one whole year doing this. Yes siree!

During this period of a year and a half we sent telegrams to the Sab'a front each night on any movements of the army we observed. We might see the enemy spying at such and such a location, or we would see so and so, or their plans were such and such. The days went by in this way until one night we had an extraordinary number of reports to make. There were rumors that the enemy was approaching. 'Asmat Ainunu came over and sent word to Funkers, alerting him of the enemy's approach and requesting replacements and supplies, since what they had on hand were not sufficient to ward off the oncoming enemy. Funkers replied that there were no replacements or supplies available and that we would have to do our best to hold the front.

He still needed more troops but they refused to send them. That night the messages flew back and forth: "I need more men." "Keep fighting, we don't have any men to send you." We were outnumbered fifty thousand to one hundred. That same night the British attacked us. Funkers continued advising us to keep on fighting. He also told them to arm the front and prepare the guns, but not to shoot. The next morning he gave permission to fire. In retaliation planes came over and the British opened fire on us. We were opposed by a huge British army on the Sabʻa front. They took over the plain and started up the Sabʻa mountain. We were now outnumbered seventy thousand to one hundred! "Keep fighting" came the reply. The battle raged on until sunset.

Just about this time I came down from my post. Orders were given to burn all the rations so they poured fuel on them and lit them. For the heavy baggage they sent us trucks which were loaded up and we began retreating. All communications with the front were now cut off. An envelope arrived, yes indeed! We sent it on horseback, God forgive us, while the shells were falling on Sabʻa. After Sabʻa we found ourselves in the middle of ferocious gunfire for there were four guns in the mountains shooting down on us. The British guns and planes erased that corner of the earth in just under an hour. Communications were now cut off between Sabʻa, the front and ʻAsmat Ainunu. Another message was sent by land (on horseback) to the front, advising them to keep fighting until sunset and then retreat under cover of dark. The next thing I knew ʻAsmat Ainunu and his staff general came riding on horseback through the marketplace of Sabʻa as it was burning down on all sides, the storehouses, grain, everything. ʻAsmat Ainunu and his general continued on until we could no longer see them. Since I had come down from the mountain, there was no longer any means of communication. At the front all the troops were prepared to flee, as fire was consuming everything in sight. When I looked around I saw two riders galloping toward the commander's headquarters. I followed them as they raced toward the chief's office. They saluted the commander-in-chief, who was standing with maps lying all around him. One of the horsemen addressed him, "Bey Affandi, the enemy is surrounding us and about one thousand of their troops have entered Sabʻa, each carrying long guns of about an arm's length." The commander, who was not in uniform, reached for his jacket and his headdress. He grabbed a few things and left the others behind. There was one last German phone operating and I cut its cord. We all lost our heads when the English came. I had left my horse downstairs ready to escape, but when I arrived at the spot I found someone had taken him. I began running toward the station with a whole crowd of people. It was about a kilometer away from Sab'a. The guns and planes continually bombarded us. Just halfway there I could hear gunfire behind me. I looked back and to my horror I saw about one hundred and fifty British soldiers on horseback shooting at us. I nearly died of fright. They were shooting to kill. We stopped running and raised our arms over our heads, surrendering. Two of the English soldiers continued after the commander-in-chief who had escaped on horseback, while the rest stopped. They caught up with the chief, killed his horse and took him prisoner. They also arrested the hospital attendant and took his gun. They made him sit with the others. We all sat. The sun by that time was high in the sky. There were about a hundred of us sleeping and sitting all over the area. British on horseback were everywhere...a huge army. We sat around until past sunset. They made us sleep in the plain that night, while they set up a telegraph post. By morning the British had completely taken over and our whole army was imprisoned without exception. For the one time we defeated them they surely enough got back at us. They had said they would take their revenge.

Morning came and both generals and troops were prisoners of war, some on the plain and some at another point. In the distance we spotted a British commander on horseback coming toward us. On horseback, next to him, was an Egyptian translator. He came up to us...we officers were on one side and the troops on another. He told the officers that the supplies for the army had not yet arrived and he apologized for not having given the soldiers anything to eat. But he did have two baskets of bread the officers could share among themselves. They brought us the two baskets. Meanwhile the Egyptian gave orders to the soldiers that they were to stand up four at a time to be counted. My goodness they all started getting up together without any kind of order like a herd of goats. Some had their heads covered with bags, others were crawling with lice and most were dirty and in a terrible state. Our senior officer at the time was Fakhri al-Barudi, God rest his soul. You would think they'd be able to march in rows of four but it was a hopeless case. The Egyptian then ordered one of our officers to give the order "Four by four." A Turk stood up and shouted out the orders in Turkish, "*Dardar, dardar, daranz*." No one paid any attention. Everything was out of control. Meanwhile the British officer watched from atop his horse...after awhile he was so disgusted that he just turned away and walked off mumbling something under his breath. He sent some of the cavalry over to us and they made all of us, prisoners, soldiers and officers, march at the rear of the British army. We walked until we came to Bir al-Sab'a where we found a large inn with two men guarding the door. They made us enter four by four. We walked in and sat on one side with the soldiers following. Finally they were able to count us! There were a few boxes of bread left there and the British officer ordered that they be given out. He had two of our soldiers carry them in. An Egyptian officer began giving out the bread but no sooner was he about to give out the second piece than the starving soldiers could contain themselves no longer. The boxes went flying. The Egyptian officer cursed them and in the end, poor fellow, he found himself engulfed by the horde. He finally managed to get out, and then just tossed food at us. They gave us water to drink too. We stayed at that inn until sunset at which time we were ordered out. Outside there were two rows of soldiers, one on either side of the entrance. We were ordered to walk out between the rows in fours! "March!" they said. And we walked all through the night and until morning. Noontime came and we were still on our feet. It was a long road with British soldiers everywhere. At the next camp there were about one hundred thousand cavalry. The British had such large horses which were orderly and didn't fight with one another, and were as obedient as lambs!

We kept walking until we reached the public train station in Ghaza, all of us starving and thirsty. There we found a man-made pond filled with water from the pipes coming from the Nile. Next to it were four tanks. They told us we could drink and wash from it, ten to a tank. We did, to our fill! Next to the station was a large plain where the British started stacking boxes and cartons, one on top of the other. It looked as though they were doing it for exercise. The trains stood there whistling and though they had passenger cars they were all being used for shipping purposes, for cargo. In front of each of the cars standing next to one another like slabs of cheese or bars of soap stood two Egyptian privates. Each picked up a box, broke it open and passed meat and bread to our soldiers...all they could eat! Imagine, such orderliness and the meats were even canned! They would break open the boxes, give each soldier as much as he wanted, throwing it in his lap. In that way they passed food out to the whole army at the same time.

The soldiers began eating. We thanked God and drank water. After the food was gone we sat around for about an hour and a half and none of us could move. Next thing we knew the British officer was with us again, ordering us to start moving. We walked over to one of the coal cars of the train and got on. There were three of those cars on the train. We were forty plus forty plus forty, that is, one hundred twenty officers including myself and, God rest his soul, Fakhri al-Barudi.

They shut the car door. About one hundred or two hundred cars were used for the soldiers. The whistle blew and we were off. Each train had fifty cars, three for the officers and the rest for the enlisted men. We were all on the train in less than an hour just as it should be. The whistle blew and the train started. It was wide not like the narrow gauge train in the Hijaz. The train followed the coast by the desert of desolation and all along the way we could see camps, stockyards, goods, tents and hospitals, all belonging to the British. At each stop there were orderly, organized military installations.

The British were all half-naked walking around in shorts. It was hot and the sun burned down on everyone. They would walk up to us and in English say "Hello!" or give us a piece of chocolate candy. We kept going until we reached Rafah. At Rafah they let all the officers out. We got off and went directly into quarantine tents with wooden boards to sleep on and encircled by a ribbon signifying a three-day quarantine.

Fakhri Bey al-Barudi's relative from the Bakri family had been caught up in Faisal's revolution in the Hijaz where Faisal's father was King. So they sent word that Fakhri Bey should be sent to them as soon as possible. When we reached Rafah they asked if Fakhri al-Barudi was present. When he said yes, they told him that the commander wished to speak with him. He went with one of the guards. We waited for him to come back but in vain. We assumed that the British had beaten and shot him. It was not until later that we learned Prince Faisal had sent for him. Anyway we finished our three days and were given mattresses and a transfer from Rafah. There were so many of us you could sleep on one and cover yourself with another.

After the three days of quarantine we were shipped off to Sidi Bishr in Alexandria where they kept captured regular officers. The soldiers they sent to Heliopolis, you see, near Cairo. As prisoners we were put under detention in a camp especially designed for that purpose. Yes, indeed! There were one hundred twenty officers, and the soldiers numbered twenty thousand. They sent us first into steam baths after stripping our clothes off. Then they gave us each a pair of underwear, an undershirt and a black military uniform. They had us bathe in large barrels and the clothes were dry cleaned. From there we went to a camp that was reserved for Arabs only. The Arabs and Turks were kept in separate camps to avoid fighting. As though we could start a revolution in prison!

We stayed in Sidi Bishr in barracks that looked like train compartments. Once inside the door there were three beds to a room, three officers to a room. The higher the rank, the more exclusive the quarters. A lieutenant colonel had a place all to himself. A marshall had an enormous tent almost as big as a house to himself, and a deputy officer also had accommodation according to his rank. This was just temporary, however. The next day in the camps there would be tents, about twenty for the Turkish and

Arab soldiers who worked in the camps. In each camp there were twenty tents and one British officer who ran the camp, telling you to sweep this and do that. In the camps where there was sand they used to "comb" the grounds with rakes. They would put rocks in wheelbarrows to weigh them down in the sand and then would push them around, picking up any garbage they found in their path.

In short the soldiers were used for service work. Each evening they had inspections. The whistle would blow and each soldier would stand outside his room. The officers were treated like soldiers. The British officer would salute, explain that he was going to inspect the tents and then he would proceed. Afterward they would count us and send us back to our quarters. It happened that there was a Jewish officer in our ranks who, when the British officer would pass, would ask if he were Jewish. He asked him if he were Jewish!! The British officer would grimace and say, "No, no, English, English!"

And I remember, at the time, there was a lieutenant from Tripoli, Libya, with us who when the British officer passed him would stand with his feet spread apart. Another, a Turkish soldier, would not return the salute. When the British officer asked him why he behaved that way, he answered that he didn't recognize the rules and regulations of the British Army nor even the Army itself. He was a Turkish officer and would not take orders from any foreigner. They took down his name, and after inspection about fifteen minutes later, we saw some British soldiers gathering in the middle of the camp. They put up a tent and ripped a big hole in it, about a meter and a half wide. Next they encircled the whole thing with barbed wire. The British officer with two soldiers ordered the Turk into the tent and gave him a mattress. They kept him inside the barbed wire for three months, and after that sent him away, God only knows where. But it was a good lesson to us all.

We stayed at that camp for eleven months. At one point some officers from the army of Sharif Hussain came and joined us in captivity. Apparently, they were introduced into our ranks to let us know that an Arab government had been formed. Whoever wanted to join could apply to the English authorities for permission to leave. We started signing up and submitting our applications to the camp's headquarters. We said we wanted to join the Arab army and fight the Turks. The following day Nishan, an Armenian translator for the British authorities, came and called off the names of those selected. He called off about thirty-five names and told those men to be ready the next day before dawn. We were told that the guards would open the gates for us and we should steal out without letting the

Turks notice. Our men and the Turks began swearing back and forth at each other.

There were three posts next to each other about ten days apart. We were at the third post. They put us all in vehicles and sent us off to Suez. There, representatives of Faisal met us, one a Damascene, Hassan Fahmi Bey, and the other from Beirut, Hassan Hamada Bey. They were sent by Faisal to receive the prisoners from the British. The British officer went to one of the hotels in Suez and signed a document testifying to the fact that he had delivered us. So we were free at last in Suez. We were told where to eat and sleep while we waited for our uniforms, courtesy of Prince Faisal and the Hijaz army. By the way, they gave us each fifty pounds sterling to spend. We occupied our time going to the tailor and getting fitted. Room and board were also courtesy of the prince.

Sixteen days went by and then we received our orders to prepare to march. Two large trucks came for our baggage. We each had one or two boxes. The Egyptian soldiers loaded our things onto the trucks and from there we went straight to the railway station and found the train waiting. From the station we boarded a train for 'Aqaba. At 'Aqaba we were met by Prince Nassar, Prince Faisal's brother, who was very kind to us. We were each given a tent...thirty-five new tents!

From then on it was a different story. We stayed in the tents for three days eating and drinking. Then we received our orders, camels came, and we travelled for three days overland until we reached Aba al-Lisan mountains opposite Ma'an where the newly formed army was camped. They were very near a Turkish post. Each day we and the Turks would have skirmishes near a place called Janubiyya and Northern Sukhna. The army was formed of Arabs and tribal leaders. The overall leader was Nuri al-Sa'id, and the high ranking personnel were mostly Iraqis, Syrians and Lebanese. It was a colorful army. They gave us mattresses, tents, rice, sugar...all the food you might wish was available. Things changed for us then. Our salary was good, paid in full. I received eight gold pounds. My cousin Tawfiq al-Tergeman was an officer in the war. My brother had been imprisoned in 'Aqaba with the Turkish army. They both signed up with the new army. My brother was now a petty officer. My cousin Tawfiq had become an officer, as had Subhi al-Muhtashim, the husband of my niece. In other words we formed a battalion with each one hundred men led by an officer and my cousin leading the lot. As I mentioned we skirmished with the Turks every day, near Ma'an.

Soon after, Faisal formed a small camel corps of officers from all over. He took us down to Dar'a where, along with the British in Nablus and

Palestine, they began their assault on the Turks. The British took Palestine and we had the Hijaz. Next stop was Damascus. Faisal and his camel corps with a few hundred officers entered Damascus with the British. They entered from one gate as the Turks fled from another.

My cousin's battalion, including myself, had stayed behind in Aba al-Lisan. When Damascus fell we made a move on Ma'an, took it over and watched the Turks flee. We found the town empty and stayed there for two days. "March on Karak," they told us so we took the Mecca road used at the time of the pilgrimage. On that road we travelled for five days until we reached Amman. The road itself was in bad condition. We stayed in Amman until things had settled down in Damascus. The officers all the while rode on horseback while the soldiers marched on foot. At night we set up camp and slept. During the day we marched. When the government was formed in Damascus they sent us replacement officers and we moved on to Damascus.

When we arrived there we were received by the head of the army at that time, Yasin Pasha al-Hashami. Each of us was given a new assignment. They sent me to the house of 'Azat Pasha al-Abid. They sent me to the leader of the division in charge of technicians. He was from Homs and his brother was an officer. I worked for him in Abis's palace. There were about one hundred men working on electric and telephone lines. I was put in charge of the telephone and telegraph division.

I was given an order to change all the electrical wiring in the Citadel prison, so I took my ninety men and went. I also received an order to reinstall the electrical grid in the University in Hamadiyya. I changed it all from one end to the other. I also replaced the telephone lines for all the telephone company officers.

I was in uniform until the year 1920. While I was still in the army they decided that all officers and aides should attend the War College. Our turn came and my brother and I completed our schooling there. The college was located near the Mosque of Dankiz. There was another one behind the Bahsa Mosque in Rushdiyya, but that was for those who wanted to join the armed forces but had not enlisted yet. When young men finished there they gave them their uniforms and sent them on to the War College where they got their military training. There was a civilian college also by the name of Maktab 'Anbar, near Suq al-Ahad (the Sunday market). During the Turkish rule judges and mayors graduated from there.

At the War College we had courses in warfare. Yasin Pasha al-Hashami was a field marshall at the time. He gave lectures as though he were addressing the official War Council. The best student in our class was a very intelligent Iraqi corporal by the name of Fahmi. God knows, he was really something! They gave us lessons on military engineering. Nishan gave us lessons in religion. Abd al-Qadar al-Mubarak gave us Arabic lessons. We were at the school for about six months.

My brother and my cousin on my mother's side, Tawfiq al-Halabi, got leave from the military and went on to Maisalun. Meanwhile Tawfiq Bey al-Jundi who was in charge of technicians needed men. So he asked the head of the War Council to take me out of the college and sent me to him. Well...the orders came and, by God, I found myself back in the same old job. Yes, indeed! The Dean of the college then was Admiral 'Ubaid, may the Prophet bless his soul. So I joined my assigned company in the 'Abid building. I was sick of the whole thing. Being an officer's aide was not at all what I wanted since I should have been a technical officer with the wire and telegraph office. I applied for a job with Hassan Bey al-Hakim, who was postmaster general for military installations. He accepted my application and passed it on to the War Council for approval:

> The assistant officer here named wishes to work at the general military post office. Would you be kind enough to give us some background information on his conduct during his years of military service, what skills he has, his origins and whether there might be objections to hiring him.

Well they refused my request. I applied again but was stopped in my tracks. I quit my job as an officer's aide and was left without pay for two or three months. They told me that since I had quit I shouldn't ask for anything. Tawfiq Bey al-Zaliq, the paymaster, refused to give me my salary. I went without it for six months and finally went to the War Council to protest to Yassin Pasha. I said I was an Army employee who had been robbed of his pay. Of course, I protested against Tawfiq Bey al-Jundi. Yassin Pasha passed my protest on to his chief of staff, Yussif Bey al-'Azmi, who wrote to the head of the War Council. He advised them that I should be paid since I had worked the specified time as head of the technical division. So they gave me the money they owed me for those six months: eight gold pounds for each month. After that they permitted my application to the post office to be processed and I was given the job. The only problem was that by that time the postal service was no longer under the administration of the War Office and so I was informed of my new job through a private emissary of the post master. Now I started work at the post office but as a civilian.

I remained in that job until I reached the age of retirement. We were then living in the neighborhood of Birka. Once out of the military I was living alone with my mother at our house in Birka in Bab Sarija. That is where your mother and I got married. Then, we moved to Suq Saruja to the house at the top of the hill at Juzat al-Hadba, near the bakery.

—But, Father, you forgot to tell me about the bedouin you met during Safar Birlik. Tell me about him and his story, where you met him and when...

—I met him at the Jaruf al-Darwish station. When the train stopped, the bedouins would come up and beg. One of them who was missing a leg came up to me and asked for a piece of bread. I looked at him and felt sorry for him, wondering how the poor man had managed to lose his leg, I asked him who had amputated his leg. He said, "Leave me alone, brother, it's too long a story!" I told him that I would only give him the bread he wanted if he would tell me his story. At that time on the road to Medina a loaf of bread meant a lot to anyone. We used to sell a packet of cigarettes for a quarter of a majidi. It was pretty good business on that road. I used to make about fifty gold pounds a round trip selling odds and ends here and there. At that stop, though, the people were particularly poor and miserable and we couldn't buy or sell a thing. It was a small station. The poor fellows were half dead anyway.

By God, daughter, he told me his story like this:

—I fell in love with a girl of my tribe but her parents refused to allow me to marry her. She loved me, though, so we eloped to a place in the mountains where there were no other human beings around. We found a cave where we lived. Every day I would go and steal a lamb or something for us to eat. One day the shepherd caught me and accused me of stealing. I confessed but he kept hassling me. Finally I got back to the cave only to find a huge snake wrapped around my wife choking her. He had almost cut her in half. I lost my mind and pulled out my sword to kill him. That only made him attack my wife more fiercely, tearing her to shreds. I was in a frenzy and the animal fled. I buried my wife and wandered off into the desert. Soon after I was surprised by a camel charging at me. In the desert if your camel becomes rabid, you abandon him in the middle of the desert and he becomes wild. When he saw me he came after me. Finally I climbed up on some rocks where I was safe from the camel. He watched me as I stood there. Then I heard a sound and looked behind me to find a large scorpion. I was paralyzed with fear and couldn't move in any direction. Then as the scorpion advanced toward me, he slipped on the rocks and fell straight at the camel's feet. The next thing I knew they both lay dead at the foot of the rocks, the scorpion stinging the camel just as the camel crushed him. They had each poisoned the other. I jumped down beside them and kicked the camel in the leg to make sure he was dead. Well I made the mistake of kicking his wound and the poison from the scorpion was now on my leg. I knew that if I didn't act soon I would be as dead as both of them so I amputated my own leg. From that time until now I've been begging from Arabs who came along as you see me now.

—That was his story, daughter!

*   *   *

My mother 'Aziza, daughter of Shaikh Ali Qasim al-Bahlul al-Jazairi, then turned to me and in her pretty Damascene accent told me about her memories of Damascus in the days of Safar Birlik:

—When the days of Safar Birlik came I was quite young, Siham, only about thirteen or fourteen years old. My, oh my, that was also the year my father died. He had been upset by something and suffered a stroke. He had never been sick a day in his life before that. He was only fifty-five or sixty years at the time, still young. We were living at my father's house in the 'Asqalan area. I was still very young when one day a bulldozer came to our street to make some sort of road. Well just when they tried to start it, it wouldn't move. Almost every man on our street tried to make it go but in the end it didn't start until they sacrificed a lamb and read the Mulid prayers in its name. Finally the elders came and read a prayer for it to work...and it did in the end. It was a little boy, in fact, that started it up. It was in the Maidan quarter and I think they may have wanted to construct a railway line through there.

During the war my family never went hungry because they were in the wool business. They would buy the raw wool and have it spun by their own workers. My mother, her sister Badriyya and her sister-in-law all stayed together during that time. My uncle Abu Rashid, my mother's brother that is, was absent for the four years of the war. A lot of people were in the wool and cotton business then. When the men were away, that was one of the best ways for women to make money.

When the men went off to the army the prices went way up. People were selling the shirts off their backs. Bread was rationed and people would stand in line outside bakeries starting at midnight hoping to get even a burned loaf of bread.

The bakers worked day and night to send bread out to the front. The mosques became recruitment centers to round up the young men to send them to the front. The Ras Bath in Sanjuqdar was used for the men to bathe and get a shave before joining the other soldiers on the front. They would pick up all the able men between the Mu'alaq Mosque and the Sadat Mosque and send them to draft headquarters. In the end they took all our men and left us no one under eighty.

Straw merchants used to sell rushes to the women who would make little rush-bottomed stools and sell them in Bab Missala, Maidan and Suwiqa. The women would gather around the Midawara fountain. You want to know where it is, Siham? Well, let me tell you. Do you know the lane you used to take to get to Khan al-Zait, by the railroad tracks. That's where it was. And do you remember the corner between Suq al-Atiq and Suq al-Hal at the Zarabiliyya intersection? Well there, on that corner, used to be an old woman who sold stuffed zucchini in tomato sauce. She was an older woman whose sons were all away in the army. Her face was usually hidden by a veil. Across from the fort in the next street over was a woman who sold roasted kibbi. Another sold fried liver at Bab al-Jabiyya. In Maidan they made straw mats. Those were not your usual mats but were thick and well-made with a very nice design on them. People used them when they went on picnics in the fields and such. There was practically nothing that women didn't sell at that time when they took all our men and left us no one. Even the seventy-year-olds were gone!

The Mosque near Suq al-Hal, the Mu'alaq Mosque, was another recruitment center. The councils would meet, names would be listed and the men would be sent off to assigned areas. It was all a matter of luck where you got sent. The Germans, the Austrians and the Turks were all in on this. Whatever was written down for someone, happened!

Oh, how those poor Damascene women suffered! I'll tell you why. The Turks could get goods from cooperative stores. The Turkish women got all sorts of meats, sugar and flour. The rest of us when we saw a single cube of sugar knew it either came from the black market or from smugglers. In fact my mother had to buy flour from the smugglers. If sellers were caught, their goods were confiscated. So people began hiding wheat and only selling it on the black market. At that time you would always find women roasting corn in the street to feed their children. People were forced to become beggars. It was filthy everywhere. Onions were impossible to find anyplace in the whole country. Ask your father! When we got married he told me how he used to hide little bags of salt in his shoes because salt was so scarce and because he was afraid people might steal them from him.

Oh, my, how they suffered!

When the war was over and the Turks fled with the Germans the people of Damascus killed any Germans left behind because they had conspired with the Austrians and Turks. During the war the Germans had confiscated all the fruits and vegetables available, canned them and sent them to their soldiers on the front. They didn't leave us, who were the people of the country, a single piece of fruit. We were left to starve in the streets. One day you would see someone looking for food in the street and the next day you would see the same poor creature dead in the street.

Children died in alleyways. Some died, some were orphaned and some were abandoned. There was no order whatsoever in the country. The children of the poor were everywhere, in Suq al-Khail following soldiers around hoping to get a crust of bread. That's basically all they got, too. They never saw a whole loaf of bread. The situation stayed like that until the British came and chased out the Germans and the Turks in the sixth or seventh year of the war. They also tried to take all our gold. They loaded it on trains but when the trains got to Dummar, the people there attacked the train and killed any German or Turk who tried to escape.

That day we had gone up the road a piece to the public bath where we used to bathe. We were washing ourselves with no idea that the Germans had been defeated and were on their way out. Somewhere nearby they blew up an artillery depot and the whole bath began shaking around us.

That night the army attacked and when day came the British were in the city. It had been the British who had blown up the artillery depot, Siham, because the people of the city had risen up against them. They blew up the depot to try and stop the revolt but the people only stole British weapons and started killing the British with their own guns. That night, three boys from the Nuri family died. Oh, it was awful!

In short, it was a very black night and by the next day the British had taken over the city. Their horses stood tall and erect like royalty all over the city and the British would fill their hands with sugar to feed their horses. When the people saw that they went crazy. They ran around offering their services to the British and for that they were rewarded with gold pounds. Two or three months later our soldiers began coming back and Faisal appeared on the scene. The British were very generous, bringing us goods and arranging celebrations for Faisal's arrival. Oh, the celebrations that took place when Faisal came...I've never seen anything like it since, seven days and seven nights of continuous celebrations with singing and dancing in the streets. The country was saved and the people had food, sugar, rice and wheat. Whoever died, died, and whoever survived, survived. Faisal stayed on for two years. My mother took me down to Marje at the time to see his coronation.

Such a celebration as took place when Faisal arrived was never witnessed anywhere else before that, I am sure. All the soldiers who had survived the war were there. I saw Faisal crowned on the balcony of the city hall at Marje Square. Oh, the cheers, the joy, the decorations! Daughter, I tell you I never saw such a celebration before, for seven days and nights in a row! Rugs were hung out, beds carried into the street and decorations hung everywhere in Bab al-Jabiyya, Maidan, Shughur, 'Amara and Qanawat...everywhere. By God, I remember seeing a clown in Qanawat near the house of the Sharif. What happened at that time was out of this world, totally unique! Never before had Damascus seen such decorations or heard so many cannons go off. The prisoners were freed from jail and those on death row were given reduced sentences. The British were there. If you so much as wiped an Englishman's shoe he rewarded you with no less than two gold pounds. The British kept everyone busy. Their horses were shining clean...you know they had such big horses you wouldn't even believe they were horses! They walked like princes!

We saw some very black days back then that we never want to live through again! God spared Damascus and its people. The British, the Germans, the Turks and the French...they all left, and God alone now guards Damascus.

But, tell me, daughter, what made you think to ask about Safar Birlik?

APPENDIX A

Peddler's Calls

Duma grapes: Beautiful, white like diamonds; the red ones stain.

Halawani grapes: Halawani, Dairani,[1] grapes!

Dairani grapes: Are they Dairani or Halawani?

Black grapes: The blacks came to us out of the night.

Baladi grapes: Country grapes, home grown!

Apples: Nirbani,[2] O Jinani.

Red apples: Product of Izmir. What comes from Izmir, reminds us of the sea. Eat and nourish your heart with this apple, O satisfied one! Can you tell if it's Golden or Starken?

Sakarji apples: O, satisfied one, use it like incense! The apple from Zabadani.

Sweet Apples: The sugar apple comes from Zabadani.

Raisins: Like the dried date with the color of henna, oh, raisins like coffee beans; oh, raisins!

Hab al-Ass:[3] This plant is worth a lot when it's green!

Bananas: The pound for one hundred, but never mind, they're delicious! Eat the one with the black spots.

Tangerines: Product of Tripoli, as fine as a king's head. This affandi is a food

---

[1] Dairani means coming from the town of Dair al Zur in the east of Syria.

[2] A rhyming word.

[3] Date fronds placed on graves.

Oranges: A skin smooth and thin has this orange from Jaffa. Product of Acre and Tyre. This Jaffa orange is without skin.

Moroccan Oranges: Sweet Moroccans, these oranges!

Navel Oranges: Oranges, Abu Surra!

APPENDIX B

Proverbs

His eye is on the dish and his ear listens to whomever speaks.
    (A gossip neglects the business at hand)

The pregnant one is coddled, the one in labor spoiled, but bringing up the child well is the great burden.
    (The difficult task is unacclaimed)

The bald woman has two combs; the blind woman has two mascara brushes.
    (The handicapped focus on their afflictions)

Let it wound your heart rather than go out and cause a scandal.
    (Keep it to yourself if you don't want others to know)

A deaf woman puts her ear to the door to listen.
    (A person with an incurably bad character)

You in a hurry, stop, I want to tell you something.
    (A good-for-nothing hinders the progress of others)

An hour for you and one for your God.
    (Live your life but don't forget what you owe God)

If you want to cause him confusion give him a choice.
    (Make things easier by defining the right way)

If you want to exclude him ask him.
    (Don't ask someone if he wants this or that, for then he will have to refuse both)

The bald woman shaves the crazy woman.
    (Only a mad person trusts a person who is excessive to do for him that thing in which he is excessive)

Is the tree in my courtyard for me or my neighbors?
    (Something rightfully belonging to someone)